Joomla! 1.5 Content Administration

Keep your website up-to-date and maintain content and users with ease

Tracey Porst

[PACKT] PUBLISHING

BIRMINGHAM - MUMBAI

Joomla! 1.5 Content Administration

Copyright © 2009 Packt Publishing

All rights reserved. No part of this book may be reproduced, stored in a retrieval system, or transmitted in any form or by any means, without the prior written permission of the publisher, except in the case of brief quotations embedded in critical articles or reviews.

Every effort has been made in the preparation of this book to ensure the accuracy of the information presented. However, the information contained in this book is sold without warranty, either express or implied. Neither the author, nor Packt Publishing, and its dealers and distributors will be held liable for any damages caused or alleged to be caused directly or indirectly by this book.

Packt Publishing has endeavored to provide trademark information about all of the companies and products mentioned in this book by the appropriate use of capitals. However, Packt Publishing cannot guarantee the accuracy of this information.

First published: October 2009

Production Reference: 1201009

Published by Packt Publishing Ltd.
32 Lincoln Road
Olton
Birmingham, B27 6PA, UK.

ISBN 978-1-847198-04-4

www.packtpub.com

Cover Image by Parag Kadam (paragvkadam@gmail.com)

Credits

Author
Tracey Porst

Reviewer
Toivo Talikka

Acquisition Editor
David Barnes

Development Editor
Amey Kanse

Technical Editor
Neha Damle

Copy Editor
Sanchari Mukherjee

Indexer
Rekha Nair

Editorial Team Leader
Gagandeep Singh

Project Team Leader
Priya Mukherji

Project Coordinator
Ashwin Shetty

Proofreader
Sandra Hopper

Graphics
Nilesh R. Mohite

Production Coordinator
Adline Swetha Jesuthas

Cover Work
Adline Swetha Jesuthas

About the Author

Tracey Porst is a creative industries practitioner and teacher in the field of visual and online design technology, who enjoys the challenge of developing creative, commercial, and educational projects.

After a number of years working in management administration, the need to work within a creative environment took hold. Tracey applied her skills and background in this area after completing full-time study in visual design and new media technologies, to develop her own successful freelance design and digital media studio. She has enjoyed a successful career as a freelance visual communication designer ever since.

Having worked consistently to develop her own freelance practice, Tracey's client base includes an interesting and diverse range of businesses, for which she has produced websites, logos, and other promotional material.

Tracey takes a collaborate approach to working with her clients, listening to their requirements and combining them with the technologies and principles she believes will deliver results. Her clients often report that they are happy to have digital and technologies explained to them in practical terms and without the jargon often associated with this field.

As a Sessional Academic and Research Assistant with a leading Australian university, in addition to the teaching aspects, Tracey also enjoys the opportunity to develop her knowledge base and stay in touch with the changing face of digital media theory and practices.

Acknowledgement

Thanks to John, as well as my family and friends for your support, encouragement, and patience. I would also like to acknowledge the Joomla! development team and community for their ongoing commitment towards improving and developing this CMS, and for sharing their knowledge with anyone who is interested in developing websites with Joomla!

Please support the development team with a donation if you are able.

About the Reviewer

Toivo Talikka lives in Sydney with his wife Maja, their son Mikko, and dog Marlo. Toivo has worked on applications based on Joomla! for two years and provided support at the Joomla! forum to reach the level of Joomla! Ace. His tips and observations can be found at his blog `http://toivo.talikka.com`.

Toivo's career in computing started in the early 70's in an air conditioned room filled with 7-foot-tall tape drives, hard disk drives looking like top-loading washing machines, paper tape, and card readers connected to a GE-115 computer. He punched his first assembler programs onto 80-column cards and had at his disposal 16 KB of ferrite core memory and 5 MB of disk space.

Toivo's expertise in Retail Point Of Sale systems gained at ICL Finland led him to work for the company in Australia, England, and Sweden. He returned to Sydney to work with NCR. Then Burns Philp offered him a position in Papua New Guinea in its Merchandise division, from where he moved to the shipping subsidiary and, subsequently, to Shipping's head office in Sydney. His next job was IT Operations Manager for a CBD law firm. After that, Toivo ran a one-man consultancy in Sydney for five years, helping clients in legal services, wholesale, and aged-care industries to manage their computer applications and networks. His company, Total Data Pty Ltd, provided remote systems administration, internet security, and onsite hardware maintenance and installations, covering both Windows and Linux servers.

For his own use, Toivo installed Linux servers and firewalls and got an introduction to Apache, MySQL, and PHP (LAMP), the tools he then used to write a web-based customer-billing application accessible from his Nokia cell phone. His interest in Open Source applications and Joomla! led to a full-time job as a web developer, responsible for websites based on Joomla!, its extensions, and their integration with web-based services, at one of the Australian subsidiaries of a French global company, Schneider Electric.

> I thank Maja, my wife, for her encouragement while reviewing this book. I am also grateful to the Joomla! developers for producing an excellent content management system.

Table of Contents

Preface	**1**
Chapter 1: Exploring Your New Joomla! Website	**7**
Where to begin	**8**
Logging into the Control Panel	8
Getting around the administration	**10**
Site	10
Menus	10
Content	10
Components	11
Extensions	11
Tools	11
Help	12
Related toolbars	**12**
Organizing your site	**12**
Understanding Sections, Categories, and Articles	13
What are uncategorized articles?	14
Site wide settings	**14**
Leave it to the experts	14
Overview of the extensions	**16**
Components	17
Modules	17
Plugins	18
Summary	**19**
Chapter 2: Creating, Editing, and Organizing Content	**21**
General tips on writing content for the Web	**22**
A note on copyright	**23**
Making your home page engaging	**24**
The Article Manager	**25**

Filtering the display of Articles	26
Column headings	27
The toolbar	28
Archive and unarchive Articles	28
Publish and unpublish an Article	29
Move or copy an Article	29
Trashing an Article	30
Edit, New, and Parameters	30
Editing an existing Article using the text editor	**32**
Opening the Article	33
Editing the Article	33
Creating a new Article	**34**
Adding text	35
Adding a table to an Article	35
Breaking up Article content	**37**
Adding a Read More link	37
Adding a page break	38
Using the JCE text editor	**39**
Authorization and publishing from the frontend	**40**
Adding content for approval through frontend access	41
To submit an Article from the frontend	42
What are Article parameters?	**45**
The advanced parameters—but only if you really have to!	46
Metadata information is what search engines like	46
Summary	**47**
Chapter 3: Managing Images and Videos	**49**
Media Manager	**50**
Accessing and using the Media Manager	50
Creating a new subfolder	51
A note on copyright	51
What you should know about image and video files	**52**
Choosing the best image file format	52
Adding and managing images	**53**
Uploading a new image	53
Deleting an image	54
Updating a Simple Image Gallery	54
Changing the Simple Image Gallery's dimensions	56
Using video files	**57**
Choosing the best video file format	58
Uploading a video	60
Updating videos—AllVideos plugin	60
Changing to a different video file and format	61

Updating a YouTube video	62
Changing the YouTube video dimensions	64
Audio files	**64**
Summary	**68**
Chapter 4: Backing Up Your Website	**69**
What's the Control Panel and where is it?	**69**
Manually backing up your site	**71**
Backing up the database using the phpMyAdmin interface	72
Backing up the site files using the Backup Wizard	74
Using an external FTP application to download and upload your files	76
Restoring your website manually	**77**
Backing up and restoring with the JoomlaPack component	78
Understanding the restoration process	78
Summary	**87**
Chapter 5: User Management	**89**
The big picture: Who are users?	**89**
Frontend users	90
Frontend user definitions	90
Administration users	91
Editing the frontend Login Form	**91**
Lost usernames and passwords	91
Allowing new account registrations	92
Adding custom text to the Login Form	94
Directing registered users to a certain section of the site	96
Managing your users: The User Manager	**97**
Creating a new user	97
Adding a new user as a site contact	98
Adding a new contact Category	98
Adding the new user to your list of contacts	99
Adding a new customer manually	102
Editing existing users	103
Editing a user profile	103
Updating the linked contact details	104
Resetting a username and password	106
Dealing with problematic users	106
Deleting a user	107
Blocking a user	107
What if a new user can't log in?	108
Sending e-mails to a group of users	**108**
Sending a private message to a user	109
Summary	**110**

Chapter 6: Making Your Site Popular — 111
Overview of Search Engine Ranking — 111
What is metadata? — 112
General strategies for SEO — 112
Updating content frequently — 113
Link building — 113
Adding an external link to an Article — 113
Adding an internal link to an Article — 114
Social media — 116
Using social media for marketing — 117
Facebook — 117
Twitter — 118
StumbleUpon — 118
Delicious — 119
Reddit and Digg — 119
RSS feeds — 119
Social media on your site — 119
Customizing Stalker — 120
Making the most of Google — 122
Setting up a Google Account — 122
Setting up Google Analytics — 124
Research keywords — 126
Google's keyword tool — 126
Adding lots of content — 127
Pay per click traffic — 127
Keyword tips — 127
Creating a new, search engine-friendly Article — 128
Summary — 131

Chapter 7: Security—Precaution and Recovery — 133
Precautionary measures — 134
Keeping up-to-date — 134
Upgrade to the latest version of Joomla! — 134
Localhost environments — 135
Installing the upgrade patch — 135
Review your hosting account — 138
Change the administration username and password — 138
Why change the administration username from "admin" to something else? — 139
Reset the FTP login password — 140
Other precautions — 140
Installing and configuring jSecure authentication — 140
Downloading jSecure — 141
Installing jSecure through the administration control panel — 143
Configuring the jSecure Plugin to change the administration login URL — 144

What should I do if my site is exploited?	145
Help, I can't log into the administration panel!	**145**
Generate an MD5 hash value	146
Reset the "admin" user password in the database	146
Log into the administration interface	147
What else should I do?	148
Check for any new or suspicious files	148
Run diagnostic scripts	148
Advise your hosting provider	148
Review the Raw Access Logs for your site	149
How do I recover my site after a serious compromise?	**150**
Summary	**150**
Chapter 8: Menus, Modules, and Components	**151**
Extending a menu with a new link	**152**
Creating the Article	152
Reordering menu items	156
Removing a menu item	156
Adding Web Links	**157**
Setting the Web Links global parameters	157
Adding a Category of links	159
Adding the links to the Category	160
Editing and deleting web links and Categories	161
Adding the web links page to the (top) menu	161
Advertising banners	**164**
Setting up banner advertising	165
Adding a banner Category	165
Adding a banner client	166
Setting the banner parameters	166
Adding the banner	167
Enabling the banner module	169
Managing and editing banners	172
Latest news module: Updating and adding	**173**
Setting up the content	173
Enabling the module	173
Managing your latest news	174
Random images module	**175**
Change the files in the image folder	175
Redirect to a different image directory	176
Installing third-party extensions—modules, components, and plugins	**177**
Position of modules	177
Plugins	178

[v]

Table of Contents

Installing an extension	178
Configuring the component	180
Adding the new component to a menu	182
Additional third-party extensions	184
VirtueMart	184
JCal Pro	184
DOCman	184
Letterman	184
Core modules	**185**
NewsFlash	185
Who's online	186
Polls	188
Feed display	188
Summary	**189**
Index	**191**

Preface

Often a company hires consultants or web developers to build a Joomla! website, and then takes over running the site in-house. If you are a content administrator concerned with creating and maintaining the product of a content management site, and not modifying its code, this book is all you need.

This practical, hands-on guide will give you all the knowledge needed to maintain and edit your website as a content-rich place that visitors return to again and again. There are many books available to help you administer a Joomla! site, but this is the only one specifically for content administrators. It is a quick-start guide that best serves content administrators and editors and doesn't cover designing or creating a site. However, anybody who has built their own site but needs help with article management, multimedia management, search engine optimization, and more will also benefit from it.

To explain all the features, we will work on developing and maintaining the content and structure of a fledgling website for a fictitious company, "The Party People." As your skills develop, you will work through techniques for making the site search-engine friendly and securing it against potential malicious attacks. All of these techniques and processes are explained step-by-step, and by the end of the book you will be able to take advantage of your new-found knowledge and skills and maintain your Joomla! site with ease. Keeping your content fresh and engaging becomes easy, once you know how, and that's what this book aims to do. It will help you become a more effective and efficient manager of Joomla!-based websites.

What this book covers

Chapter 1: Exploring Your New Joomla! Website covers accessing and navigating the backend or administration interface of a Joomla! website. We will also understand the overall structure and the hierarchy of the content.

Chapter 2: Creating, Editing, and Organizing Content covers the Article Manager, which is used for creating, editing, and organizing content.

Chapter 3: Managing Images and Videos covers the Media Manager. We will learn how to upload and manage audio, video, and images. We also learn how to select the best file formats for our media files.

Chapter 4: Backing Up Your Website covers the backing up and restoring of a Joomla! website in case your site is maliciously attacked or compromised. We'll also outline how to use the JoomlaPack component through the administration interface to create an archive file that can be uploaded and unpacked to restore our website.

Chapter 5: User Management covers the user management system within the administration interface that allows us to effectively manage our website users and their profiles. We will learn to establish and edit new user accounts, manage username and password issues, and deal with problematic users.

Chapter 6: Making Your Site Popular outlines how search engines find websites based on keywords and page descriptions. It also explains how we can apply them to our website and increase the chances of a better ranking in the index page of a search engine result. We also look at some ways we may be able to improve the success of our search engine ranking.

Chapter 7: Security–Recovery and Precaution covers precautions to make it harder for hackers to compromise our website. It explains how to recover from a malicious attack and what to do if your site is exploited

Chapter 8: Menus, Modules, and Components covers applying some of the key components and modules that are a part of the core Joomla! installation, as well as looking at an overview of some third-party extensions such as VirtueMart, JCal Pro, DOCman, and Letterman.

What you need for this book

You will need to have Joomla! installed and a website of your own to go through the instructions in the book. Throughout the text we address a number of optional applications such as local host servers or ftp programs and information about them is provided in context.

Who this book is for

If you are someone who wants to quickly and easily manage content and users for a Joomla! website, this book is ideal for you. You could be a content editor, proofreader, graphic artist, feature editor, or anyone else concerned with managing content on a Joomla! installation. If you can browse the Web and use a word processing software package, this book will help you develop the skills to efficiently manage your website and gain a solid understanding of the Joomla! content management system.

Conventions

In this book, you will find a number of styles of text that distinguish between different kinds of information. Here are some examples of these styles, and an explanation of their meaning.

Code words in text are shown as follows: "We can include other contexts through the use of the `include` directive."

New terms and **important words** are shown in bold. Words that you see on the screen, in menus or dialog boxes for example, appear in the text like this: "clicking the **Next** button moves you to the next screen."

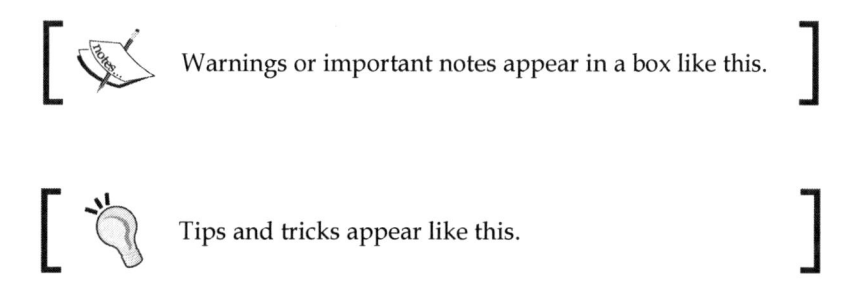

> Warnings or important notes appear in a box like this.

> Tips and tricks appear like this.

Reader feedback

Feedback from our readers is always welcome. Let us know what you think about this book—what you liked or may have disliked. Reader feedback is important for us to develop titles that you really get the most out of.

To send us general feedback, simply send an e-mail to `feedback@packtpub.com`, and mention the book title via the subject of your message.

If there is a book that you need and would like to see us publish, please send us a note in the **SUGGEST A TITLE** form on `www.packtpub.com` or e-mail `suggest@packtpub.com`.

If there is a topic that you have expertise in and you are interested in either writing or contributing to a book on, see our author guide on `www.packtpub.com/authors`.

Customer support

Now that you are the proud owner of a Packt book, we have a number of things to help you to get the most from your purchase.

Errata

Although we have taken every care to ensure the accuracy of our content, mistakes do happen. If you find a mistake in one of our books—maybe a mistake in the text or the code—we would be grateful if you would report this to us. By doing so, you can save other readers from frustration, and help us to improve subsequent versions of this book. If you find any errata, please report them by visiting `http://www.packtpub.com/support`, selecting your book, clicking on the **let us know** link, and entering the details of your errata. Once your errata are verified, your submission will be accepted and the errata added to any list of existing errata. Any existing errata can be viewed by selecting your title from `http://www.packtpub.com/support`.

Piracy

Piracy of copyright material on the Internet is an ongoing problem across all media. At Packt, we take the protection of our copyright and licenses very seriously. If you come across any illegal copies of our works, in any form, on the Internet, please provide us with the location address or website name immediately so that we can pursue a remedy.

Please contact us at `copyright@packtpub.com` with a link to the suspected pirated material.

We appreciate your help in protecting our authors, and our ability to bring you valuable content.

Questions

You can contact us at questions@packtpub.com if you are having a problem with any aspect of the book, and we will do our best to address it.

Exploring Your New Joomla! Website

Today it's generally expected that an organization, company, or even an individual (for example, think of creative professionals such as photographers or musicians) have a website which will serve as a tool for promotional purposes or to generate an income. It may simply be a one page portfolio, or possibly a blog that allows you to share your opinions, or a comprehensive e-commerce operation such as eBay or Amazon. As a content management system, Joomla! has the capacity to accommodate all of these applications. Also, whatever you or your website developer's reasons for choosing Joomla! to power your site, one of the great things about it is the ease with which you can manage and update your content, keeping your users interested in you and your activities or products. Learning how to keep your content fresh and engaging becomes easy once you know how, and that's what this book aims to achieve.

In this first chapter towards understanding how to manage your Joomla! website, we'll refer to a mock up of a website called **The Party People** to cover:

- Accessing and navigating the "backend" or administration interface of your new website
- The overall structure of the site and the hierarchy of content
- What the overall configuration settings mean to the presentation and delivery of your site

Where to begin

What you see in the web browser is referred to as the *frontend* of your site and presents the online face and personality of your organization. Managing this pleasant face is easily achieved when you access the *backend* of the site. The kind folks at Joomla! have made this as fuss free as possible by providing a graphical and easy to navigate administration interface.

It is also important to mention here that editing your website can be done through the frontend of the site as well, depending upon the level of access the user has been granted. There are also certain extensions to Joomla! that allows access to particular areas. Chapter 5, *User Management* looks at the level of access in detail.

However, access to the administration requires logging in and your website developer will have provided you with the appropriate level of authority to do so. The administration interface called the Control Panel, is a "members only" area.

> If your developer has not given you the level of authority as a user to do this, you will need to approach them and ask them to change your user profile. The developer should allocate access to you as a manager at least for administrative rights. Chapter 5, *User Management* covers user management in a detailed manner.

Logging into the Control Panel

Access to the Control Panel is through a link relative to the website address. Using the Party People example, the content editor will type in `http://partypeople.com/administrator/` and be presented with the login panel to enter a **Username** and **Password** before proceeding to the Control Panel.

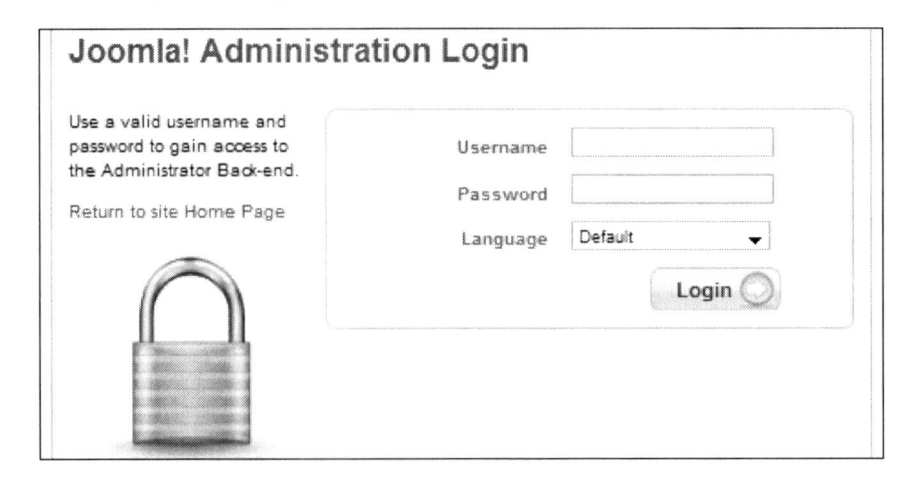

Having logged in successfully, you are presented with the Control Panel screen (the central hub for managing your content). This is where you begin creating and managing articles, uploading images, as well as a host of other functional activities. Clicking one of the icons (as seen in the following screenshot) gives you access to various sections of the administration interface. We'll address these progressively throughout the chapter.

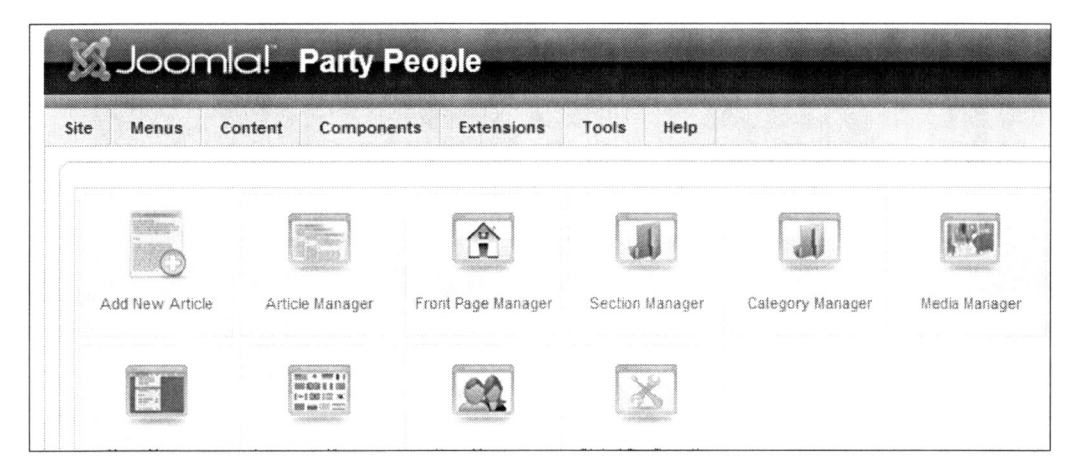

The icons presented are quick links to the most frequently accessed content editing and management activities and are supplementary to the main menu structure located at the top of the administration interface. Use either the icon or the menu to take you to the section.

The icons on display are determined by the level of authority the website developer has created for your role.

As the Control Panel is the central hub of the administration interface, it can also be accessed from other areas of the site through the top menu.

Click the **Site | Control Panel** link from anywhere within the administration interface to return to this screen. You will need to close or save your current updates in order to enable the link.

Exploring Your New Joomla! Website

Getting around the administration

Navigating the administration interface from anywhere within the backend of the site is made easy with a global menu bar to guide you through the various areas of the administration. Located at the top left of every screen (which is why we refer to it as global) the links are named according to the areas they lead to. The global menu bar is as shown in the following screenshot:

Site

This contains links to all of the key site settings, which include the following:

- Control Panel
- User Manager
- Media Manager
- Global Configuration
- Logout

Menus

This links to the section where you can organize the management of the menus established on your site. The menu manager link takes you through a list of the menus presented on the frontend of your site, where you can manage them by clicking the links.

Content

All the information presented on the site can be accessed through here, as there are links to the following:

- Article Manager
- Article Trash
- Section Manager
- Category Manager
- Front Page Manager

We'll cover the details later in this chapter.

Components

Components are a section of your site that provide a specific functional feature, such as the Newsfeed or a Poll. Any components built into your site can be accessed using this link. Components are covered at the end of this chapter and Chapter 8, *Menus, Modules, and Components* covers some of the more popular ones in detail.

Extensions

Extensions are extra functional features your site has installed within to customize it. They are referred to as Modules or Plugins. They are also addressed at the end of this chapter and Chapter 8, *Menus, Modules, and Components* covers some of the more popular ones.

The site template and languages can be managed through here; however, they are for more advanced users and generally best left to your developer to make changes to.

Tools

This menu provides access to a number of useful administrative tools. For example, the administration interface provides the capability to leave messages for other users and they can be accessed through here. The specifics of what users can do are addressed in Chapter 5, *User Management* in detail, but the **Tools** menu includes links to the following:

- **Read Messages**: Any message sent to you from other users can be accessed.
- **Write Message**: A link to send a message to another user.
- **Mass Mail**: The link for a Super Administrator to send a message to a group of users.
- **Global Check-in**: Allows a user to check what content items are locked or checked out by other users (which can make these items inaccessible to others).
- **Clean Cache**: Allows you to clean any cached files from your web server, thereby updating the frontend presentation with any recent changes to your site. The settings are established within the Global Configuration of your site.
- **Purge Expired Cache**: This deletes all of the stored cache files on the web server.

Exploring Your New Joomla! Website

> Cache files are generated to assist with the efficiency of presenting your site in the web browser. They are files of HTML, images, or other media elements stored for later reuse, making the site load faster the next time it is accessed. However, if changes are made to a site, clearing the cache in the browser (*Ctrl+F5*) is required to update the content.

Help

A comprehensive list of terms and key phrases are contained within a database of information. This is the site-wide **Help** database and contains broad information for all areas of the site.

Related toolbars

When you access a management screen (for example, Article Manager) there is a toolbar to the top right-hand side of the screen, which typically looks as shown in the following screenshot. It may include icons to **Publish**, **Edit**, and **Archive** content. This toolbar displays relevant contextual icons to assist you with creating, editing, and managing your content. As we work through the various content editing processes throughout the book, we'll use these tools in context.

The **Help** icon in this toolbar is contextual as well and offers insights into topics relevant to the area you are currently within.

| Unarchive | Archive | Publish | Unpublish | Move | Copy | Trash | Edit | New | Parameters | Help |

Organizing your site

The structure for organizing content within your Joomla! site is based on a hierarchy of **Sections**, **Categories**, and **Articles**.

Sections are created first and established as the highest level of organization, separating the content of the site into the broader topic areas. **Categories** are then created and allocated to **Sections**, to sort the content into more specific subject areas. **Articles** are allocated to **Sections** and **Categories** and present the details on these areas on the frontend of the website.

Chapter 1

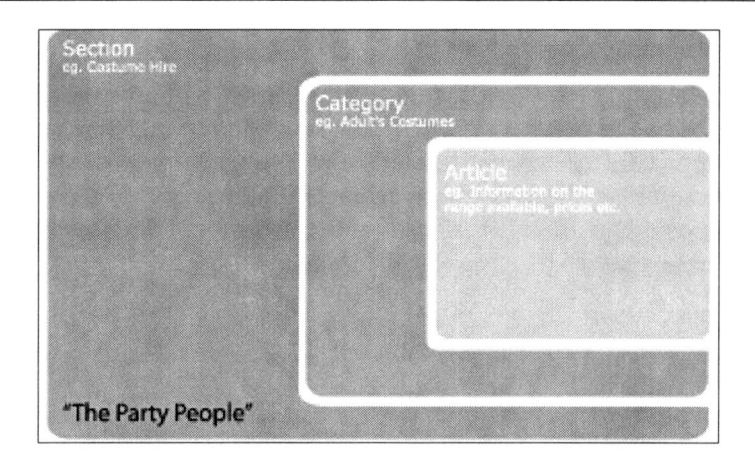

Understanding Sections, Categories, and Articles

To access the individual manager screen for **Sections**, **Categories**, or **Articles**, use either the Control Panel icons, or go to **Content | Section Manager | Category Manager | Article Manager** from the menu.

Using the **Section Manager** as a guide, we can edit and manage all the **Sections** created for your site. Double clicking the name of the section provides access to the details.

Use the icons on the toolbar to create a new **Section**, delete an existing one, or publish/unpublish them.

The **Category Manager** and the **Article Manager** are accessed the same way.

Within the Party People website, there are five **Sections**, each with at least two **Categories** within them. Articles are then created and allocated to each depending on their content.

When your developer established your site, he/she would have created a Section and a Category for the content to be allocated. Chapter 2, *Creating, Editing, and Organizing Content* looks at this in a detailed manner when we create and allocate content to **Sections** and **Categories**.

What are uncategorized articles?

Articles generally used for content that is not associated with any particular Section or Category are saved as uncategorized. They are content items that are used in certain locations, where the content remains the same and doesn't require user input or regular updates. Content that requires updating regularly and may include enabling a user to add comments is allocated to a category. For example, a "Welcome to the Site" message may be listed as a static item.

Site wide settings

So that your site performs as intended, there were a number of important operational (or system configuration) settings established by the developer during the setup phase. These settings include how often the site cache files are cleansed and whether users can register on your site or not.

Leave it to the experts

The **Global Configuration** screen can only be accessed by users with Super Administrator access and presents all the fundamental settings required to ensure that your site runs smoothly. It can be accessed from the Control Panel or the site menu: **Site | Global Configuration**.

Having said this however, it is best to leave any changes to this section to your web developer.

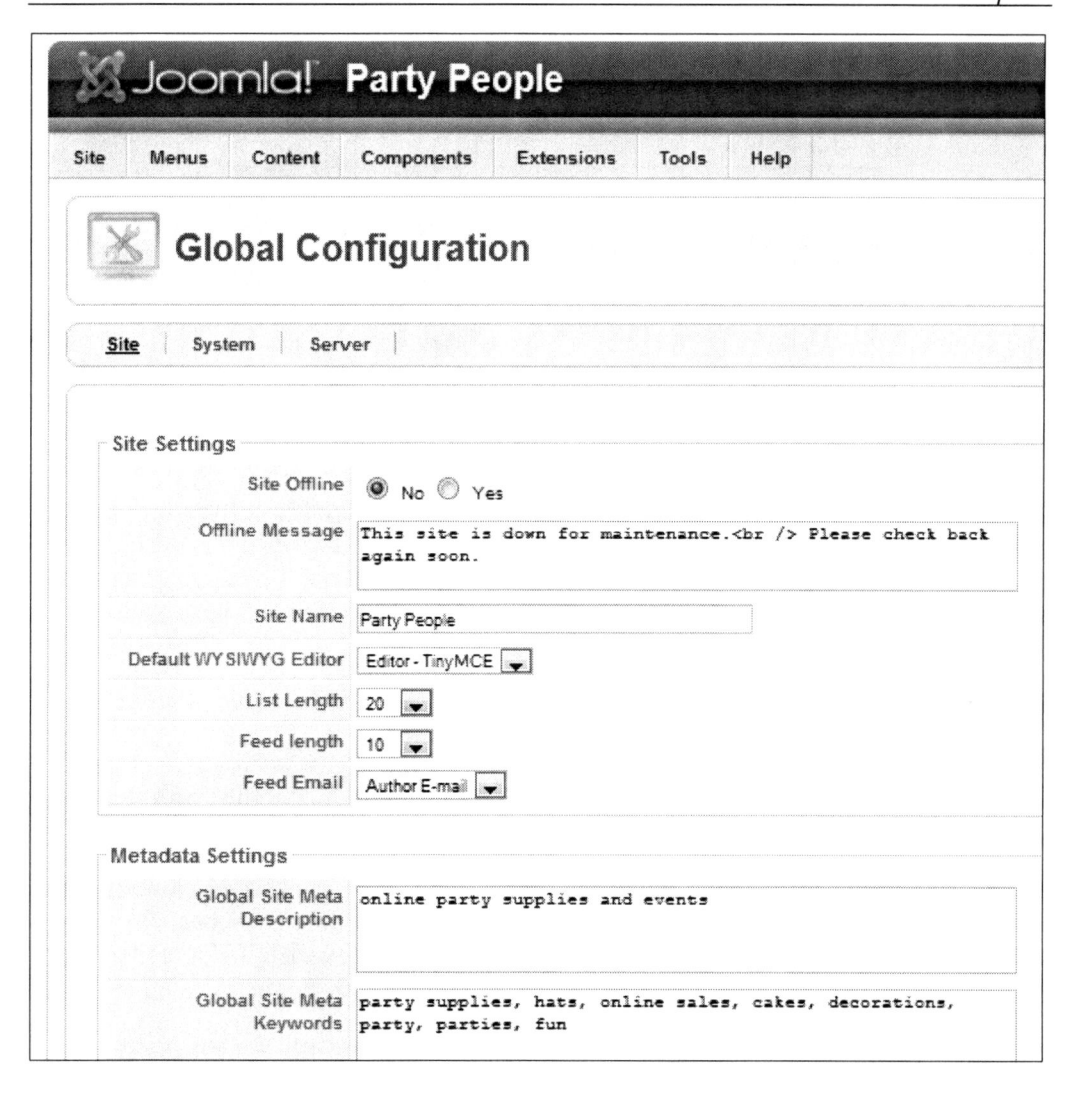

There are three tabs within the **Configuration** screen: **Site**, **System** and **Server**. All of the settings within have been set up by your developer and should be left as they are. If they are changed, the front and backend of the site may go offline or some of its functionality will be affected. Approach with extreme caution if you are not familiar with any of these settings.

Outside the scope of the previous screenshot, which shows the three sections within the **Global Configuration**, within the **Site** section there is also the **SEO Settings**, seen in the following screenshot:

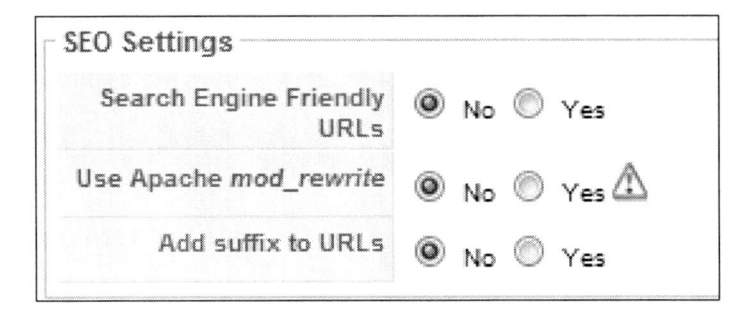

```
SEO Settings
         Search Engine Friendly   ◉ No   ○ Yes
                          URLs
         Use Apache mod_rewrite   ◉ No   ○ Yes ⚠
             Add suffix to URLs   ◉ No   ○ Yes
```

These settings were established by your developer and should be left as they are. Enabling settings that are set to **No** without some in-depth technical knowledge of .htaccess among other things will most likely result in the incorrect presentation of your site.

Overview of the extensions

Similar to the way Sections, Categories, and Articles are organized, your website operates around a hierarchy of extensions that add to the functionality and the presentation of your site.

A number of key Components, Modules, and Plugins were applied when your site was initially installed and customized. Some work behind the scenes ensuring your website operates as it should, whereas others may have been installed in order to customize your site for your target audience.

Beyond these three types of extensions, there are others to cover the templates applied to your site and the languages it presents information in. These extensions are beyond the scope of what we need to cover here and their management should be left in the hands of your website developer.

Chapter 8, *Menus, Modules, and Components* works through the updating and editing of a number of popular and core Components, Modules, and Plugins, whereas in this chapter we just identify them for you.

Components

Being the most sophisticated extension, Components provide a specialized functional element and are mostly displayed within the main body of the website, that is within the middle column. They include features such as the **Contacts** page, **Advertising Banners**, a **Web Links** list or possibly an image gallery, or a **Web Poll**. The following screenshot shows how the **Contacts** section of the **Party People** website sits in the middle of the layout.

All components can be managed from the **Components** link on the menu bar.

Modules

These are smaller extensions that generally appear in the header, footer, or side columns. They may also work with a particular **Component** to extend its capabilities. There are a number of core modules installed behind the scenes that are required to make your site work, but there are also some modules included that may be activated on your site to present a **News Flash** feature or a **Most Read Content** display. The following screenshot shows the main menu and **Login Form** modules enabled on the Party People website.

All modules can be managed from the **Modules** link on the menu bar.

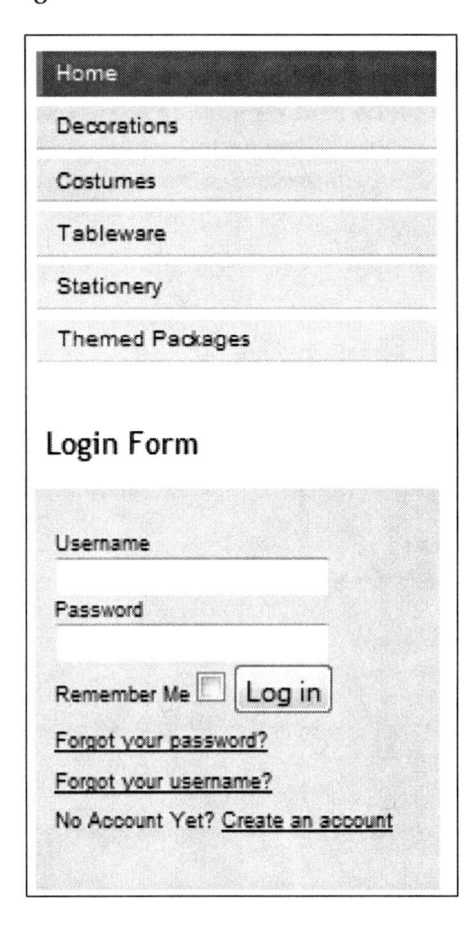

Plugins

Smaller again and task related, Plugins offer behind the scenes functionality. They intercept information from the code of a web page and manipulate it so that the information is presented correctly. The installation of a video feed from YouTube, or, as the following screenshot illustrates, a plugin that changes the link to the administration login address will be covered in Chapter 7, *Security – Recovery and Precaution* on security.

Plugin: [Edit]	

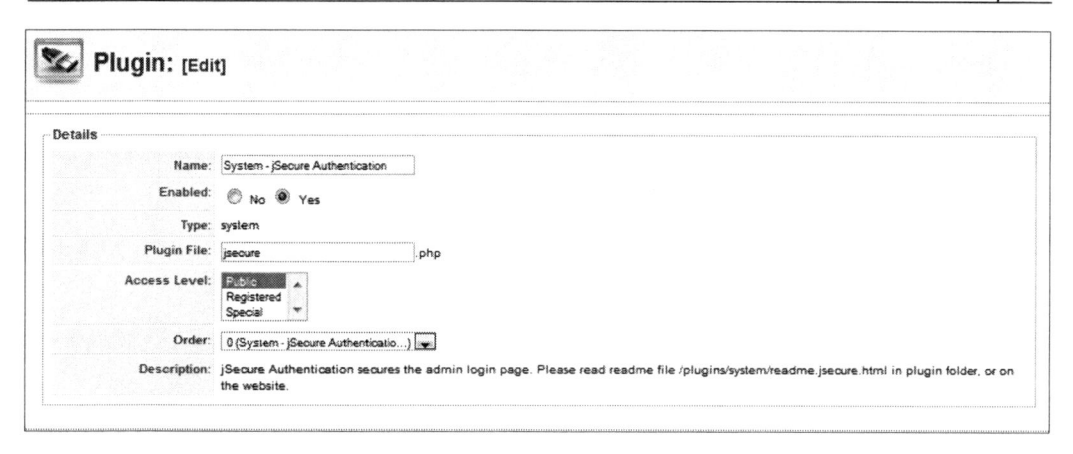

Details

Name:	System - jSecure Authentication
Enabled:	○ No ● Yes
Type:	system
Plugin File:	jsecure .php
Access Level:	Public / Registered / Special
Order:	0 (System - jSecure Authenticatio...)
Description:	jSecure Authentication secures the admin login page. Please read readme file /plugins/system/readme.jsecure.html in plugin folder, or on the website.

This is how part of the plugin parameters appear in the administration interface. The **jSecure Authentication** plugin is an example of a system plugin that operates in the background of your site.

Summary

Accessing the administration area of your new website can be a little intimidating at first, but once you make yourself familiar with the navigation and how your content is organized, things get a lot easier.

It is important to remember that access to the Control Panel and the Global Configuration are privileged and changes should only be made by users who you are confident have the necessary knowledge.

Understanding the structure of your site allows you to manage and edit your content, and we'll refer to the Party People website through the book to illustrate how you can get things done.

2
Creating, Editing, and Organizing Content

The content of a website is what drives users to visit it in the first instance and keeping them coming back is the key to a successful website. Content should be written for its intended audience and delivered in a well presented and easy-to-read layout. Writing and presenting content for the Web is different from writing for printed material, and this chapter addresses a number of ways content editors can do this successfully. The Wired magazines website (`http://www.wired.com/`) recently won a "Webby Award" for the exceptional quality of its editing/copyediting. If you want to know more about The Webby Awards, take a look at their Wikipedia page at `http://en.wikipedia.org/wiki/Webby_Awards`. They award exceptional websites within categories.

Articles are an important part of the Joomla! website framework as they present the various items of news and information a user seeks. They contain text and multimedia like images, videos, and audio files and updating them is a relatively simple process.

The article editing application within Joomla!'s administration framework is a simple text editing application referred to as a **WYSIWYG** editor. Basically, **What You See Is What You Get** because the editor shows content creators how the new material will look as it is being developed.

The Article Manager provides the central point of access to managing the articles, the presentation of which can be filtered to show only articles of a certain nature, such as published articles.

Articles can be created from the front or backend of a site, depending on the user group the creator belongs to. Authors are allowed to create and edit their own Articles from the frontend of the site and must log in to do so. Refer to Chapter 5, *User Management* for more information on user groups.

Other users are given access to the backend and will be registered as a Manager, Administrator, or the Super Administrator. The role of a Manager or an Administrator is assumed for the purpose of creating and editing content as the website owner and content editor.

In this chapter we'll look at:

- General tips for writing well for the Web
- Making your frontpage engaging
- How to use the Article Manager
- How to add content for approval as a frontend only editor

General tips on writing content for the Web

Writing an Article for a website isn't the same as writing printed material; in fact, around half the number of words works best for online content. Website users are looking for specific information and want to find it quickly, so don't make them work for it; otherwise, they will go elsewhere.

There are many theories and guidelines on writing for the web. This list covers some of the general principles for new website content for editors to work with:

- Keep the writing style succinct and to the point. Use links to external websites or other pages, if necessary, to further build an understanding of the point.
- Know the target audience—who they are and what they are looking for on the website. Make sure the content suits the audience.
- Avoid jargon, unless the target audience knows the language.
- Use short, eye-catching headings that have meaning outside their context. Headings break up the information and make reading quick and easy. Use subheadings and bullet points for easy scanning.
- Website readers mostly scan a page rather than ponder over each word. Use bold formatting on keywords so that they stand out.
- Make the first sentence your topic for the paragraph. Don't include any more than one topic per paragraph.
- Avoid metaphors unless it's a complicated subject being communicated to a general audience. Explaining a metaphor and then explaining its relevance, means more words.

- Don't forget to proofread! Nothing turns away a potential customer faster than a hastily edited article. Poor spelling and grammar makes a site appear unprofessional and creates an impression of untrustworthiness.
- Don't plagiarize other people's work. Instead, quote or reference something you are referring to and perhaps use it as an opportunity to set up a reciprocal link, which helps with search engine ranking—more on this in Chapter 6, *Making Your Site Popular*.
- Keep the formatting of your text simple. Make the headings stand out from the body of the text by making them slightly larger and bolder. Avoid using italics for large portions of text, as it is harder to read.
- Use the article title and headings within as a way to assist with search engine optimization. Name your article titles succinctly (you don't have to display them on the page—more on this in Chapter 6, *Making Your Site Popular*).
- The first sentence of your article is also important, not only for assisting with search engine rankings, but also to make the reader want to continue reading.

A note on copyright

Copyright is an important factor when considering content for your website, whether it's written material or an image you have found that perfectly suits your needs. To put it briefly, using other people's work without reference or their permission and/or claiming it as your own constitutes copyright infringement.

You can avoid copyright infringement by:

- Approaching the owner of the material and requesting their written permission to use it in your website. Potentially, if you request permission, you may gain a new reciprocal link to and from your site at the same time.
- Including a link to the original work and its source. The Creative Commons website (`http://www.creativecommons.org`) is a great source of information around copyright and using the content of others. The site explains what the Creative Commons project is and the rules around using and editing other people's work, when they have licensed their work under Creative Commons. The website has a number of easy-to-use tools and links to download copyright badges.

Creating, Editing, and Organizing Content

Making your home page engaging

The front page of your website should be considered one of, if not the most important section of your site. As a an example, the Adidas site (`http://www.adidas.com/au/homepage.asp`) also won a Webby Award recently for its exceptional home page design.

The content within the home page screen "real estate" sets the tone and all-important first impression of your online presence. Not only should it load quickly, the content within should be up-to-date and reflect the interests of your visitors.

The following are some general guidelines to help you in deciding what content should appear on your home page:

- Include any recent developments or good news up front. Have you won an award or received some kind of accolade that will enhance your visitor's perception of you and/or your organization? Include copy on the details and an image to accompany it—perhaps a photo or a logo—with a link behind it to another website.
- Include any new information about a relevant topic that is related to your industry, profession, or interests.
- Add recent comments from your forum users. Positive and negative comments can be used as a means of conveying information. For example, is there a contentious issue around your area? Use any posts around this to address the topic yourself as the moderator and clear up any misconceptions.
- Visually engaging material always works. Consider a slideshow or short video to capture your visitor's attention and get them interested.
- Include a **Read More** link to the most often accessed content on your site.

The content on your home page can be managed through either the link on the top menu, **Content | Front Page Manager,** which also includes the **Article Manager,** or the icon on the control panel interface, as shown in the following screenshot:

Now that we have some ideas about what to include in our content, let's look at using the **Article Manager** in the **Party People** website to build some new content.

The Article Manager

The **Article Manager** screen located within the Administration section is the place to manage all of the Articles within your Joomla! website. The specifications of each Article are laid out in columns to make it easy to sort them, which is especially useful when there are many.

Creating, Editing, and Organizing Content

The following screenshot shows the overall layout and the contextual toolbar at the top right, which also assists you with managing your Articles in the broad sense. You can also filter the display of Articles using the parameters within the drop-down menus.

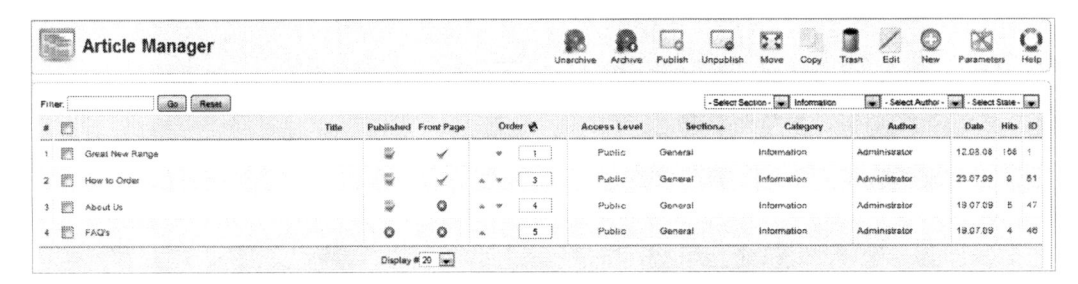

Filtering the display of Articles

Above the main table of Article parameters there are four drop-down menus that allow you to filter the Articles you can see in one view. This is especially helpful when trying to find a particular Article if you have a large number of them.

To use the filter options, you can select one or more of the filter options.

We'll filter the Party People Article Manager to retrieve only published Articles within the **Costumes** category, within the **Products** section.

1. Navigate to the **Article Manager** through the top menu or by clicking the icon on the Control Panel.

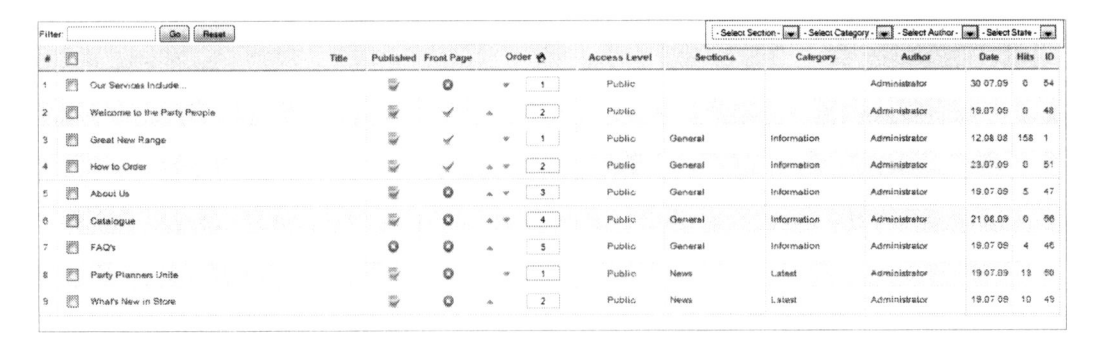

2. Open the **Section** drop-down menu and select **Products**. From the **Category** drop-down selection, click **Costumes**. Making these selections automatically updates the display.

[26]

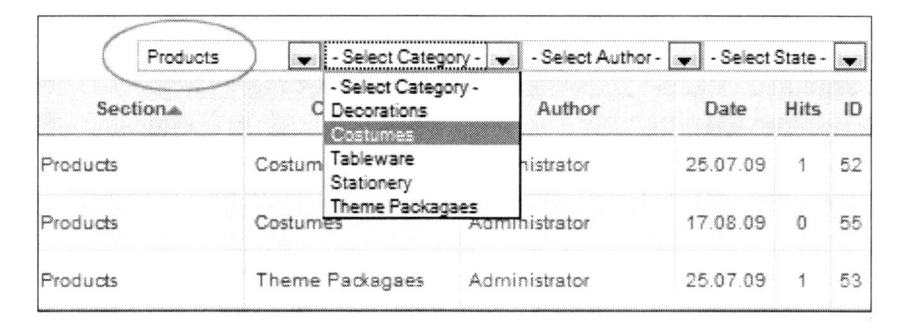

3. Open the **Select State** drop-down menu and choose **Published**. Here, we can now see the filtered display:

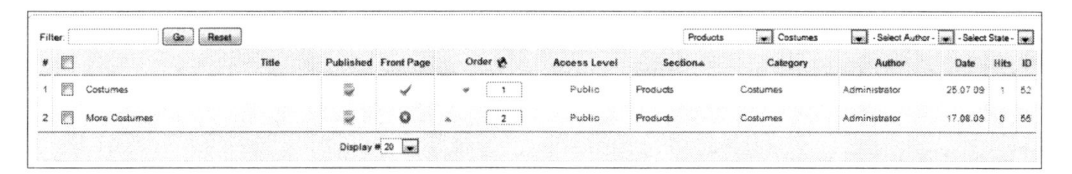

Column headings

As we can see, the Article Manager lists all of the Articles in rows. You can order the Article listing by clicking the column values (headings). Here, we have clicked the **Front Page** column heading to display those Articles appearing on the front page at the top of the list.

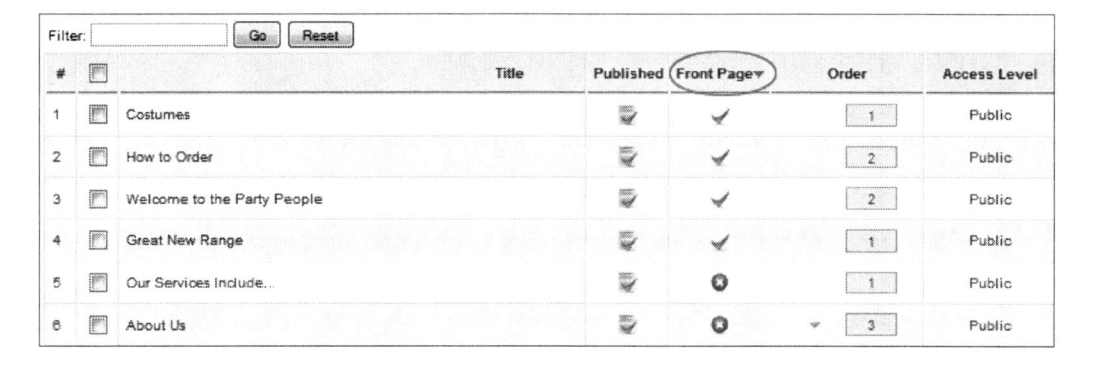

Each of the column values has its own parameters. They are as follows:

- **Published**: A green tick means that article is currently published; a red cross means it's unpublished. Click the tick or cross to change its state.
- **Front Page**: It indicates whether the Article appears on the front page or not.
- **Order**: This shows the order in which to display the Articles. The list can be sorted by this column. Changing the order here can affect the Article display order on a page of the website. To change the order either click on the arrows or enter numbers in sequential order and click the disk icon to save the new order.
- **Access Level**: This reveals who has access to this Article. **Public** means it is seen on the site; if set to registered, then only registered users of the site have access.

The **Section**, **Category**, and **Author** columns are self explanatory.

The toolbar

The icons at the top right toolbar provide access to the general functions associated with maintaining and presenting Articles. To use these functions in relation to a particular Article, select the checkbox next to the Article title.

Archive and unarchive Articles

Articles that are no longer current can be archived, rather than "trashing" them in case you want to refer to them at a later stage. To archive an Article:

1. Select the Article no longer required using the checkbox next to its title.
2. Click the **Archive** icon. The Article still appears in the list, but has been archived and listed as published.

    You can then use the **State** drop-down filter to only show published or unpublished Articles.

To reinstate an Article:

1. Click the checkbox next to the archived Article.
2. Click the **Unarchive** icon on the toolbar. The Article is listed as unpublished, so you will need to click the red cross icon in the **Published** column.

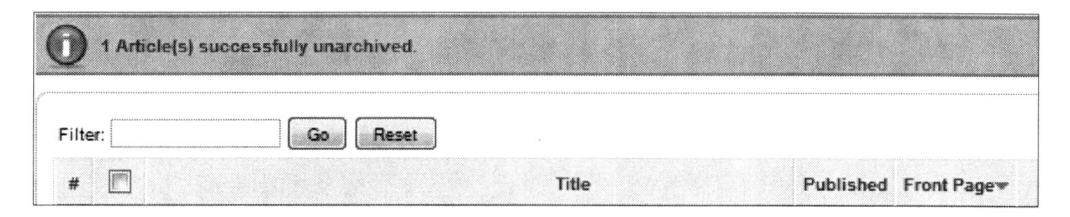

Publish and unpublish an Article

These buttons provide another way to publish and unpublish your articles. You can also click the icons in the **Published** column in the Article row.

Move or copy an Article

If you want to move the Article into a new **Section** or **Category**:

1. Select the Article and click the **Move** icon on the toolbar.
2. Select the new **Section/Category** and click **Save**.

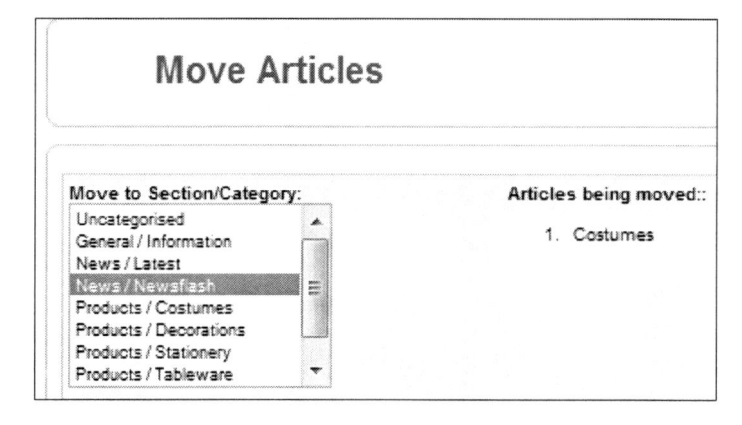

To copy an Article into another **Section/Category**, follow the same steps, but select the **Copy** button.

Trashing an Article

If you have one or more Articles to trash, select them and click the **Trash** button. To restore an Article, navigate to the **Trash Manager**:

Select **Content | Article Trash** from the top menu.

To restore a trashed Article, select the **Trash Manager**, then click the **Restore** button.

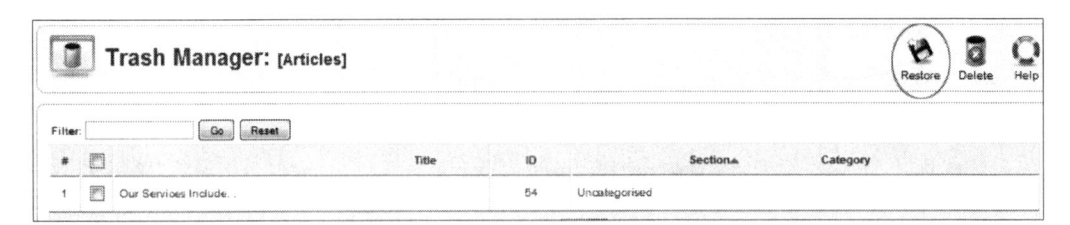

Edit, New, and Parameters

These three buttons relate to the management of your Articles.

You can use the **Edit** button to open an article and edit it.

Use the **New** button to generate a new Article, while the **Parameters** button allows you to set the general default settings for all your Articles. A pop-up **Global Configuration** window opens, as seen in the following screenshot:

Select any of these items to make a feature of your Article appear by selecting the **Show** radio button. Select **Hide** if that element should not be displayed.

Creating, Editing, and Organizing Content

The following screenshot shows what the **Home** page Article of the Party People website looks like with some of these elements set to **Show**. You might notice that things can start to look a bit cluttered if you have too many options showing. It's best to show only what you really need here.

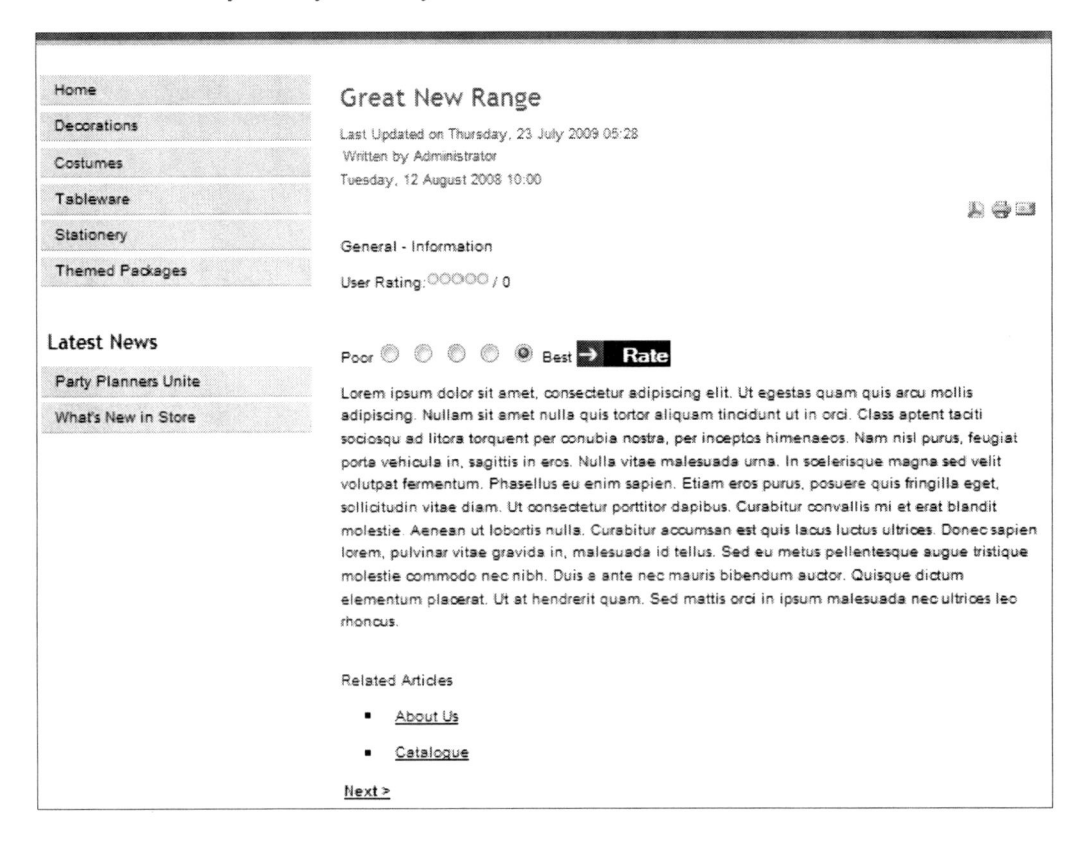

So, now that we know how to locate Articles using the Article Manager, let's look at managing them, including editing and creating new ones.

Editing an existing Article using the text editor

Editing an Article within Joomla! is similar to working on a document within a word processing environment. The core Joomla! installation comes with a standard text editor; however, there are a number of other editors that can be installed to assist you in your Article writing/editing and formatting. One such component is the JCE WYSIWG text editor which we will look at later in this chapter in the "Using the JCE text editor" section.

[32]

Opening the Article

- To open an Article, double-click the title within the Article Manager.
- The editing screen displays the details of the Article—its **Title**, **Alias,** and the **Section** and **Category** it belongs to. Unless the Article should be moved or displayed on the front page if it's not already, then leave them as they are.

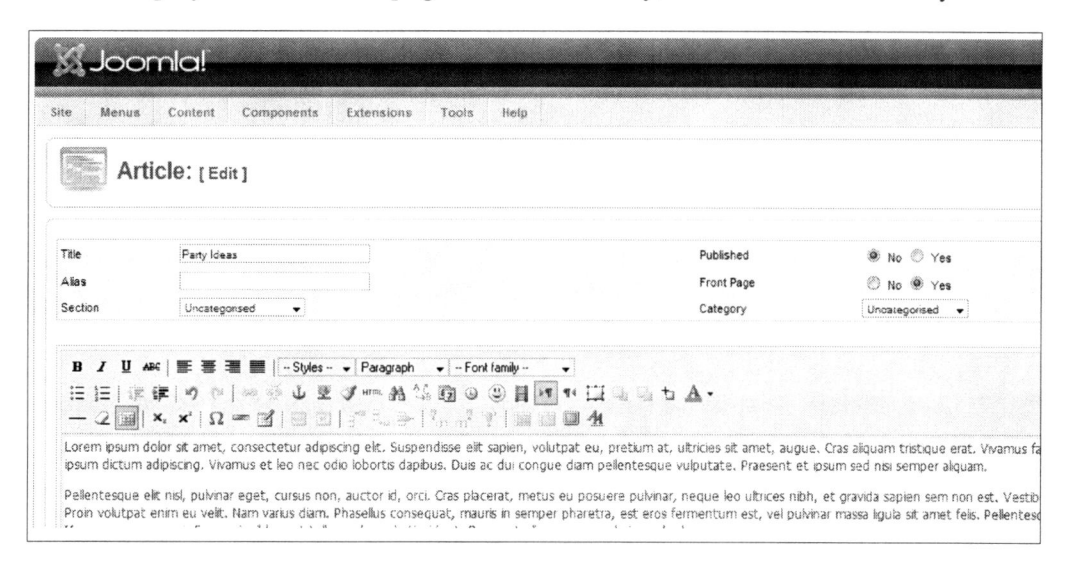

Editing the Article

The text editing section displays the formatting options and the text for editing.

Within the text editor highlight the relevant section and edit your new material. Apply formatting—bold, italics, underlining, paragraph justification, bullet points, and numbering, as required.

There are also a number of preset styles for headings to choose from. They are similar to a word processing package and the icons for each should be familiar. There is also an option to add a table, which is covered later in this chapter.

> **A Word of Caution!**
>
> Copying and pasting text directly from a word processing package into this editing screen can cause the text to format itself in an undesirable way and the ability to edit HTML code is required to correct it.
>
> To avoid this, type the original text in a plain text editor application such as Notepad, then copy and paste it from there. Apart from this, it's not a bad idea to keep a backup copy of the material anyway. Also the JCE text editor has a button that allows editors to copy and paste directly from Word, which is covered in this chapter under "Using the JCE text editor".

Once the new content is ready, preview the changes before you commit it to the site, by clicking the **Preview** button at the top right-hand side of the interface.

If all is okay, click the **Apply** button to save your work and stay at the article editing screen to make further changes. If the edit is complete, save the new version using the **Save** button to save your changes and return to the Article Manager.

Closing the Article without a preview or without saving means the changes made to the content are lost.

On the right side of the editing screen, you can reset the number of hits to the Article to zero using the **Reset** button, to indicate how many views there have been (as your edit).

When you have finished editing, click the **Close** button, returning you to the main **Article Manager** screen.

Creating a new Article

Adding new content to a website is important to keep it interesting for the target audience—and, more importantly, it keeps them coming back! Creating a new Article is a good way to add new information while retaining the earlier Articles, which can be unpublished to make room within the existing framework.

Chapter 2

Adding text

The following steps show how to add text:

1. Click the **New** button within the Article Manager.
2. Type in an Article **Title**, remembering that it may appear on the site (depending on the global settings), so name it something relevant or interesting. Leave the **Alias** name blank, as Joomla! does this automatically.
3. Decide whether the Article should appear on the front page or not and then allocate it to an existing **Section** or leave it as unallocated. Select a **Category**, or if the section is uncategorized, this will automatically be completed as uncategorized. The following screenshot illustrates an uncategorized Article, published to the home page of the Party People website.

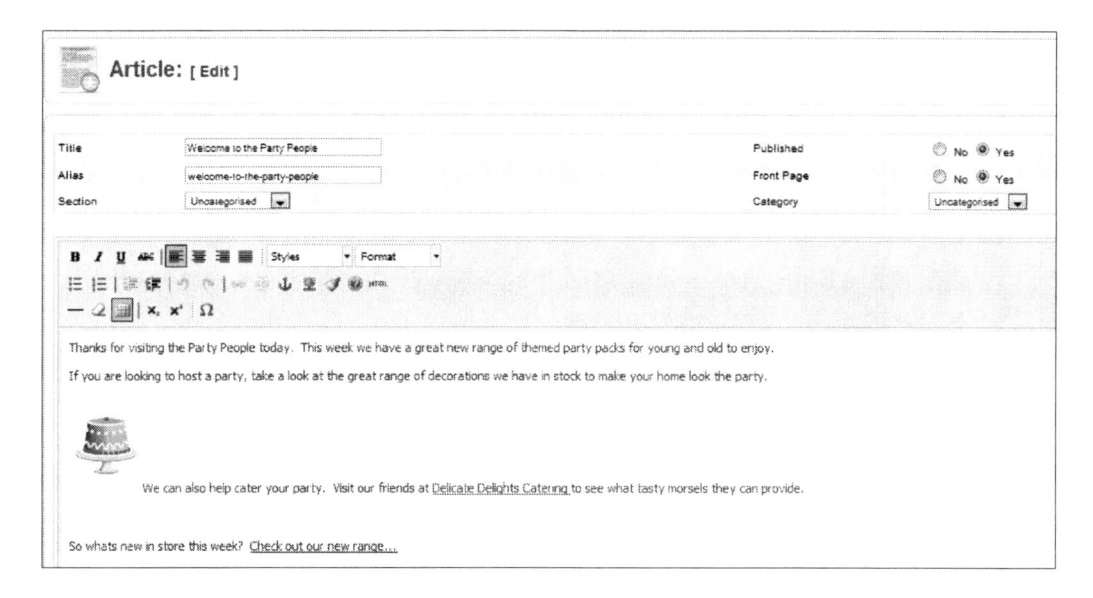

Adding a table to an Article

Within the text editor, a table can be applied to the Article page to assist with the layout of information. Consider using a table to section content so it's easier to read or scan quickly.

1. Click inside the text editing screen or select the **Insert New Table** icon.

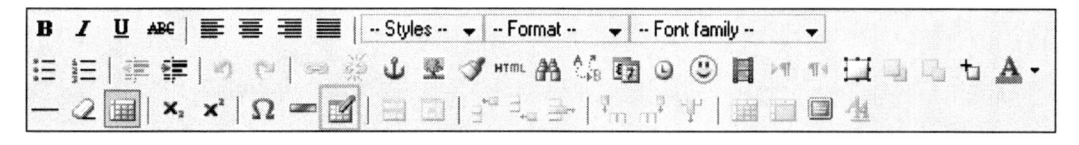

[35]

Creating, Editing, and Organizing Content

2. A dialog box opens requesting details of the table such as the number of columns and rows required, which can be altered later if necessary.

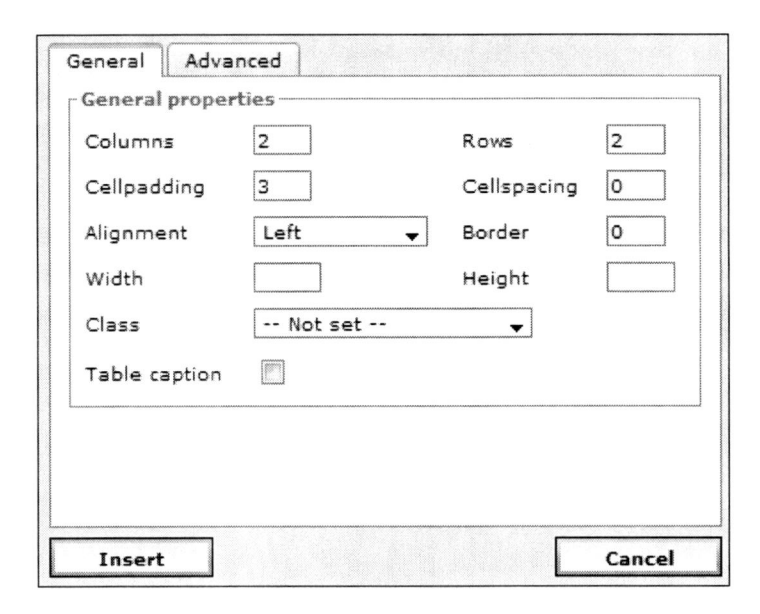

Add cell padding and cell spacing if the content should sit away from the inside edge of the table perimeter.

Set the **Alignment** to **Left**, **Centre**, or **Justify**, depending on where the table should sit within the framework of the page.

Add a **Border** to define the content of the table so that it stands out; usually one pixel will do.

Leave the **Width**, **Height**, and **Class** blank. These dimensions will be filled based on the amount of content you place within each cell of the table.

3. Click **Insert** to apply the table.

Now you can go ahead and add content to the table cells as you would in a Word processing environment. The cells are the blank spaces within each row and column.

Also, you can copy and paste a table into another area of your Article and replace the cell contents. This means you don't have to create a new table and its dimensions will be consistent with the previous table, important for consistency in presentation. Readers rely on order and consistency when reading content, as it helps them with locating information.

Breaking up Article content

If the Article turns out to be longer than anticipated, consider adding an introduction to it on the main category page for the section or the home page, with a **Read More** link to access and read the body of the Article on another page.

Adding a Read More link

Let's add a **Read More** link to a Party People Article.

1. Type the complete article; then after the first paragraph, place the cursor at the end of the paragraph (or at the beginning of the next).
2. Click the **Read More** button located at the bottom of the text editor. A line will appear between the two paragraphs within the text editor.

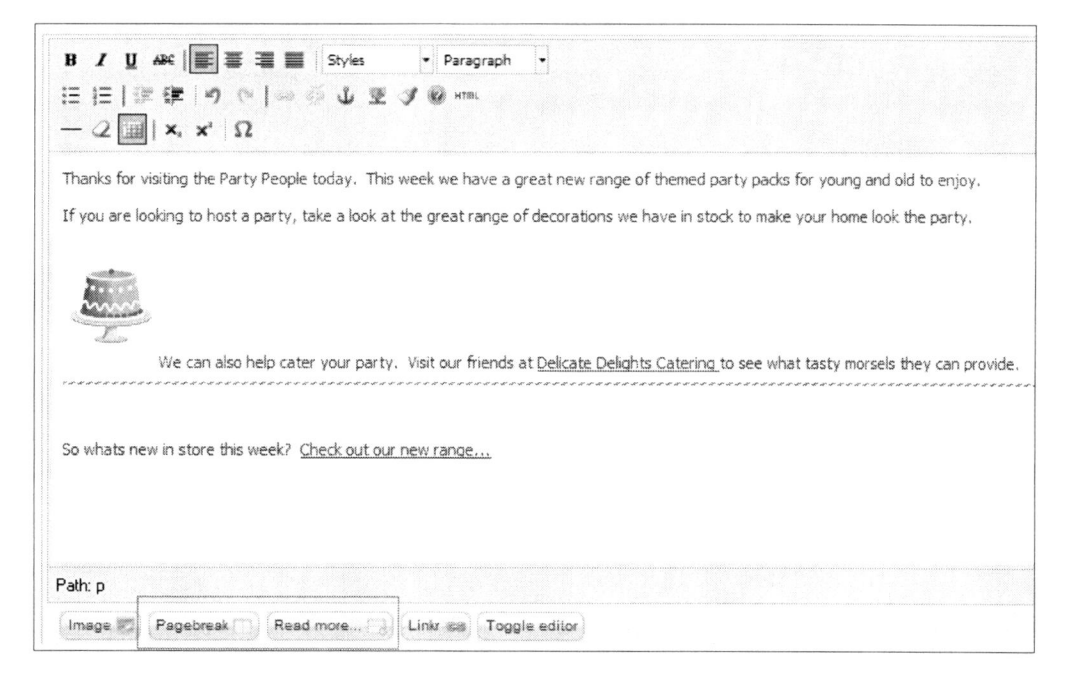

As you can see, the home page of our site is now updated with the "Welcome to the Party People" Article which includes a **Read More** link.

If your target audience is into some serious reading, say you're publishing part of a report or a journal, a long Article can be broken into several pages using the page break function.

Adding a page break

Page breaks provide navigation within the Article itself, using **Next** and **Previous** links. Think about where to insert the page break—following a complete heading or subject area works well.

Adding a page break is similar to including a **Read More** link. The button to use can be seen in the previous screenshot.

Within your Article text editor, execute the following steps:

1. Place the cursor at the end of a paragraph and click the **Page Break** button located at the bottom of the text editor.
2. A dialog box appears to enter a title for the new page (say page 2). The **Table of Contents** field is optional and can display the contents for the page when it is a multipage Article.
3. Click **Insert Page Break**.
4. From the frontend of the site your table of contents is presented as a small box to the upper right of the article and contains links to the different pages. Its appearance is determined by the site style template.
5. When you access the site from the backend, you can publish Articles immediately. Once the Article has been edited and is ready for publication on the site, the Article parameters can be set or checked.

Using the JCE text editor

This is a very useful component that can be downloaded from the developer's website at `http://www.joomlacontenteditor.net/`, which is embedded within the Article editing framework and allows you to add new elements to your text and offers some useful tools to assist with the development of your Articles. The screenshot shows how it appears with the Article editing screen. If you can see any of these icons, then its already installed. If not, then you can download the package from the website and install it yourself, following the instructions given in Chapter 8, *Menus, Modules, and Components*.

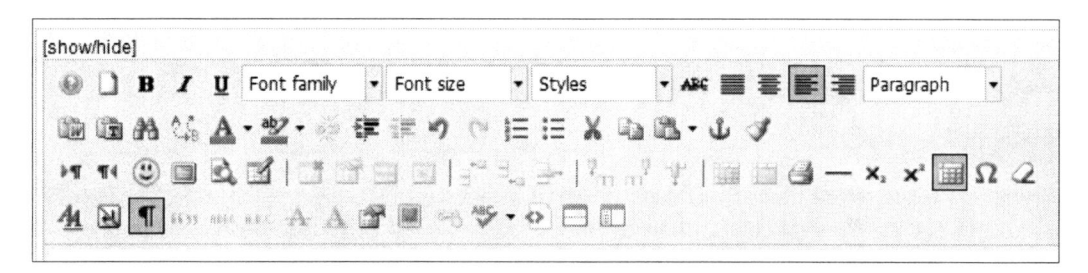

The icons within the core text editor are accompanied by some extra icons offering tools such as:

- **Paste from Word**: This allows you to copy the text taken from Microsoft Word and paste it into your Article, without any extra HTML tags (which can affect the formatting of your text on the website).
- **Search and Replace**: This allows you to find and replace a word or phrase.
- **Choose a Text Color**: You can change the color of your text to highlight certain keywords or phrases. Don't go overboard with this one though, you could end up with a patchwork effect if there are too many colors.
- **Select a Background Color**: You can add a background color behind your text to highlight certain areas. Just select the text and click the icon.
- **Emoticons**: You can add them to your content as you would in a text message.
- **Toggle Fullscreen Mode**: Allows you to make the text editor consume the whole screen rather than a small portion, which is good if you are vision impaired.
- **Code Edit**: If you're familiar with the code behind your content, you can edit it here within an interface similar to other, more comprehensive code editing software.
- **Edit the CSS**: The **CSS** is the **Cascading Style Sheet** your site refers to in order to present your site with the colors and layout it does. Be cautious when changing this one as stylesheets are part of the site template structure.

Any of these extra functions can be used to enhance the appearance of your content or make your writing more efficient.

Authorization and publishing from the frontend

Frontend users must have their new content approved by a user with a higher level of access before the Article can be published. Users with only frontend access can edit their material by logging in using the Login panel (a special module enabled).

Adding content for approval through frontend access

While Chapter 5, *User Management* covers user management in detail, you can create a user account for a content editor who only submits content from the frontend of the site, never having access to any of the information in the backend.

The Party People website has a frontend-only Author called **FrontEditor**, as shown in the following screenshot. We'll show you how that user creates content by logging in through the frontend of the site and how the **Super Administrator** publishes it.

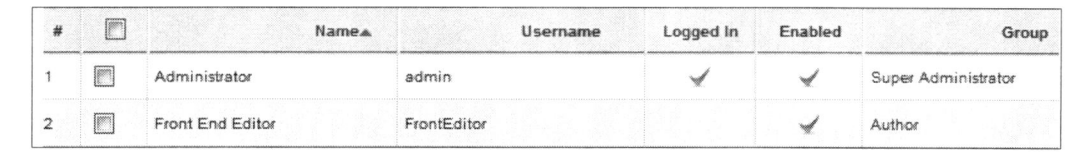

#		Name▲	Username	Logged In	Enabled	Group
1		Administrator	admin	✓	✓	Super Administrator
2		Front End Editor	FrontEditor		✓	Author

The first step is to log in as **FrontEditor** using the **Login** module on the home page.

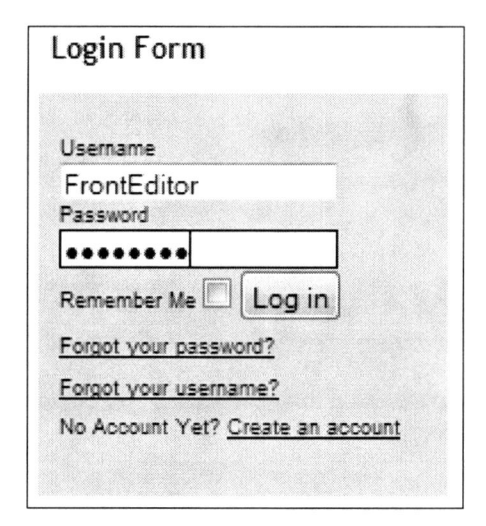

Having logged in, the user can edit the user details or submit an Article or a weblink to the site, if you have that component enabled.

To submit an Article from the frontend

Follow these steps to submit your Article from the frontend:

1. Click the **Submit an Article** link to display the Article editing screen within the frontend interface.
2. Type in a **Title** for the Article and add the content using the text editor. We have installed the JCE text editor to our administration configuration. This is a useful component that offers a broader range of content editing options.

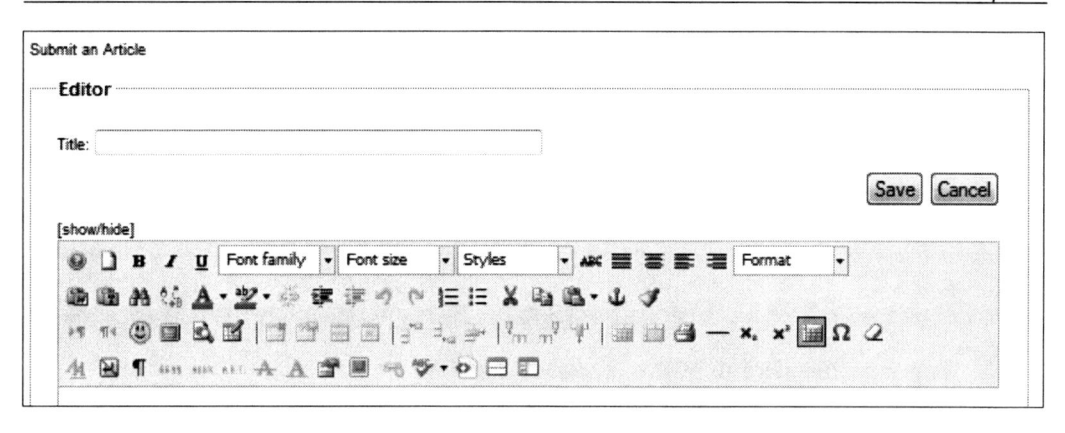

3. Scroll further down the page to enter the **Publishing** parameters and the **Metadata** information. Chapter 6, *Making Your Site Popular,* on search engine optimization outlines some useful ideas on generating words and phrases for this section.

   The sections and categories established for the site will be included in the drop-down menus.

4. Save your content and a message appears:

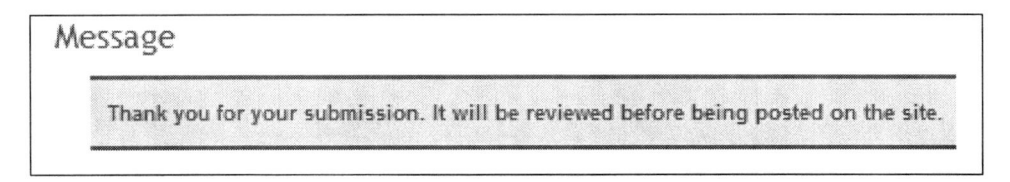

> Message
>
> Thank you for your submission. It will be reviewed before being posted on the site.

Now that a new Article has been submitted, the Super Administrator will approve it:

1. Log into the administration panel of the site.
2. Navigate to the **Article Manager** where the new Article appears in the list, marked as unpublished.

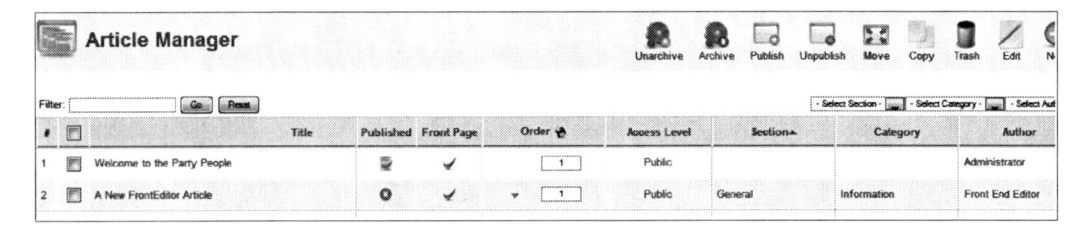

3. Click to open the Article and review its contents.
4. Publish the Article by clicking the **Publish** icon or the checkbox next to it and the **Publish** button on the top toolbar.

Further, the Super Administrator will also have a message in his/her inbox advising about the new Article.

What are Article parameters?

Articles also contain information to identify them and the content within them. This information can be changed and can include a range of options as seen in the following screenshot:

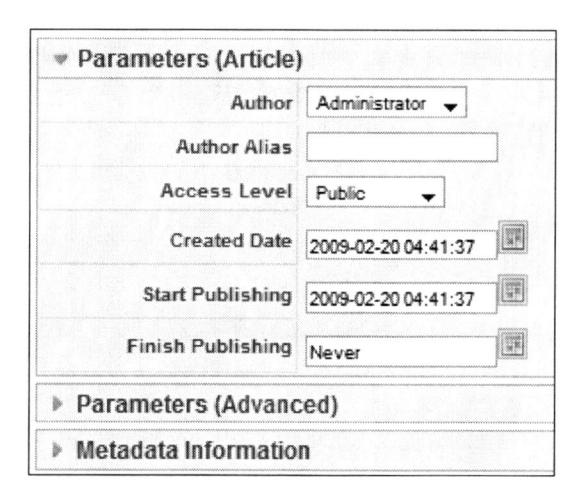

- **Author**: The Author is by default the current user, but can be changed to another.
- **Author Alias**: A different Author can be allocated to the Article, if required.
- **Access Level**:
    - **Public**: Everyone who can see the site can read this Article.
    - **Registered**: Only registered users can view the Article.
    - **Special**: Only those users with Author status or higher are given access.

   These levels mean the Article can be published for a range of audiences and the Article levels can be changed by opening the drop-down menu to reveal the choices.
- **Created Date**: Defaults to the current date, however, this can be changed by clicking on the calendar icon to change this.
- **Start Publishing**: The date and time to commence publishing the Article, which means the Article can be created and set to be published from that date. It will then appear automatically when scheduled.
- **Finish Publishing**: The date and time to finish publishing the Article. This can be set to change the content to an unpublished state at a future date and time.

The advanced parameters—but only if you really have to!

All of these parameters would have been established by the website developer, but can be overridden here.

If the parameter is set to **Use Global,** then the setting has been established from the **Global Configuration** or the Menu item itself. They can be changed by selecting from the drop-down menu for each item.

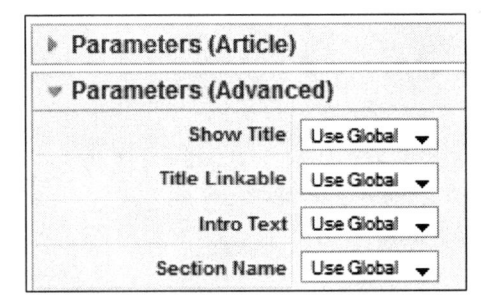

Metadata information is what search engines like

Metadata is information about the Article which is not displayed on the frontend of the site, but it makes it easier for search engines to classify its content in their ranking. The entries here are optional and information can be entered.

A detailed outline on how to generate and add keywords and descriptions to make your content more search-engine friendly is covered in Chapter 6, *Making Your Site Popular*.

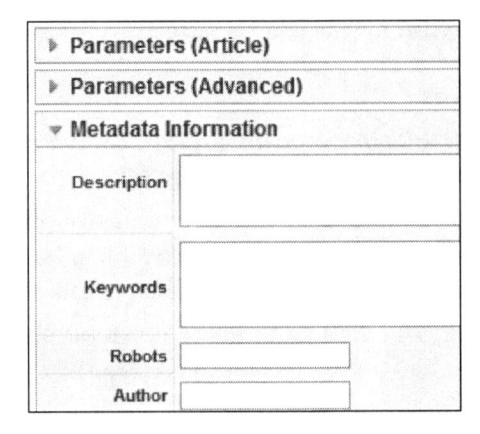

- **Metadata Description**: A brief description of the Article.
- **Metadata Keywords**: Individual tags to describe the content of your Article, which must be enclosed in quotation marks and separated by commas (for example, "clowns" or "pony rides"). They can be upper or lowercase and both match, that is, "CIRCUS" matches "circus."
- **Robots**: Software that browses the Internet and catalogs content from websites. You may not need to be concerned with this, but the option to include tags is here as well.
- **Author**: An option to add the name of the **Author**'s with the metadata. This is useful if any of your Authors has a profile of a well-known writer.

Summary

The old adage that "content is king" is true when it comes to giving your website users what they want. The more the interest in your content, the more likely you are to increase your hit rate, which can lead to better sales opportunities or advertising on your site.

In this chapter, we have learnt how to write some solid content for your Articles, with consideration for copyright and how to make your home page interesting. We also accessed the Article Manager and used it to manage our content, including creating new Articles and managing existing ones.

The next chapter covers applying videos and images to your Articles, which can add a whole new dimension to the level of engagement your users have with your site.

Managing Images and Videos

Images and videos are a great way to attract interest in a website. Also, when they are used in the right way, they can make an impact where text alone can't (not just in terms of aesthetics, but conveying a message quickly and with impact). Communicating visually with your users means that you can convey a theme or message about yourself or your organization without the need to write any text.

Videos can be prepared quickly using digital cameras and edited and uploaded using many free and low budget software applications, those that often come bundled within your computer's operating system. Photos can easily be retouched and cropped using high end and free software applications and applied to your articles with little fuss. The same applies to audio files as well.

The **Media Manager** within the administration interface allows you to update the visual and audio content of your website to give it a fresh appeal. New content will always be welcomed by your users and is one of the reasons for them to keep coming back.

In this chapter, we'll look at the following:

- Accessing and using the Media Manager to upload image and media files
- The various image and video file formats, what is available, and what you should know about them
- Uploading and managing image and video files
- Managing a Simple Image Gallery and videos played with the AllVideos and EasierTube plugins
- Adding an MP3 audio file to the Party People website

Media Manager

As its name suggests, the Media Manager is the place to keep track of and organize all your media files within folders and subfolders. You can use it to upload files, delete old material, or create new folders.

Accessing and using the Media Manager

The interface within the Media Manager is graphical and similar to other file explorer programs you will have definitely used within a Windows environment.

Like any of the sections of the administration control panel, you can access the Media Manager either by:

- Clicking **Site | Media Manager** from the top menu
- Clicking the **Media Manager** icon on the Control Panel

You can switch your view of the files within the Media Manager to suit your preference, as both provide the same level of functionality:

- Click **Thumbnail View** to see small graphic versions of your files, handy when you want to find an image
- Click **Detail View** to see the names of your files along with the dimensions and sizes

The following screenshot illustrates the use of the thumbnail view:

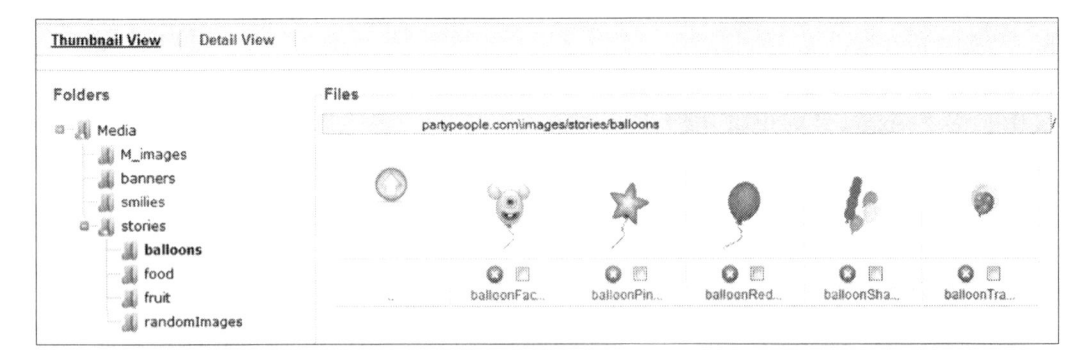

The **Folders** section to the left of the Media Manager interface displays the site folders. Click one to open and reveal any subfolders within it.

Within your site there will most likely be a subfolder within the **images** folder called **stories,** that is, **images | stories**. This is generally where the site images will have been placed and is where the **Image Upload** button defaults to when you add an image to an Article, as outlined in Chapter 2, *Creating, Editing, and Organizing Content*. You can also create new folders in here to store additional media.

Using the Party People website, we have created a new article and now need to add an image that doesn't fit in with the established folder structure.

Creating a new subfolder

It may be that after adding a new **Section** and/or **Category**, none of the existing image folder structures apply. Here we'll create a new subfolder called **glassware** to accommodate the new material:

1. Navigate to the **Media Manager** through the top menu or by clicking the **Media Manager** icon on the home page of the Control Panel.
2. Click on the **stories** folder in the Media Manager. Note that the Media Manager opens directly into the **images** folder (this is set in the **Global Configuration** area and can be changed if necessary).
3. Type in **glassware** as the name of the new folder and click the **Create Folder** button. The new subfolder will appear instantly.

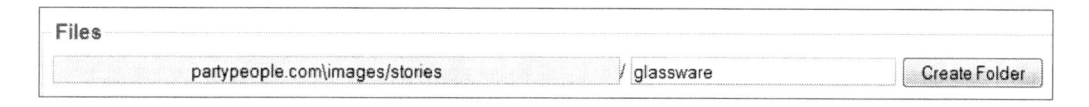

Now that we have the new **glassware** subfolder we can upload a new image to store in it using the **Upload File** tool.

A note on copyright

While you may have your own images and videos to use on your website, if you are considering using another artist's material and content, always ensure you have copyright permission or the license to do so in order to avoid breach of any copyright laws. You should refer to your local authority for full details.

Many website developers and owners regularly purchase and use stock photography, illustrations, and videos. If you choose to purchase any material for your site, ensure you are purchasing it with the right license, as there may be restrictions on its use even after paying for the material. This may, in fact, be a license fee and not a transfer of complete ownership. Sites such as `http://www.istockphoto.com/license.php` have a page dedicated to licensing agreements around purchasing their material.

What you should know about image and video files

Have you ever visited a website where a large image takes forever to download? Or the video takes forever to start playing? Chances are that you gave up and left the site.

While it doesn't happen quite so much now, take care to avoid this wherever possible. As a general rule, the larger the file size, the longer it takes to download into the browser, and not all users of your website may have fast download speeds.

To ensure your images are downloaded as quickly as possible, ensure your files are formatted and compressed into as low a resolution version as possible (without losing the quality) and the dimensions of the videos displayed kept to minimum viewing sizes. There is a trade-off between quality of the image and download speed; compromise is the key here. Audio, video, and animation files can be referred to collectively as multimedia, especially when they are combined within a project.

Choosing the best image file format

Images come in a variety of file formats and some are smaller in size than others. There are other image file formats, but the following are often used within websites:

- **.jpg** files are great for highly detailed images such as photographs. As a result, their file size is generally bigger due to the amount of information they require to present the detail.
- **.gif** files are suited to images requiring less detail, such as drawings or diagrams, and are smaller in file size as a result.
- **.png** files are similar to .gif files, as they are also low resolution images. They often have a transparent background so you can place them over a colored background and the color will appear behind the image.

Remember the following when applying images to your website:

- Use images with a purpose—to enhance or illustrate your content.
- Keep file sizes as small as possible. Consider a `.gif` rather than a `.jpg` if the image isn't a particularly detailed one.
- Use photo editing software to reduce the resolution of your image to 72dpi for fastest download time. Anything higher is pointless, as computer monitors only present a certain number of colors and drop the excess. If you don't have access to software such as Photoshop, there are a number of free possibilities. One is a program called GIMP (`http://www.gimp.org`). It's a free program that allows you to retouch photos and create and edit images. The website has tutorials as well.

Adding and managing images

Having covered editing and adding text to an article, updating and/or adding new images or other media to your articles is easy too.

In this section, we'll work on adding and deleting images and cover some general information on how they can work best for your site.

Uploading a new image

The **File Upload** tool within the Media Manager makes it easy to move your images from your computer into your website folders.

- Select the new **glassware** subfolder within the **Folders** structure. This places us in that folder.
- Click the **Browse** button under the **Upload File** section.
- Navigate to the image file in the pop-up window and click **Open**.
- Click the **Start Upload** button back in the **Media Manager**.

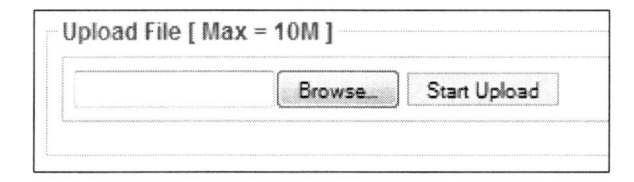

Now we have an image within the **glassware** folder, it's ready to be used within an article, as outlined in Chapter 2, *Creating, Editing, and Organizing Content*. Note that the following screenshot presents the **Details View**.

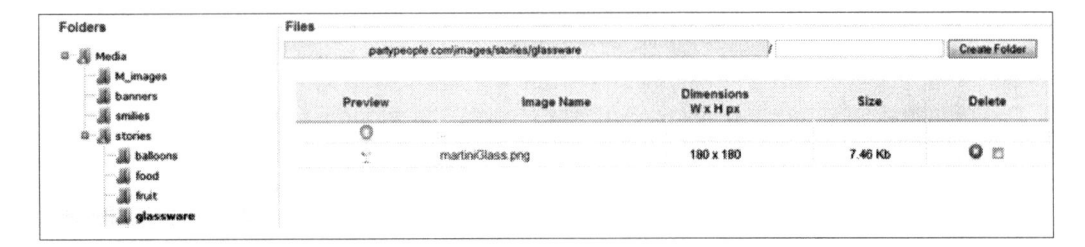

Deleting an image

You might find that as your website consumes more space on the server, you may have to delete some image files. However, be careful doing this, as you don't get a warning! Ensure your site does not require the image anymore, as you will end up with a blank area with a red square in it where the image should be, and that looks unprofessional.

Using Thumbnail View within the Media Manager, select the checkbox under the image thumbnail or next to the filename. Click the red "x" icon next to it in order to immediately delete that file, as shown in the following screenshot. You can also use the **Delete** button in the contextual toolbar at the top right.

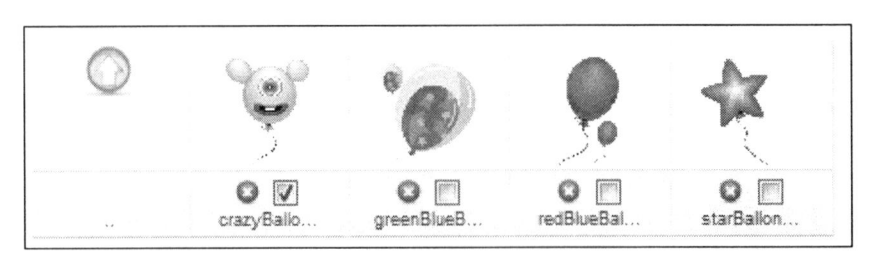

Updating a Simple Image Gallery

Rather than a single image, you might have an article with a Simple Image Gallery embedded within it that presents a selection of thumbnail images to the browser through the article. The gallery plugin parameters can be accessed through the **Extensions | Plugins** menu along the top of the administration interface. The following screenshot is an example of how one looks on the Party People website.

> **New Ballons in Stock Now!**
>
> Latest News
>
> **We have a great new range of Balloons in store now...**
>
> The Party People have a terrific range of novelty balloons for that special party. Below are samples from our new range in stock now.

Using the Party People website, we'll update this **New Balloons in Stock Now!** gallery applying the **Balloons** folder we made earlier. However, remember that the authors of this plugin recommend only 16 to 20 images per gallery.

1. Navigate to the **Media Manager** and to the **balloons** folder.
2. Upload the additional images to the balloons folder using the **File Upload** tool as outlined in the *Uploading a file* section of this chapter.
3. Delete any outdated images, if necessary, by selecting them and clicking the **Delete** button, as outlined in the *Deleting a File* section of this chapter.

To display the new images from a different folder in the article, we will need to access the article through which the gallery is presented:

1. Navigate to the Article Manager and open the article containing the gallery of images. You will see something like the following code within the Article's text editor:

    {gallery}galleryNameIsHere{/gallery}

2. Change this to **balloons** as in the folder where the balloon images are kept. The following screenshot illustrates the code snippet where you should change the folder name.

Managing Images and Videos

3. Apply your changes and review them before going live.

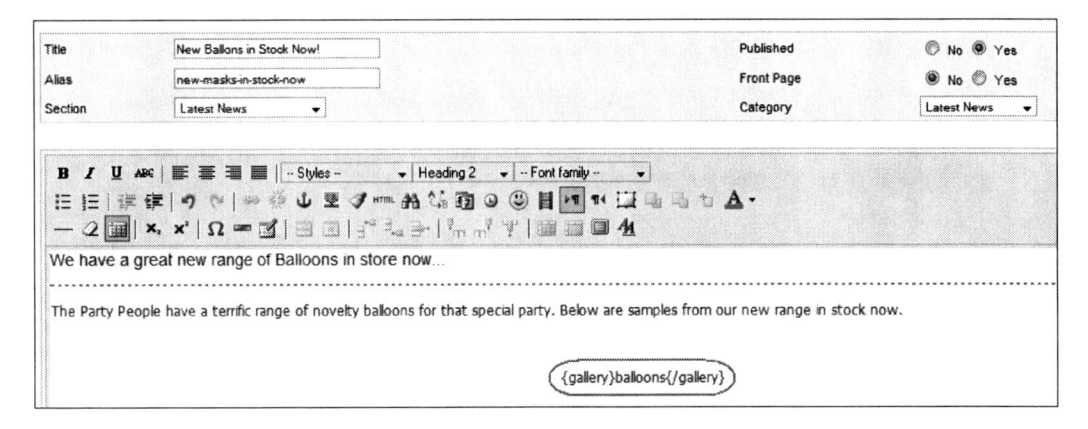

Changing the Simple Image Gallery's dimensions

If the dimensions of the image gallery, such as the height and width, need to be changed, there are the following steps:

1. Navigate to the **Extensions** menu using the global menu at the top of the screen.
2. Select **Plugin Manager** from the drop-down list and navigate through the list until you see the **Simple Image Gallery Plugin** link in the list. To make this quicker, use the **Select Type** filter and choose **Content**.
3. Ensure this plugin is enabled in the **Plugin Manager**.
4. Click the link to view the parameters for this plug-in; change them as you like.

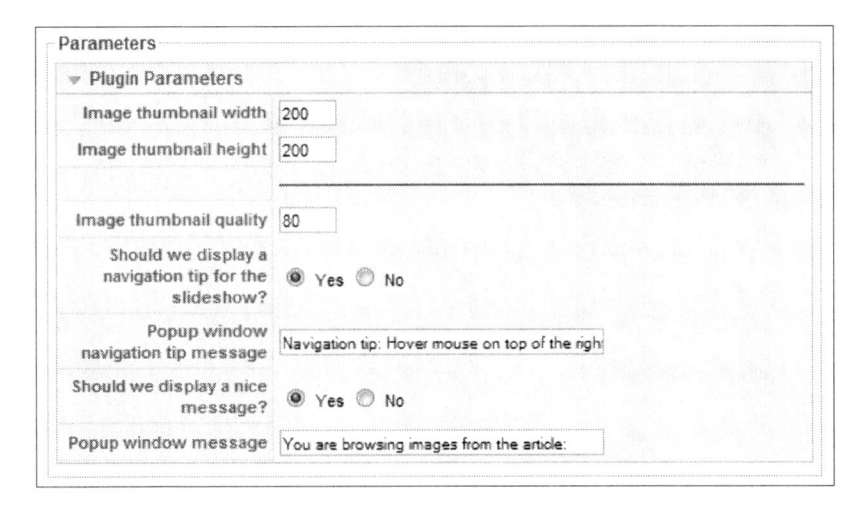

[56]

> Note that your developer may have changed the name of the module when it was installed.

Using video files

Video files are generally large due to the amount of content they contain and their length. It's beyond the scope of our book to describe them in detail, but in basic terms, they are a linear sequence of still images placed together to create a sequence of movement, usually accompanied by an audio track. Original video files are compressed using a *codec* to produce a compressed video file. The various codecs produce different results for file size, quality, and export.

Video files play in the browser by downloading the data through the Internet, progressively streaming it so the movie begins to play before the whole file has downloaded. Audio files work in a similar way, but are often not as large.

The final quality of a video also depends on the method used to capture it and how it's stored. The better the quality of the camera, the better the result. If you want to learn more about video, Wikipedia has a page at http://en.wikipedia.org/wiki/Video_formats.

Just like anything else, there are pros and cons of adding videos to your website. YouTube alone has proven there is a strong market for a more visual medium. However, there are still many people who prefer text-based content as well. Consider whether adding a video to your site will enhance your user's experience.

- Is the material promotional or instructional? Is the content better demonstrated than explained?
- Video material can broaden your target audience. Many people prefer watching a video online to reading lengthy bodies of text.
- Videos aren't that great for search engine optimization. Consider adding a transcript to the page as well, in order to increase the ability to search. Chapter 6, *Making Your Site Popular* covers search engine optimization and the use of text.

Choosing the best video file format

Video played through the Internet requires a media player, which acts as an interface between the video file and the browser. These days most Internet users have one embedded within their browser. Popular versions include:

- QuickTime, a player created by Apple
- Windows Media Player
- WINAMP
- Real Player, developed by Real Networks
- Adobe Flash Player

The following are some of the video file types that can be played through your website using third-party media players:

- **.wmv** files are a popular format developed by Microsoft and which come bundled within the Internet Explorer software package and are, therefore, preinstalled on Windows PCs. This is a format good for movies with movement within them. This format works with Windows Media Player, RealPlayer, and another called VLC Player. This format isn't very compatible with Mac or Linux computer users.

- **.mov** files are a QuickTime video platform extension that also plays back on the Windows operating system. The Apple QuickTime movie player software can be easily downloaded from Apple at http://www.apple.com/quicktime/download/. While not many browsers have the QuickTime media player installed, this format does provide very high quality video. You can always provide a link to the URL to download the software in order to play the video.

- **.avi** files are often the format of videos with smaller dimensions, played back through a website. They are a container for audio and video files (hence the name!). They can sometimes be quite large in file size, depending on the codec used to compress the video footage. They are a mainstream format.

- **.swf** and **.flv** videos are excellent for web video streaming and can also include interactive features. Most Mac and PCs have the Flash Shockwave Player installed; however, it can be downloaded from http://get.adobe.com/flashplayer/. Take note of the requirements for your individual operating system and browser preferences.

Keep the following in mind when considering a video for your website:

- Ensure the video is succinct and the file size as small as possible. Even with a high speed download, time is still required to fully download the complete file.

  Keeping the video between one to three minutes long and the file size under five megabytes
- The more the movement in a video, the larger the file size.
- Consider whether the video really enhances the message. Viewers are only interested in material that is useful to them and will resent consuming their download resources on a video that holds no value for them.
- The larger the file size, the longer it takes to upload.
- Consider your audience's data rate. Do they have high speed downloads or are there some with dial-up connections?

Video files are generally large due to the amount of content they contain. They stream (streaming is the way the Internet transfers multimedia information) through the data so the video will begin playing before it has fully downloaded itself into the browser, allowing it to be played back as quickly as possible. Audio files work in a similar way, but are not usually big files.

There are various video file formats available and most website users have a player to see them already contained within the browser. Many users have QuickTime, a player created by Apple (that also runs on PCs) and Real Player, developed by Real Networks.

Videos require a special plugin to play them through an article on your site, once you have uploaded it. Alternatively, you can embed a link from the popular YouTube site (http://www.youtube.com/). We'll look at how to do both in relation to the Party People website.

Uploading a video

We'll upload a new video, much the same way we would upload an image, to a new subfolder called **videos** within the Party People website. The steps are as follows:

1. Navigate to the **Media Manager**.
2. Select the stories folder and type **videos** into the **Files** input box.
3. Click **Create Folder**.
4. Select the new **videos** folder icon; then click the **Browse** button to choose the video from our desktop computer.
5. Click **Start Upload.**

Now we have a video file ready to be inserted into an article. The Party People website has the popular AllVideos plugin installed to do this.

Updating videos—AllVideos plugin

This is another neat plugin that works in much the same way as the Simple Image Gallery, a stablemate from this team of developers.

If you don't have it installed and you would like to present videos on your site, ask your developer to install it for you or refer to the developers website `http://www.joomlaworks.gr/content/view/35/41/` for instructions. Chapter 8, *Menus, Modules, and Components* also covers the installation of plugins and extensions.

Our Party People website has a `.mov` video on the **Products and Services** page, which we will update.

To update the video display:

1. Navigate to the Article Manager through the top menu and open the **Our Services Include...** article.
2. Change the name of the video file between the {} and {/} tags within the text editor to the new filename. Depending on the format of the video being presented, the code should look like this:

   `{mov}promoVideo{/mov}`

3. This code displays a QuickTime movie within the article.
4. Save the changes. The following screenshot shows us how the video will look in context.

Note that you do not need to include the format extension at the end of the filename, as the tag surrounding the name addresses this.

Changing to a different video file and format

The AllVideos plugin supports a number of video file formats and the developer's website lists them all at `http://www.joomlaworks.gr/content/view/35/41/`.

We'll change the video we just linked to a different one which is in the .wmv format. The steps are as follows:

1. Navigate to the Article containing the video presentation.
2. Change the tag between the { } braces to reflect the new file type, taking care not to delete any of the symbols. For example:

    {wmv}updatedServicesVideo{/wmv}

- Save the changes to your article.

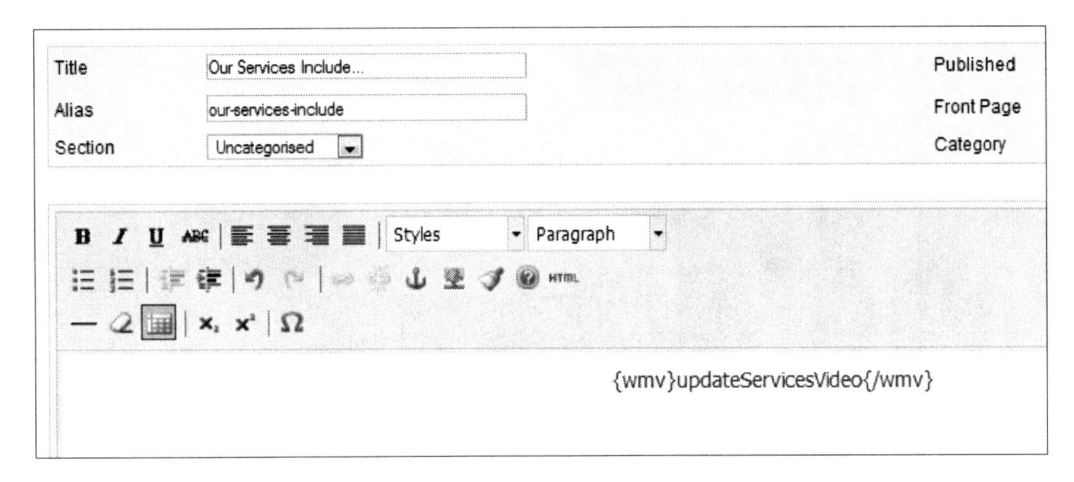

{wmv}updateServicesVideo{/wmv}

You should take care to avoid rearranging any of the formatting within the code, as this will prevent the movie from playing. That is, don't add any extra spaces, colons, commas, and so on.

Updating a YouTube video

If there is a YouTube video playing within your website, there is a plugin installed within your site to make this happen. The Party People site uses the EasierTube plugin (which is accessible from http://joomlacode.org/gf/project/easiertube/).

If you don't have this plugin installed and want to include a YouTube video, Chapter 8, *Menus, Modules, and Components* looks at installing extensions.

Here we'll update our link within an Article on the Party People website.

The code for this to happen is fed through an article and changing the link to the video will update the display. Assuming a video has already been uploaded to YouTube and used in the Party People website, we'll now update the link.

Go to www.youtube.com and copy the relevant URL code for the link.

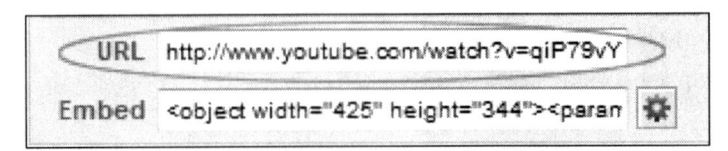

Navigate back to the Article Manager within your administration Control Panel and locate the "Party Planners Unite" article.

Highlight the code for the old video link within the text editor and paste the code from YouTube over it.

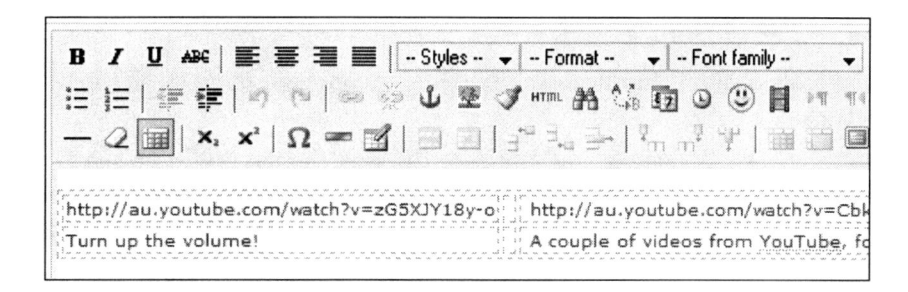

Save these changes to your Article and the new video link will play within the article in the same place as previously.

Changing the YouTube video dimensions

Say you need to change the dimensions of the video, such as the height and the width:

1. Navigate to the **Extensions** menu using the global menu at the top of the screen.
2. Select **Plugin Manager** and navigate through the list until you see **Content | EasierTube** in the drop-down list. To make this quicker, use the **Select Type** filter at the top right of the screen and choose **Content**. This sorts the plugins to show only those applicable to content.
3. Click the **Content | EasierTube** link to view the parameters for this plug-in and change them as you would like.
4. Click **Save** to make your changes and view your updates on the live site.

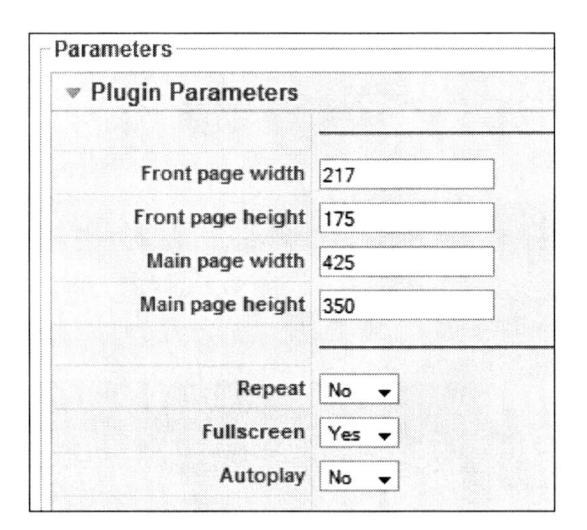

Parameters

▼ Plugin Parameters

Front page width	217
Front page height	175
Main page width	425
Main page height	350
Repeat	No
Fullscreen	Yes
Autoplay	No

Audio files

While it's not as commonplace as images and video, you can stream audio files through your website much as you would a video. Perhaps you have a recorded message for your users or you would like to play some music for them. Remember to keep your file sizes as small as possible and consider the copyright implications of the material you use.

There are various audio recording and editing software programs available to purchase and download. Audacity is a free program and can be downloaded from `http://audacity.sourceforge.net/`. This software, along with a microphone, will allow you to record sounds or speech and save it as various audio file formats, including MP3.

There are many audio file formats, just as there are images. Wikipedia has a page with details of them at `http://en.wikipedia.org/wiki/Audio_file_format`.

Here we will use the Simple MP3 Player module to play an MP3 file on the Party People website.

If you don't have this module installed, Chapter 8, *Menus, Modules, and Components* will guide you on installing third party extensions.

To demonstrate how it can be applied, we have pre-installed it within the Party People website in the left module position, under the two existing menus. Now we'll configure it to play a sound effects file.

1. Click the **Extensions | Module Manager** link through the top menu.
2. Select the **Simple MP3 Player** module from the list of installed modules, in order to enable it and configure the player.

| 19 | | Simple MP3 Player | | ◯ | ▲ |

3. Set the **Details** of the player as you require them. We'll change ours to be called **Play Me!**. Note that this is the name you will see in the **Modules** listing screen from now on.
4. Enable the **Module** and select the position.

Managing Images and Videos

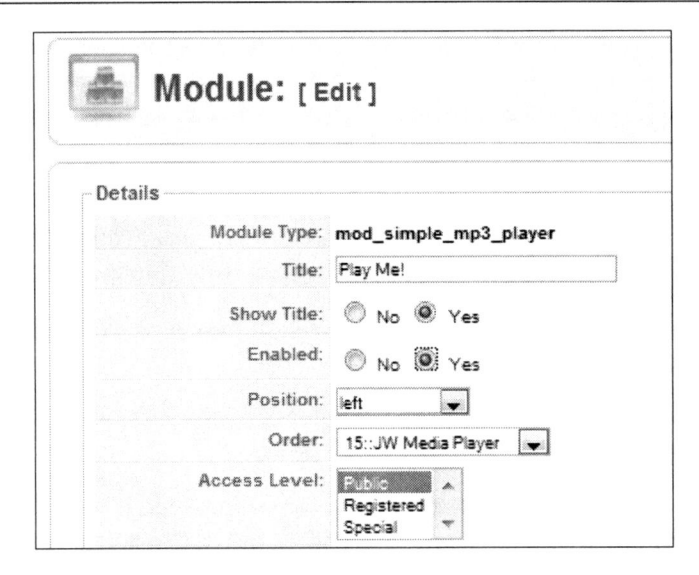

5. Type in the filename of your MP3 file, you can include more than one by typing it as:

   First.mp3 | second.mp3 | third.mp3

6. Type in the Title of each MP3 to be shown in the playlist.

   songOne :: Track 1 | songTwo :: Track2 | songThree :: Track3

   Set all of the other variables as you would like them, including a background image. Note that we have changed the width of the player to be the same as the menus above it, for a tidier layout. Consider the colors and general style of your site to make it appear integrated.

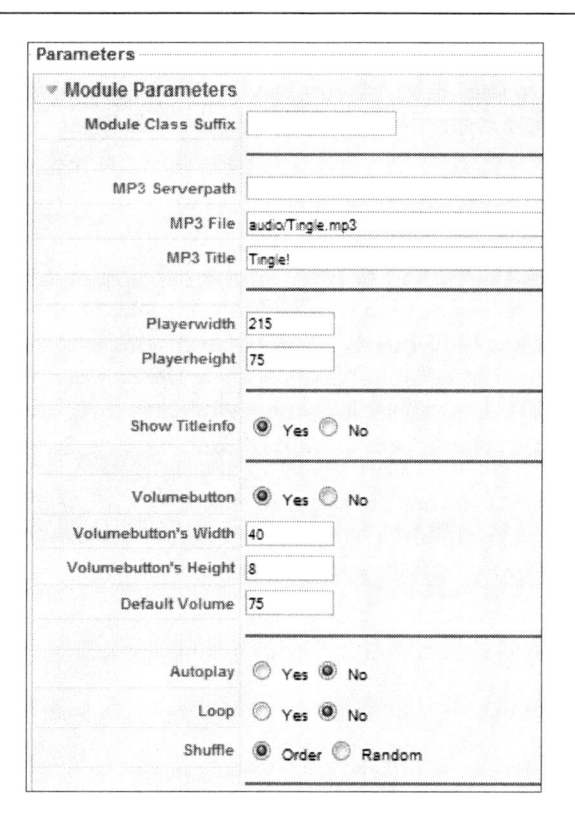

Save your settings and check the player on the frontend of your site.

Now when a visitor hits the site, they can choose to play the audio file and set the volume. This sort of user interactivity can be good for keeping visitors engaged with your site and tweaking some control works on this level.

Summary

As we have seen, it's not necessary to have an extensive knowledge of multimedia to be able to use images, videos, and audio within your site. However, it makes sense to be aware of the various file formats available and which one will suit your needs. Including visual and multimedia material on your site can certainly give it more impact and convey your message quickly and without words, which is handy when we know that users don't like to spend a lot of time reading large bodies of text.

Using the Media Manager makes adding and managing all of this quite easy and ensures your files are kept within a close-knit group of folders that can be readily accessed when you want to update your website content.

4
Backing Up Your Website

In information technology terms, a backup is a process of copying digital files, so that they can be used to restore the data, in the event that the original is lost. One of the main reasons for backing up your website is the possibility of your site being maliciously attacked or compromised. If this happens, you would want to counteract this quickly and get things up and running again. Another reason may be that you want to relocate the site to another server and you will need a complete copy of the website to do this.

In this chapter, we'll look at the following points:

- How you can manually copy your site files and database using the control panel interface on your hosting server, which is useful if you can't access the administration interface of your site through the browser.
- How to use the JoomlaPack component through the administration interface to create an archive file that can be uploaded and unpacked to restore your website.

What's the Control Panel and where is it?

The Control Panel is a graphical interface that you enter through your hosting service website. Control Panels themselves use proprietary software and are all different, but for the purposes of our outline we'll use the cPanel system. They are all similar in nature though and even if your hosting service uses a different system, this outline will still help you understand some of the terminology and areas you need to access.

The Control Panel is shown in the following screenshot:

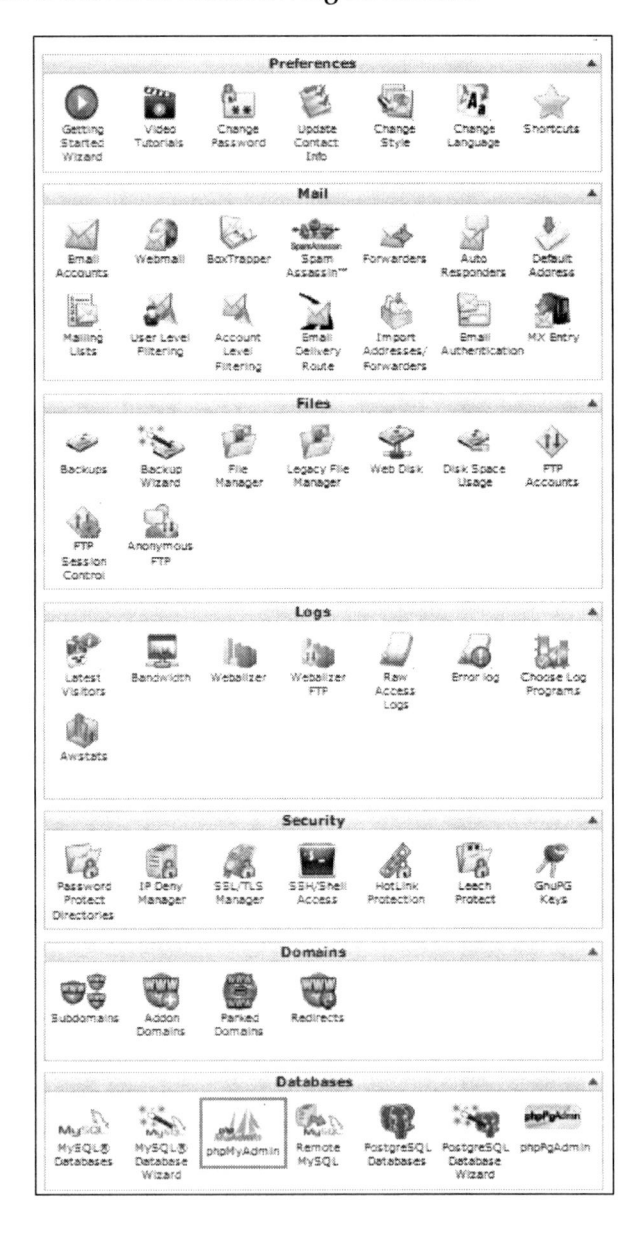

The modules we'll refer to in this chapter are as follows:

- File Manager
- Backup Wizard
- phpMyAdmin

Briefly, the Control Panel is sectioned into areas containing a number of modules, which you can use to manage your account. They are as follows:

- **Preferences**: Allows you to set certain preferences in the management of your hosting account, such as adding/changing your contact details and passwords.
- **Mail**: Set up and manage your e-mail accounts and any redirections. Here you can also usually set up auto responders and spam filtering.
- **Files**: This section contains the modules for you to manage all of the files located on your server space, including the File Manager and the FTP logins; both are important for you to familiarize yourself with.
- **Logs**: These are modules that allow you to check who has accessed your site and when. This section may include the Webalizer, which can prepare charts and reports based on certain usage statistics.
- **Security**: Here you can apply password protection to certain folders, or deny certain web addresses access to your site or the ability to link to your website.
- **Domains**: Allows you to manage your domain names and any sub domains, including a redirection of one domain name to another, or to add a "parked" domain name if you have one.
- **Databases**: Several applications are available to manage various types of databases; our Joomla! Sites use MySQL and the phpMyAdmin applications.
- **Software Services**: Sometimes programs are pre-installed into your account and you can make use of these on your sites, such as a CGI counter, a clock, or a simple guest book.
- **Advanced**: These are the applications that developers are more likely to use, as they require some background knowledge to configure.

Manually backing up your site

If you are going to manually back up your website files, the first step is to log into the Control Panel. When you set up your account, your hosting provider will have sent you an e-mail with a link to this, along with a username and password. The information contained within this e-mail is important. Ensure that you keep it secure, as it's required to gain access to your website and can potentially be used to exploit your site. It's a good idea to copy and save the information in a separate file, away from your site files as well.

Backing Up Your Website

The link to the Control Panel should look like this:

`http://partypeople.com/cpanel/`

Copy the link provided into the browser window and type in the username and password as prompted.

This leads you to the home page of your Control Panel, as shown in the previous screenshot.

Backing up the database using the phpMyAdmin interface

Database files are essentially an intricate system of fields and records, all wrapped up within a collection of interlinking tables. These tables hold the data your website presents to the end user, such as article content or product catalogue details. If you would like to know more, Wikipedia has a good overview of databases and their functions at `http://en.wikipedia.org/wiki/Databases`.

The phpMyAdmin is an application designed to administer MySQL databases, which is the database type used to run your website. We'll use this module to "export" a database in the following steps:

1. Within the Control Panel, select the **phpMyAdmin** icon to open the interface. On the left is a list of the databases hosted on your server. Select the database that runs your website. Selecting this will present you with a list of the tables set up for that database within the main frame of the interface.

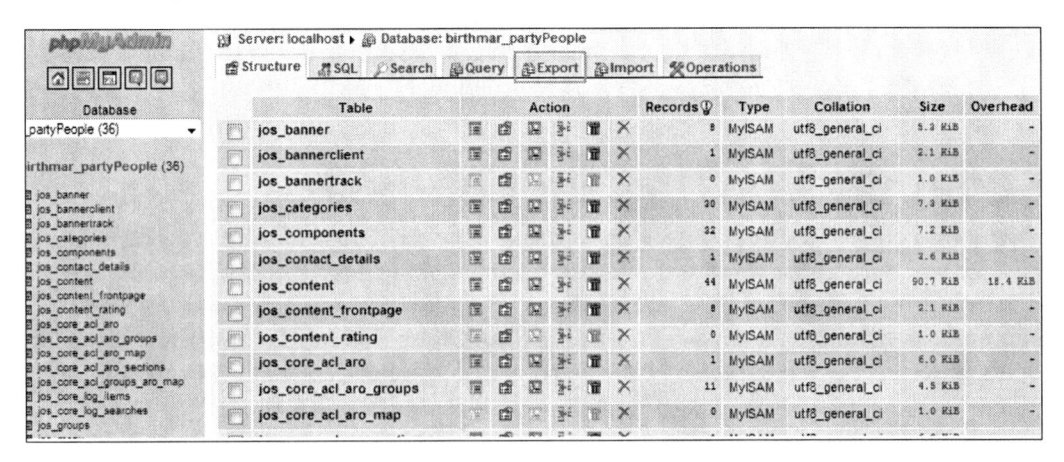

Table	Action	Records	Type	Collation	Size	Overhead
jos_banner		9	MyISAM	utf8_general_ci	5.3 KiB	-
jos_bannerclient		1	MyISAM	utf8_general_ci	2.1 KiB	-
jos_bannertrack		0	MyISAM	utf8_general_ci	1.0 KiB	-
jos_categories		20	MyISAM	utf8_general_ci	7.3 KiB	-
jos_components		32	MyISAM	utf8_general_ci	7.2 KiB	-
jos_contact_details		1	MyISAM	utf8_general_ci	2.6 KiB	-
jos_content		44	MyISAM	utf8_general_ci	90.7 KiB	18.4 KiB
jos_content_frontpage		8	MyISAM	utf8_general_ci	2.1 KiB	-
jos_content_rating		0	MyISAM	utf8_general_ci	1.0 KiB	-
jos_core_acl_aro		1	MyISAM	utf8_general_ci	6.0 KiB	-
jos_core_acl_aro_groups		11	MyISAM	utf8_general_ci	4.5 KiB	-
jos_core_acl_aro_map		0	MyISAM	utf8_general_ci	1.0 KiB	-

2. Next, select the **Export** tab at the top of the interface. Within the export page, leave the default options as they are and, in addition, check the **Add DROP TABLE/VIEW/PROCEDURE/FUNCTION** and the **Save as File** options.
3. Choose **Select All**, to ensure that you have collected all of the tables within the database.
4. Select the **SQL** radio button.
5. Finally, select the compression type of your choice. The options are **None**, **Zipped**, and **GZipped**.

   None means no compression is applied, so if the site is a small one, select this option. Select **Zipped** or **GZipped** to compress the file down into a reduced size in a zipped format.

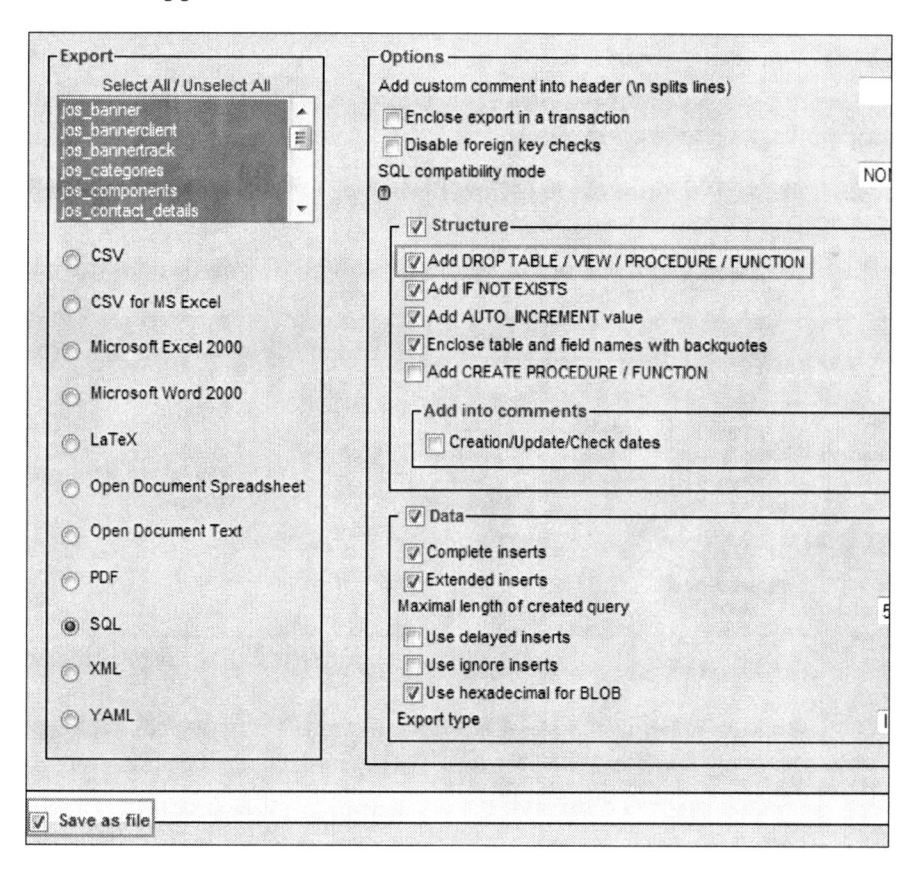

6. Click the **Go** button at the bottom right of the screen to start the export process. A pop-up window will prompt you to choose where to save your database file and give it the name of your database as the default, which you can change. Do this and the process should begin automatically, depending on your browser settings.

You now have a copy of your database saved, in the compressed format if you had selected one, at the location you nominated in step 6.

To access this file, navigate to the folder you nominated on your computer and look for a .sql file. For example, partyPeople.sql.

Backing up the site files using the Backup Wizard

Now that you have your database saved, we'll look at backing up the the actual site files using the Backup Wizard module.

1. Navigate back to your Control Panel interface (which may still be open in another tab in your browser window).
2. Click the **Backup Wizard** module option to open the interface for this module.

3. Click **Backup** to begin the steps to create a complete or partial backup of your site files. You can select a complete backup of all your files, including the database, or just your site files.

Chapter 4

Backup Wizard

Steps:

① **Backup/Restore**   ② Full or Partial Backup   ③ Download

Backup

This feature allows you to download a zipped copy of your entire site or parts of it onto your computer.

The following are backed up and included in a zip file for your convenience:

    Home Directory
    MySQL Databases
    Email forwarders configuration
    Email filters configuration

Backup →

Restore

This feature allows you to restore parts of your cPanel by uploading your partial backup zip file(s) that you downloaded from the backup feature.

The following can be restored:

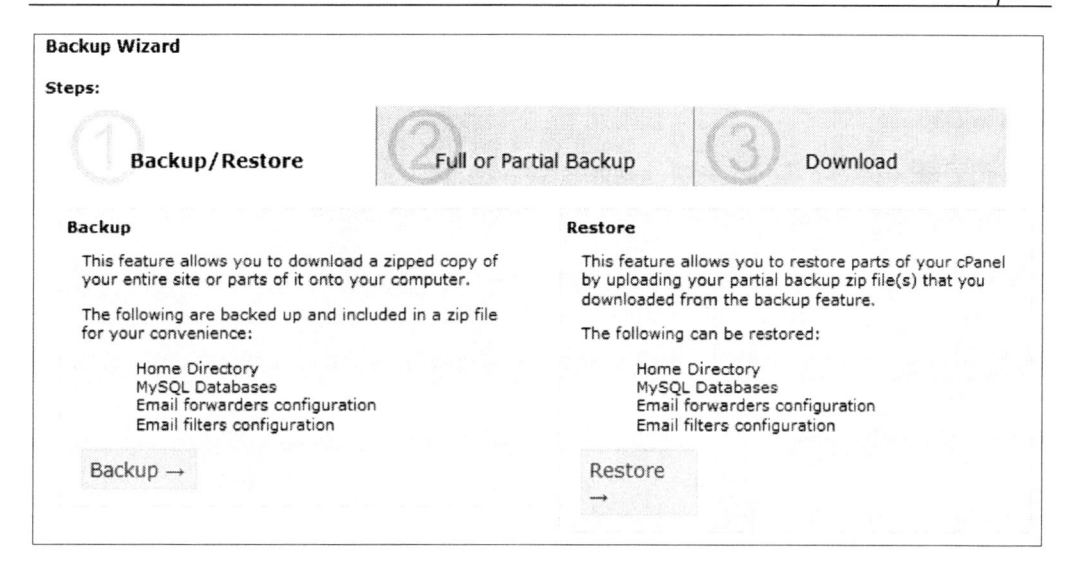

    Home Directory
    MySQL Databases
    Email forwarders configuration
    Email filters configuration

Restore →

4. Click the **Backup** button to be taken to the next step which asks you whether you want a full or partial backup of your site. We'll select a partial backup as we have already exported and saved our database file.

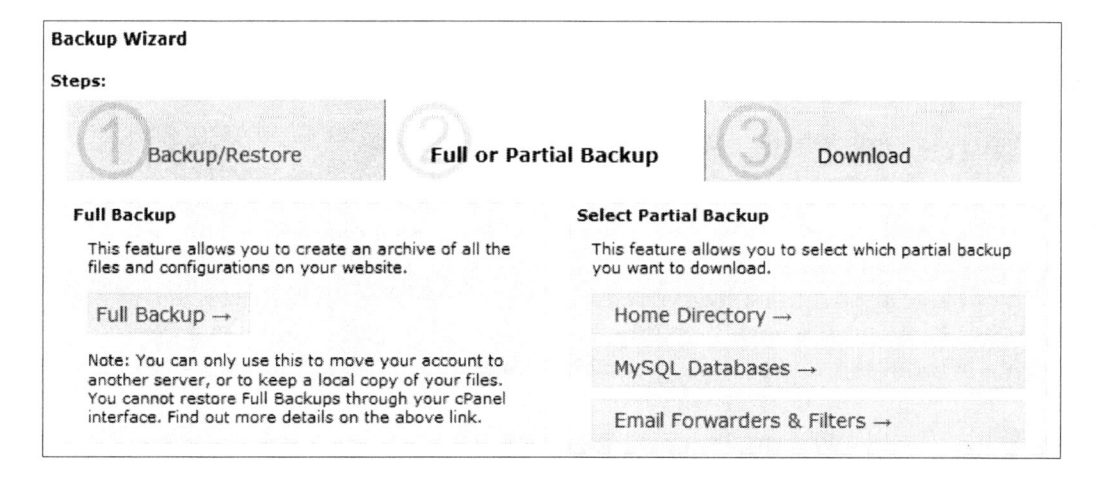

Backup Wizard

Steps:

① Backup/Restore   ② **Full or Partial Backup**   ③ Download

Full Backup

This feature allows you to create an archive of all the files and configurations on your website.

Full Backup →

Note: You can only use this to move your account to another server, or to keep a local copy of your files. You cannot restore Full Backups through your cPanel interface. Find out more details on the above link.

Select Partial Backup

This feature allows you to select which partial backup you want to download.

Home Directory →

MySQL Databases →

Email Forwarders & Filters →

5. Click **Home Directory** to select the site files. This will lead you to the final step.

[75]

6. Click the **Home Directory** button which will open a browser window.

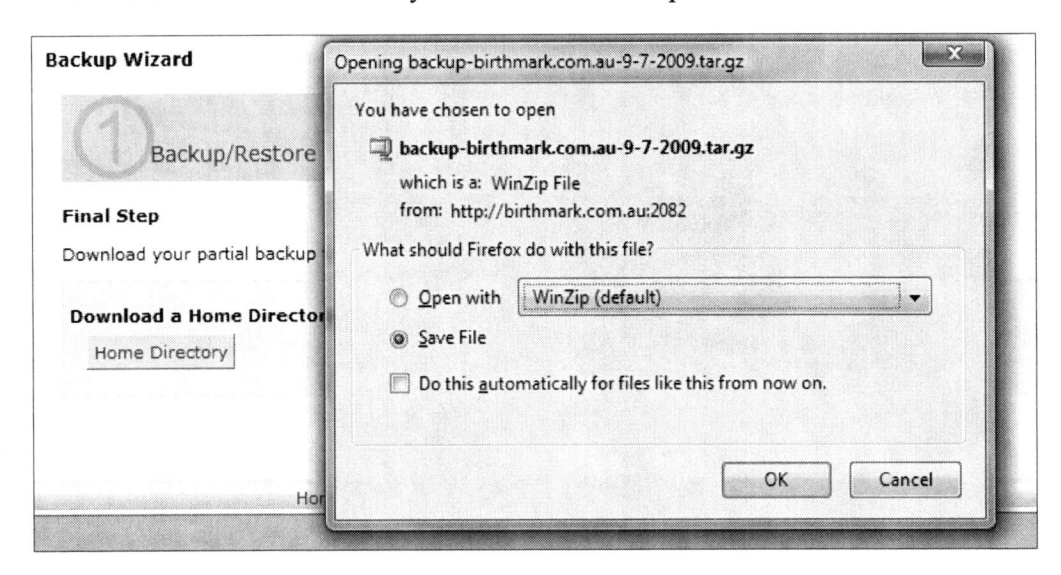

7. Select **Save File** and **OK** to save a zipped file to your computer hard drive or storage device. You can change the name of the file if you need to as well.

Using an external FTP application to download and upload your files

If you cannot find a module within your Control Panel that allows you to do this, download and install an external FTP application, such as CuteFTP (http://www.globalscape.com/cuteftp/) or FileZilla (http://filezilla-project.org/). Both of these applications have documentation available on their respective websites to assist you with installing and using them. Both can be installed within Windows and Apple Mac environments.

> An **FTP (File Transfer Protocol)** program is an intermediary application that allows you to access the server to upload and download files.

Both of these applications are free to use, although CuteFTP does have a commercial version, which offers additional functionality. There are other FTP programs available though, and you should choose one that suits your requirements.

To use these applications, you will need to enter some of the details provided by your hosting provider in the e-mail referred to earlier in this chapter, when we looked at the Control Panel access. Locate the FTP and enter the following details:

- Username
- Password
- Root Path
- The Port number used by your hosting provider. This can be either the standard "TCP port 21" or a specific port number.

Your FTP connection details are as shown next:

FTP Host:	ftp.partypeople.com (Server Address: 123.45.678.912)
Username:	aUserName
Password:	aSpecialPassword

Note that FTP passwords can be changed using the Control Panel.

> You should upload your website files to the `public_html` directory when you are logged in to the server through FTP. Please note that uploading your files to another directory will mean your site will not be visible online. Also, you should have the index page of your website named `index.html` or `index.php` (all lowercase); otherwise, you will see the default server index page.

If you would like further information on installing and using FileZilla, visit the developer's website at http://wiki.filezilla-project.org/Documentation.

Restoring your website manually

Before we look at the JoomlaPack component, you should be aware that you can manually restore your site files through the Control Panel, using the same Backup Wizard from the previous section.

This time click the **Restore** button to navigate through the quick steps to select and upload your zipped file.

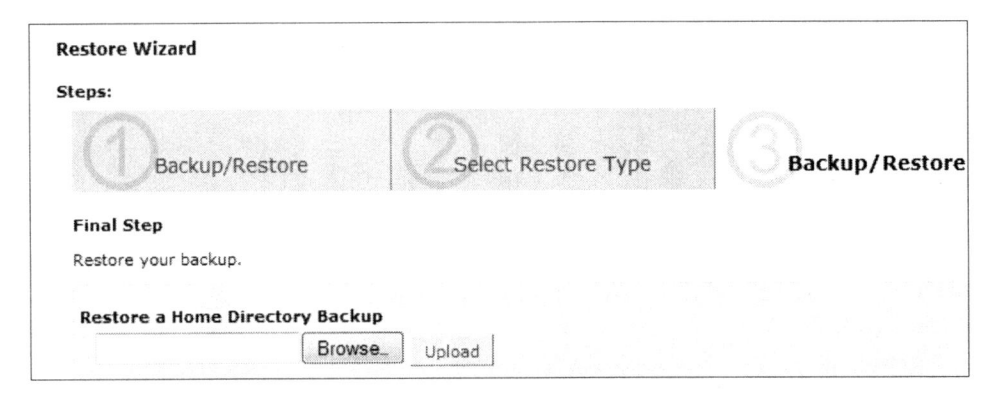

Backing up and restoring with the JoomlaPack component

JoomlaPack is a third-party extension that can be installed within the administration interface of Joomla!, offering a streamlined process of backing up your website and saving it as a compressed archive file on your computer. You can use this component not only if your site has been compromised, but also if you are relocating to a different server.

Understanding the restoration process

Using JoomlaPack is essentially a four step process. The steps are as follows:

1. Create the archive file and upload it to the server directory where your site files belong.
2. Create a new database.
3. Obtain and upload a copy of the installation extraction script called `kickstart.php` to unpack the archive file.
4. Proceed through the installation interface.

Firstly, you will create the archive file of your website, in a folder on your workstation, and upload the archive to the server. Then, you will have a copy of the entire website and a snapshot of your database to work with. Having a snapshot of the database means you need to create a new database for your website using the Control Panel. By applying JoomlaPack, the contents of the archive are imported into the new database to populate it with your content. We'll work through this process in steps, beginning with locating the JoomlaPack component.

Step 1: Create the archive file and upload

Your Joomla! developer will need to have installed the component into the administration interface of your website. If so, go to **Components** within the top menu and select JoomlaPack from the drop-down menu.

If this component is not installed, Chapter 8, *Menus, Modules, and Components* has an overview of installing third-party extensions.

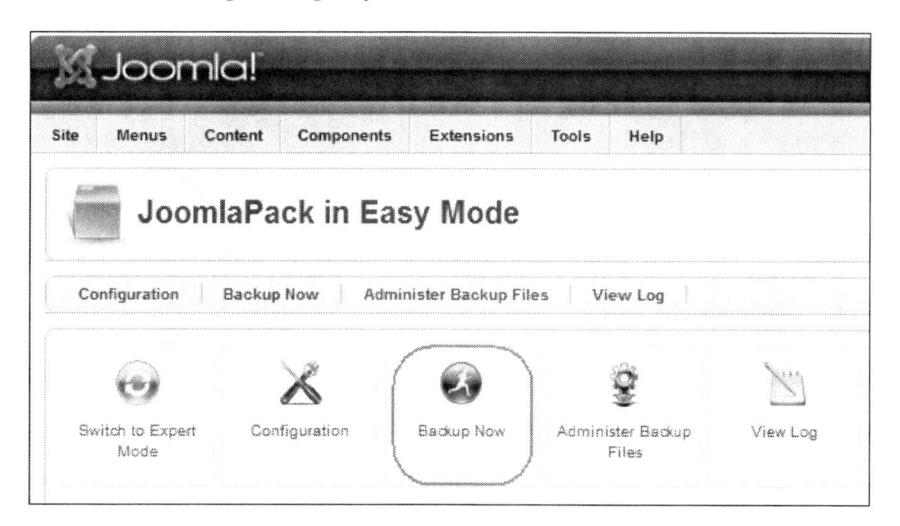

Ensure you are in **Easy Mode** and select **Backup Now**. This automatically begins the process and you will be instructed not to navigate away from the page until the backup is complete.

Once complete, go to the **Administrator Backup** page to see the archive file created as a result. The following screenshot illustrates this:

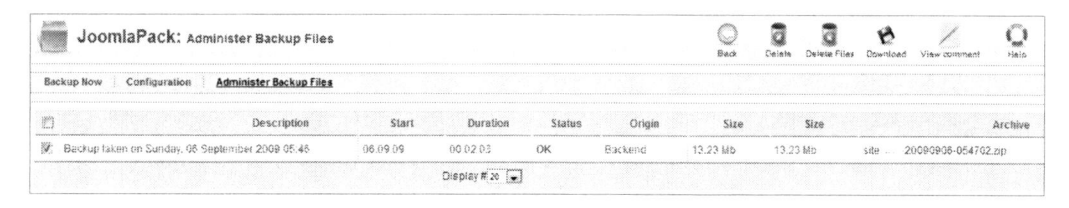

Backing Up Your Website

- Select the archive file and click the **Download** icon to save the file to your hard drive or other storage device. Now you have an entire copy of your website, including a snapshot of the database, packed into one file. As mentioned earlier, many hosting sites offer a file manager module to administer files on your site. You can use this utility to upload the archive file. This is the recommended method and for our purposes, we'll use this option, as it is usually much faster than an external FTP application.
- Log into your Control Panel interface and locate the file manager module. Within the file manager, navigate to the folder where your site files are kept.
- Having located the folder, copy (in case you need to refer back to them at any time) and then delete the existing files within, as some Control Panel configurations will not allow you to overwrite any existing files. This may affect the installation of the site from the archive file.

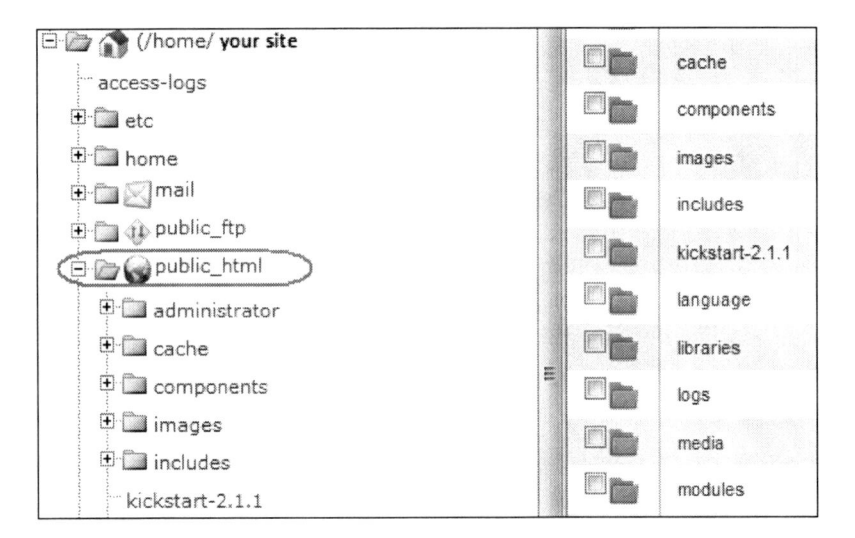

```
(/home/ your site              cache
  access-logs                  components
  etc                          images
  home                         includes
  mail                         kickstart-2.1.1
  public_ftp                   language
  public_html                  libraries
    administrator              logs
    cache                      media
    components                 modules
    images
    includes
  kickstart-2.1.1
```

- Next, move the archive file from your hard drive to the server, using the **File Upload** icon. Use the **Browse** button to locate the file and start the upload process.
- Note that the archive file will most likely be quite large. For example, our Party People website ZIP file is about 13 MB, which isn't particularly large for a whole website. So, a large site can take some time to pack up. Allow the process to run its course and keep an eye on its progress.

Step 2. Creating a new database and user

Using the cPanel system as an example, find the **Databases** section and click the **MySQL Database Wizard** icon. Other hosting environments may be a little different, so look for the appropriate module to create and manage databases for your account.

Follow these steps to create a MySQL database, adding users and passwords as required. Remember to take a record of the new username, password, and database name so that you can enter these details during the restoration process.

1. Click the **MySQL Database Wizard** icon to open the process. Step 1 is to create the database. Give it a name.

2. Add a username and a password to the database. This is the user who logs in and makes changes.

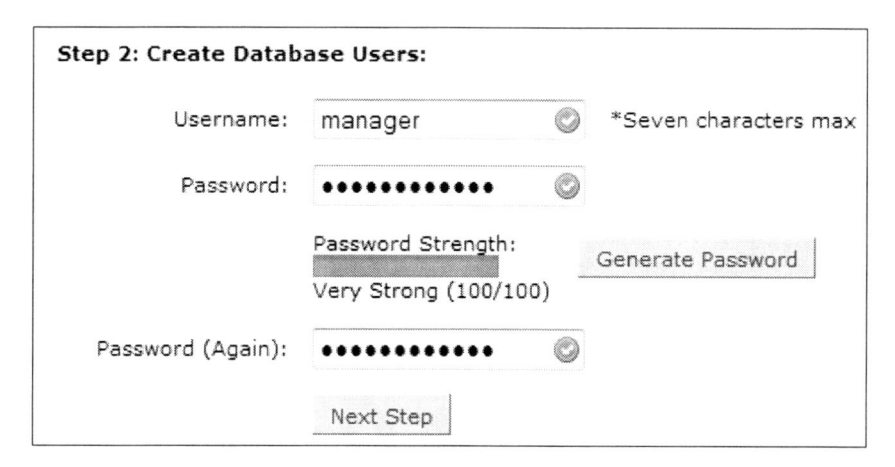

Backing Up Your Website

3. Give this user privileges to the database, that is, give them authority to make changes to manage the database.

☑ ALL PRIVILEGES ▼	
☑ CREATE TEMPORARY TABLES	☑ CREATE ROUTINE
☑ DELETE	☑ LOCK TABLES
☑ INDEX	☑ REFERENCES
☑ INSERT	☑ ALTER
☑ SELECT	☑ CREATE
☑ UPDATE	☑ DROP

Next Step

4. Click the **All Privileges** checkbox followed by **Next Step**. Your new user and database are confirmed.

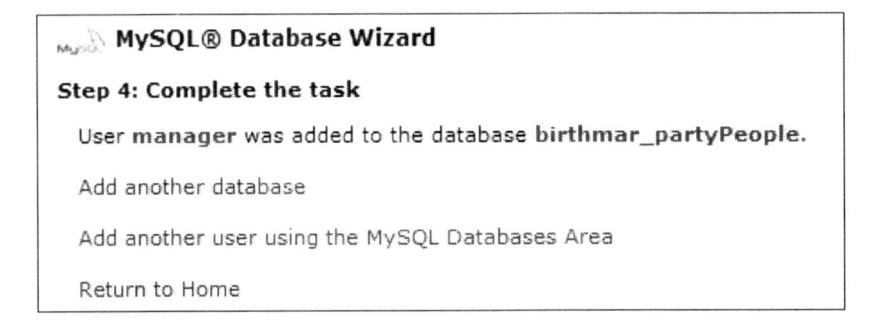

MySQL® Database Wizard

Step 4: Complete the task

User manager was added to the database **birthmar_partyPeople**.

Add another database

Add another user using the MySQL Databases Area

Return to Home

5. Click **Return to Home** to go back to the main Control Panel interface. Click the **MySQL Database** icon to see the new database and user profile.

Database	Size	Users	Actions
birthmar_partyPeople	0.80 MB	birthmar_manager ⊗ birthmar_partyP ⊗ birthmar_tracey ⊗	Delete Database

Once the archive has safely arrived at the server directory and you have created a new database, you can begin to unpack the archive using a restoration script contained within a special file, named `kickstart.php`.

Step 3: Kick-start the installation

The `kickstart.php` file contains special code to extract the archive file and present an installation interface within the browser for you to reinstall the files and connect with the database.

If you do not have a copy of the `kickstart.php` file saved with your local site files (perhaps your developer gave you a copy along with the complete copy of your site on a CD-ROM), then you can download it from:

http://joomlacode.org/gf/project/jpack/frs/?action=FrsReleaseView&release_id=9919

Download, unzip, and save the `kickstart.php` file in the same folder as your other site files on your computer.

Then within the Control Panel, upload the `kickstart.php` file into the same folder on your server space as the archive file. Use the upload function or an external FTP, as this is not a large file.

Once you have established a new database and uploaded the `kickstart.php` script, go to the web browser and type in the address of your site, followed by the `kickstart.php` file. This would look something like: http://www.yoursite.com/kickstart.php. You will see the following screenshot:

To unpack the archive file:

- Select the `.jpa` file from the drop-down menu and leave the default settings as they are. The other option is a `.zip` file. Use the drop-down menu to select your archive file.
- Click the big green **Start** button to begin unpacking the archive file.

Once this process is completed, type the address of your website into the browser to begin the final installation interface.

Step 4: Restoring your website

What you see now is the beginning of the installer interface that will walk you through the final restoration process. Each step is listed on the left and must be completed in order to move onto the next.

After you have entered the details for each screen, click the **Next** button at the top right to move on. It's during this process that you will need to refer back to the site installation settings. Ensure for possible future reference that you document all of the settings you have established somewhere, preferably away from your site files. A simple plain text file (for example, Notepad) with all of the passwords, database names, and so on is all it takes.

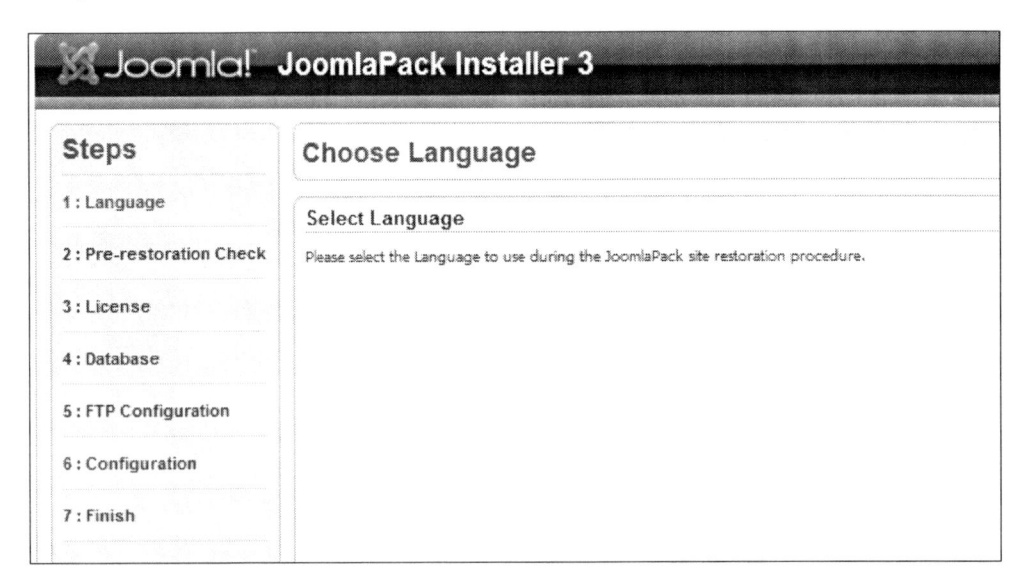

Select the language of your choice, then click **Next**.

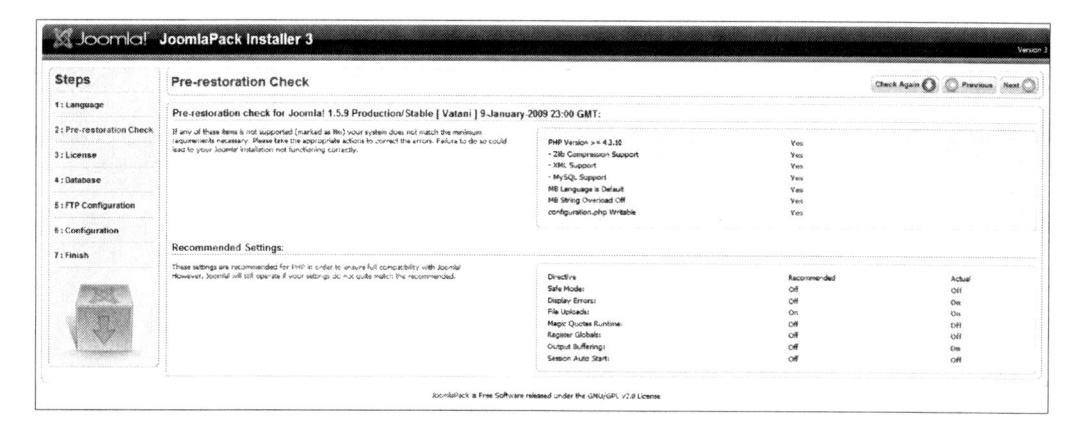

This previous screen checks the server settings.

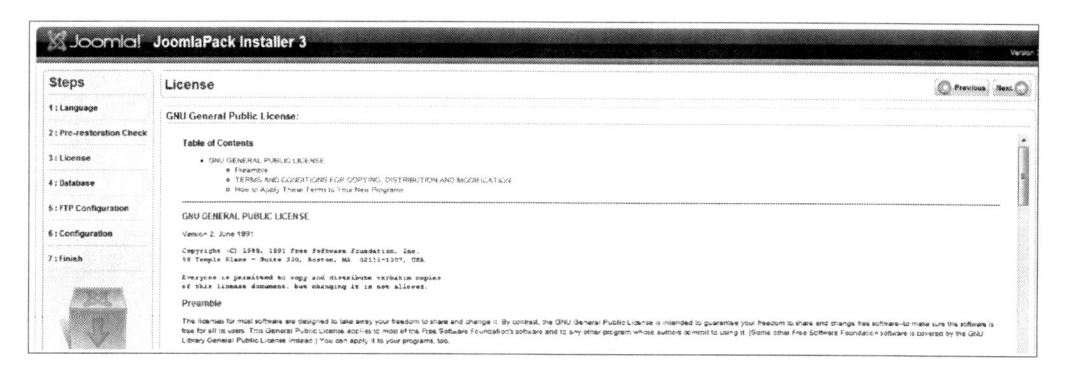

This screen outlines the license conditions and by selecting **Next**, you are accepting them.

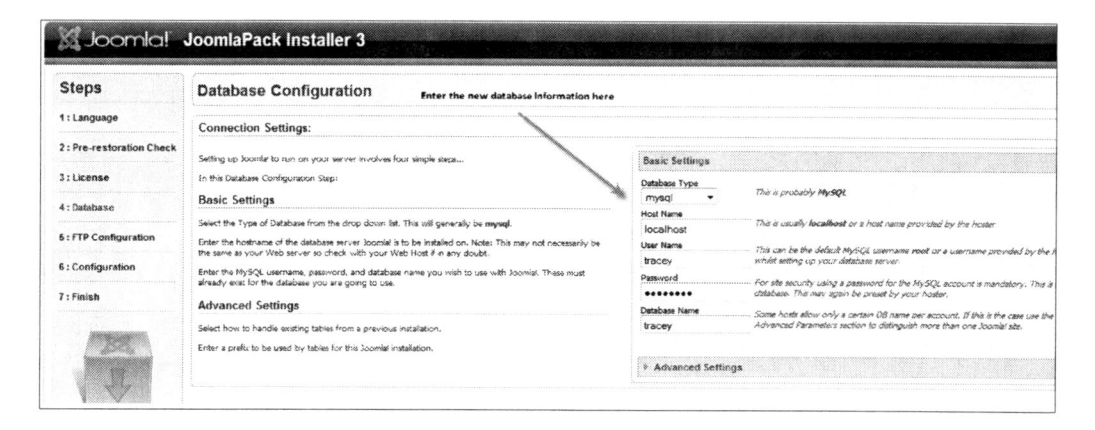

The **Database Configuration** screen requires the details of the database you created earlier.

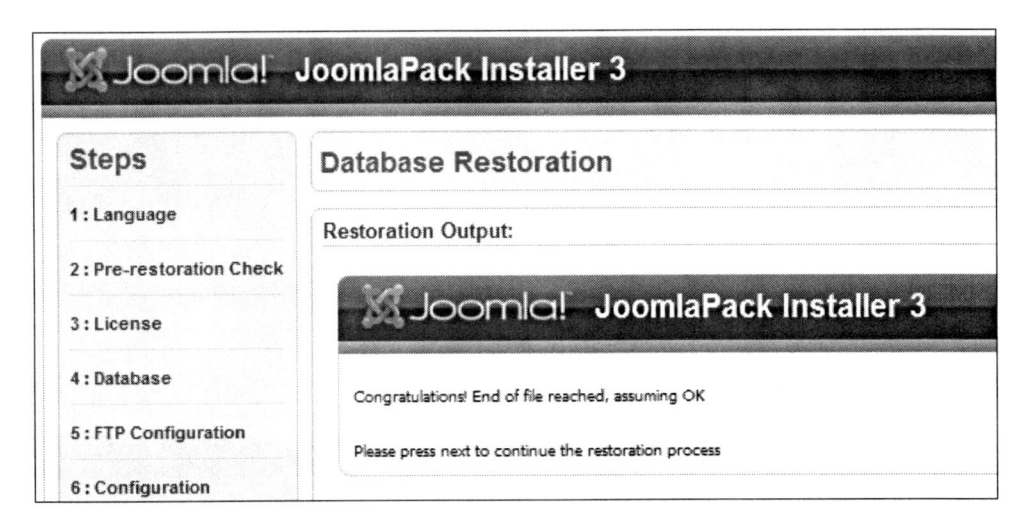

Provided you have entered the correct information, the database is restored and a congratulatory message appears.

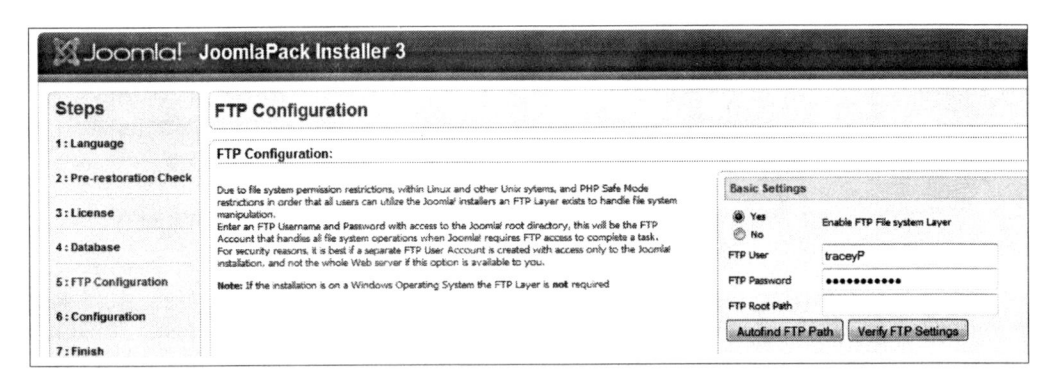

Enter the FTP details for your site. Your hosting server provider will have provided you with these details when you established your service.

Select the **Yes** radio button for **Enable FTP system Layer**.

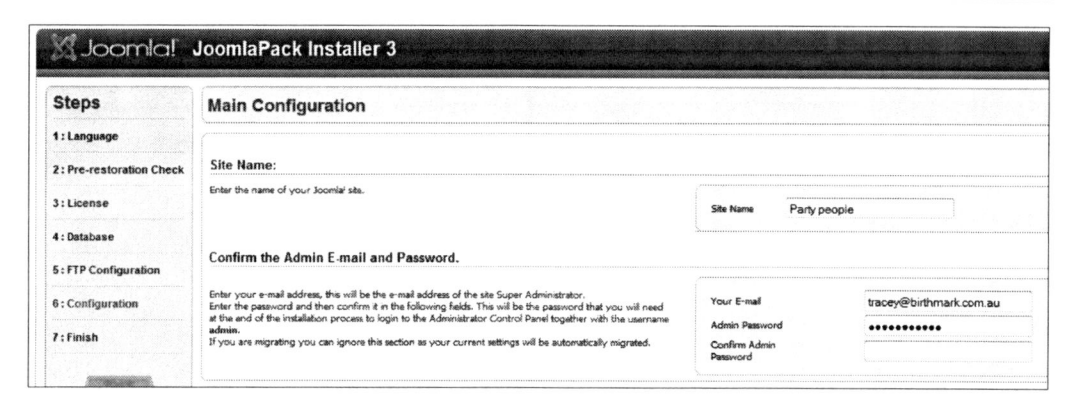

Enter the details of your site name and so on and make a note of your passwords.

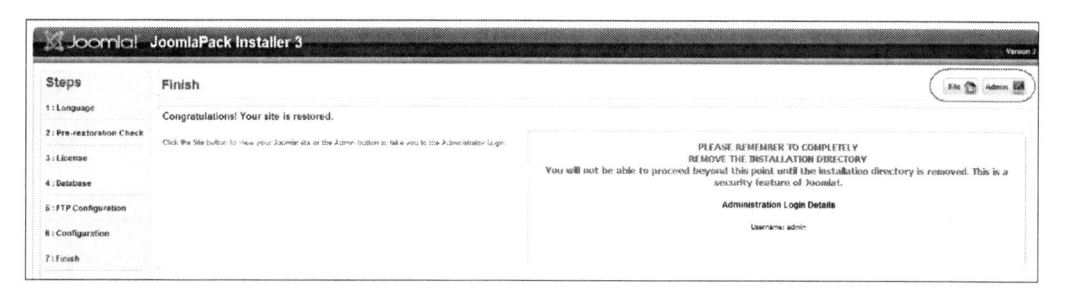

When you have successfully worked through the restoration process, the final screen will instruct you to delete the installation folder within your site files. Do this by going back into the file manager within the Control Panel. Select the installation folder and delete it. Once you have completed all the steps, go and type in the address of your website and it will appear in the browser.

Summary

As you can see, the backup and restoration process is quite lengthy, but achievable. It's very important to secure your Control Panel login and FTP details, as you will refer to them from time to time, and not just when you need to backup or restore your site.

With the availability of open source software, such as FileZilla and CuteFTP, you can manage the process without too much in the way of additional costs. Just familiarize yourself with the process and refer back to the developer's website. If you need more details, they are generally happy to answer questions. Also, don't be afraid to post a thread on their forum, but check the forum first to ensure that someone else hasn't already posted the same issue.

If you do not have the JoomlaPack component installed, undertaking the manual backup process is important and could (but hopefully not!) prove invaluable. Having a good working knowledge of your site and its functions is important as a content editor or webmaster. Working through this process, if you need to, will improve your overall understanding. Good luck!

5
User Management

Managing the registered users of your website can be a time consuming process, particularly if you have a large number of them, all of whom have various roles. Each role or user profile has access to certain information or tasks (if they're administrative) within the scope of your website. You have the tools to determine the extent of their access by using the backend interface modules. To explain, we'll use the Party People website to show you how to stay on top of managing your users and their profiles.

In this chapter, we will look at the **User Manager** to deal with the scenarios that can, and inevitably will, arise in your role as content editor and web master. These include:

- Managing existing frontend and administrative users
- Establishing and editing new user accounts
- Managing username and password issues
- Dealing with problematic users
- Tying in user profiles with site contacts
- Communicating with users

The big picture: Who are users?

Users are people who have registered their details with you and are allocated access to certain resources and information, depending on their role within the scope of your website. They can be administrators and content editors/contributors or customers who purchase goods and services from you.

User Management

This is different to a casual visitor who lands up at the frontend of your site because he/she has your website address or hopefully has found you through a search engine. You may be able to turn these casual visitors into registered users if you have something to offer them. Say you want to provide special content to only those who are genuinely interested in your services or products. Encouraging them to register allows you to collect contact information (it's best to ask only for the most relevant details, as people generally don't want to give out more than they need to) and keep in touch. Hopefully, you can convert it into an ongoing relationship with sales and benefits for your business. Generating interest in your products and services is important here and suggesting some level of exclusivity can make your customers feel privileged in terms of being privy to information not readily available to just anyone. Consider Chapter 2, *Creating, Editing, and Organizing Content* and the tips for writing good copy and using images and videos in Chapter 3, *Managing Images and Videos* to help you do this.

Put simply though, users are your website visitors, content contributors, and administrators. Depending on their role, they are essentially divided into two broad groups with smaller sub-categories within them.

Frontend users

Frontend users do not have access to the administration interface and can only access material and information through the frontend. They can be:

- Registered users, authors, editors, and publishers who have privileges to edit and update information.
- Guests or casual visitors to your site. These visitors come to your site anonymously and unregistered.
- People who register their details in order to transact with you.

Frontend user definitions

When a user is registered with you, they are allocated to a group, as per the settings applied within the Global Configuration, which we will work with later in this chapter.

They can be any one of the following:

- **Registered Users** are visitors to your site who have registered themselves in order to view certain content or transact with you.
- **Authors** can submit new content articles to the site with approval, but can't edit existing articles. A publisher or someone higher must approve these submissions.

- **Editors** can submit and edit new content articles. A publisher or someone higher must also approve these entries.
- **Publishers** can submit new content articles, edit existing articles, and publish the articles.

None of these user groups have access to the administration interface, and can only edit or add material from the frontend.

Administration users

Administration users can edit and update the content of your site by logging into the administration control panel and are those who:

- Have Administrator Manager or Super Administrator access. Each of these roles has specific access. For example, the Manager profile does not have access to the User Manager section, which is outlined in the "Managing your users" section of this chapter.
- Have various levels of access within the administration control panel, the highest level being Super Administrator.

Editing the frontend Login Form

From the frontend of your website, the **Login Form** allows users to access content that is potentially specialized and only visible to them, or to transact with you if you're running an e-commerce site.

You can also customize your **Login Form** by adding text and a link to create new accounts.

Lost usernames and passwords

The **Forgot your password** and **Forgot your username** links are important not only for users to find their password or username again, but also to help you to manage users. Rather than unnecessarily creating a new account if they have lost their login details, having an e-mail prompt sent to reset their details is a more efficient approach.

User Management

Clicking the link for either will generate a request to enter an e-mail address. A confirmation e-mail will be sent with a verification token or string of characters which allows the user to enter and reset their password. Alternatively, their username will be emailed to them.

Login Form

Username

Password

Remember Me ☐ [Log in]

Forgot your password?
Forgot your username?
Thank you for visiting again!

Allowing new account registrations

As seen in the previous screenshot, the Party People website currently allows only existing users to log in, with no option for new users to register. We'll reset the parameters of the **Login** module to add some text and allow new customers to create an account and log in.

To do this, we shall execute the following steps:

1. Navigate to the **Global Configuration** panel through the **Site | Global Configuration** in the top menu. You can also click the **Global Configuration** icon on the administration home page.

2. As shown in the following screenshot, select the **System** tab. Don't worry about the **Site** and **Server** tabs at this point, as they don't need to be edited in order to allow new registrations.

Chapter 5

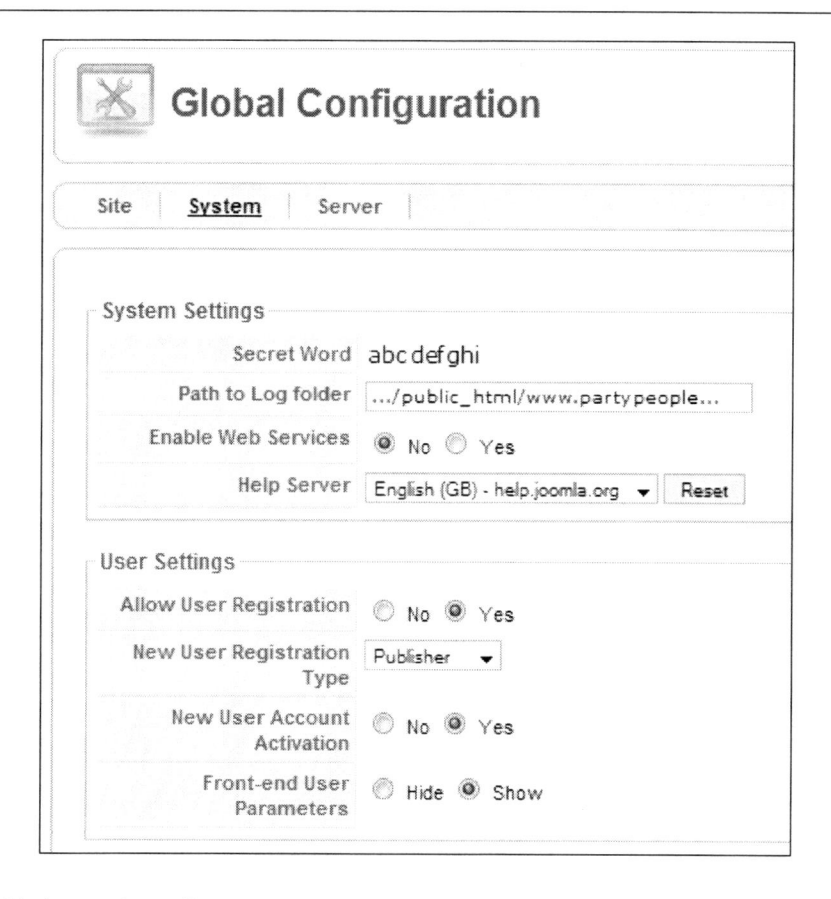

Global Configuration

Site | **System** | Server

System Settings

- Secret Word: abc def ghi
- Path to Log folder: .../public_html/www.partypeople...
- Enable Web Services: ● No ○ Yes
- Help Server: English (GB) - help.joomla.org [Reset]

User Settings

- Allow User Registration: ○ No ● Yes
- New User Registration Type: Publisher ▼
- New User Account Activation: ○ No ● Yes
- Front-end User Parameters: ○ Hide ● Show

3. Click **Yes** for **Allow User Registration**. This adds the **Create an account** link to the frontend **Login Form**. If you change your mind, click **No**, so that only previously registered users can log in.

4. Open **New User Registration Type**. Allocate these new users as **Registered** for **New User Registration Type**, as we are not allocating administrative rights (if we do, then you would be able to set it to **Authors**, **Editors**, or **Publishers**).

5. Click **Yes** for **New User Account Activation** to send an e-mail to the new user requesting them to activate their registration before gaining access. This helps with malicious and unnecessary registrations.

6. Click **Hide** or **Show** for the **Front-end User Parameters**, which provide options for the new user to set their preferred settings when they log in.

7. Click **Save**.

User Management

Adding custom text to the Login Form

We can add customized text to the top and bottom sections of the **Login Form** box using the **Modules** menu.

1. Go to **Extensions | Module Manager** through the top menu.
2. Click the **Login Form** under the **Module Name** column to open its screen. If you have called it something else, then select that name. The **Details** and **Menu Assignment** sections (as shown in the following screenshot) contain the settings, positioning, and details of the actual login form.

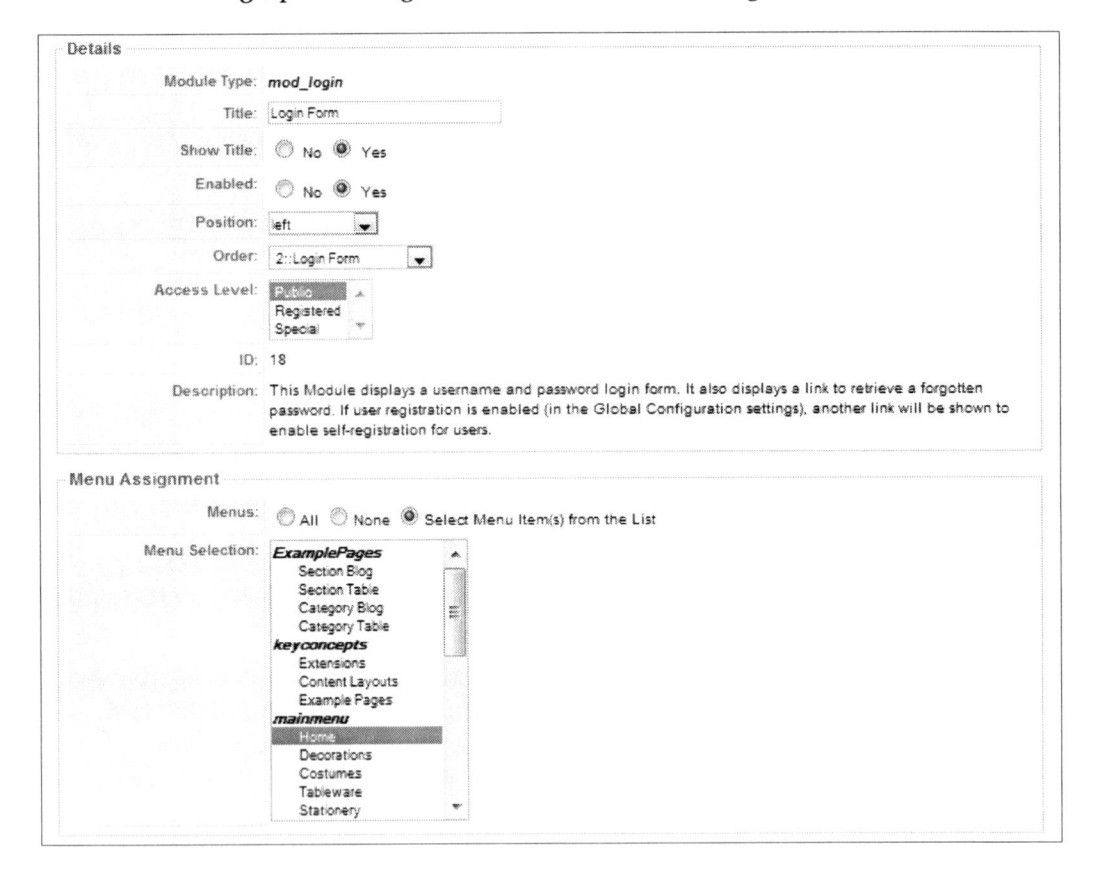

Change these settings if you need to; otherwise, they can be left as they are.

3. Go to the **Parameters** section to the right of screen, as shown in the following screenshot, and add your text in the **Pre-text** and **Post-text** input boxes.

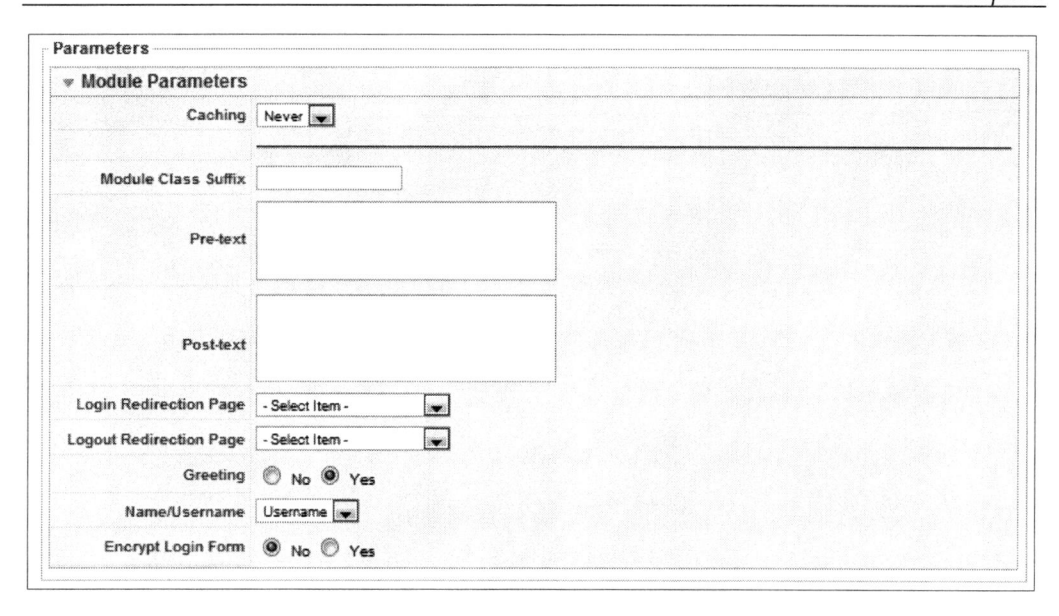

Pre-text is the text that is displayed before the **Username** and Post-text is displayed at the end. For example, enter **Login if you are already a Customer, or create a new account and order online with us.** in the **Pre-text** field and **Thank You!** in the **Post-text** field.

If you're just adding the text to the form, leave the rest of the settings, such as the **Login Redirection Page** as it is. This will be addressed in the following section.

4. Click **Save** and your new text is added to the form, as shown in the following screenshot:

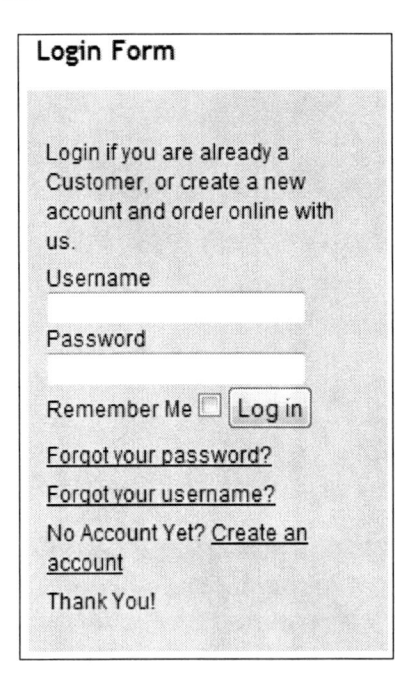

> **Login Form**
>
> Login if you are already a Customer, or create a new account and order online with us.
>
> Username
>
> Password
>
> Remember Me ☐ Log in
>
> Forgot your password?
> Forgot your username?
> No Account Yet? Create an account
> Thank You!

This adds a personalized touch to your form or you can use the space for some concise instructions or information.

Directing registered users to a certain section of the site

Within the **Login** module screen, you can also set where you want logged-in users to land after they enter their username and password and where they go after logging out. This can be a very useful tool and you can create a custom section or article for them to land up on to communicate with your users.

While you are still in the **Login Form** module:

1. Click **Login Redirection Page** in the **Parameters** section.
2. Click on the area you want your users to land on when they have successfully logged in.
3. Click **Logout Redirection Page** in the **Parameters** section.
4. Click on the area you want your users to land on when they have successfully logged out.

Chapter 5

Login Redirection Page	- Select Item -
Logout Redirection Page	- Select Item -
Greeting	○ No ● Yes
Name/Username	Username
Encrypt Login Form	● No ○ Yes

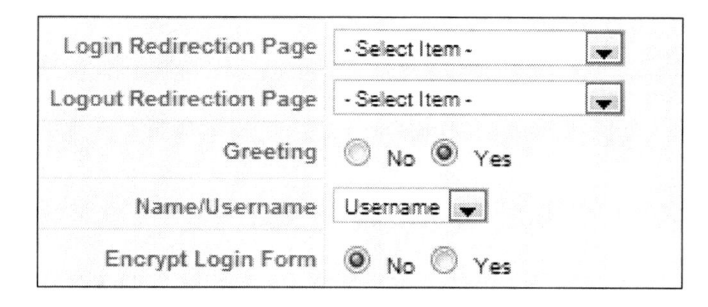

5. Decide whether to show or hide a short greeting.
6. Click **Save** for your changes to take effect.

Managing your users: The User Manager

The **User Manager** within the administration interface gives you an overview of all the registered users of your website and the ability to manage them as needed.

Only users registered as Administrator or Super Administrator can make changes here.

Creating a new user

The Party People website has only one administration user and we want to add a new user who has backend manager access. As the administrator, you can do this by accessing the **User Manager** from within the administration.

1. Click **Site | User Manager** in the top menu or click the **User Manager** icon on the front page of the administration page.
2. To add a new user, click the **New** icon on the top right toolbar.
3. Type in a name, a username, an e-mail address, and a password into the **Name**, **Username**, and **New Password** input boxes, as shown in the following screenshot. Verify the password to be sure you have entered the correct string.
4. Click on the user group that you want to allocate them to from the selection in the **Group** window. Your choice will obviously depend upon the content and access level you want them to have. We'll select **Manager** for our site.
5. Click **No** for **Block User,** as we are setting up a new one.
6. Select **Yes** or **No** for **Receive System E-mails**.

User Management

7. Save your new user.

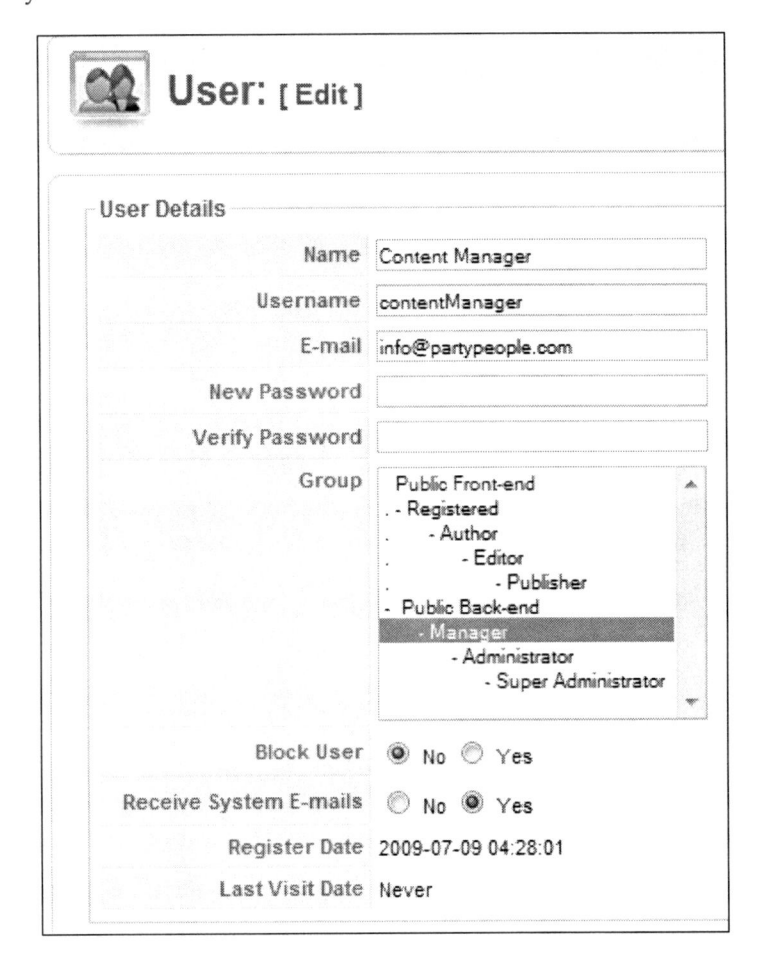

Adding a new user as a site contact

Before you add your new user to your contact list, consider whether they fit into the established contact categories. If they don't, you can add a new Category. Do this before you add the new contact.

Adding a new contact Category

Create contact Categories based on what role the user is to take within your site. It is described in the following steps:

1. Select **Components** from the top menu, then **Contacts** and **Manage Contacts** to see the **Contact Manager**.

[98]

2. To add a new contact Category, select that link.
3. In the new Category screen, give the category a name and complete the details as shown in the following screenshot. Add a brief description if you need to.
4. Save your new category.

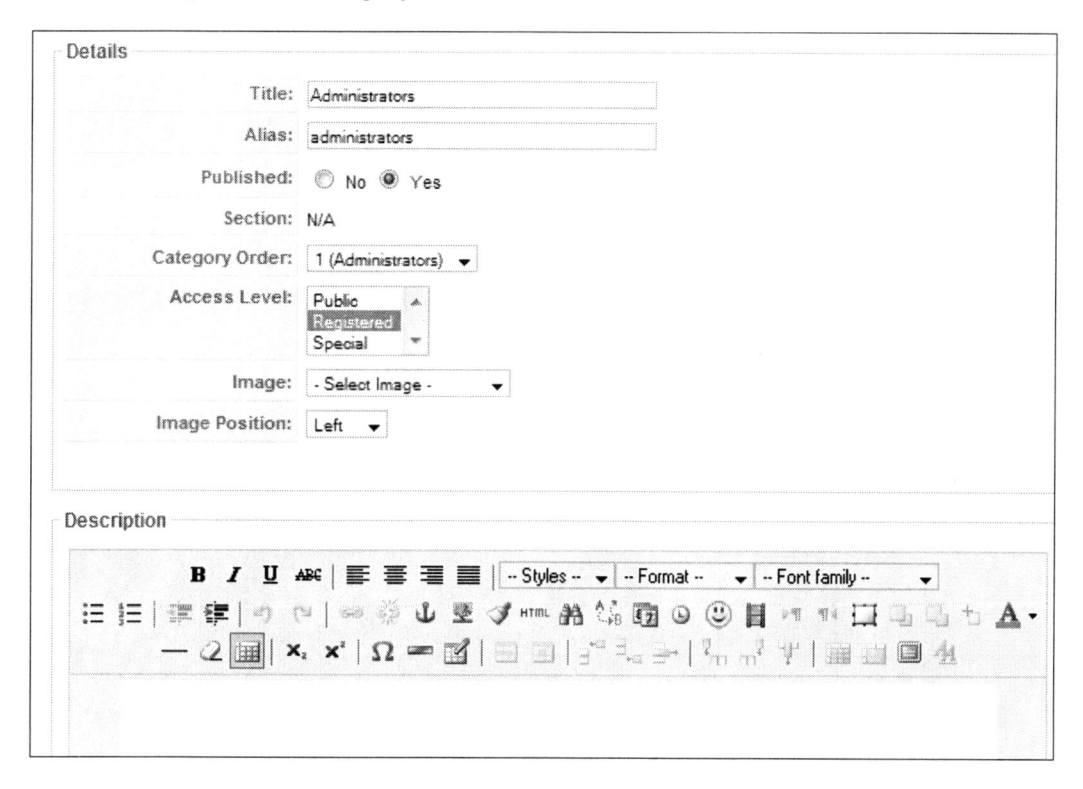

Adding the new user to your list of contacts

If you have added a new user profile, say for an employee, and also want them to be available as a site contact, you can simply do so by following these steps:

1. Click **Contacts** in the **Contact Manager** and the **New** icon.
2. Type in the name details for your user.
3. Select the **Category** of contact you just created, if necessary.

User Management

4. Click **Registered** for the **Access Level**, as the user is the administrator for the site.

Contact: [New]

Details
- Name:
- Alias:
- Published: No ● Yes
- Category: Administrators
- Linked to User: Content Manager
- Order: New Contacts default to the last position. Ordering can be changed after this Contact is saved.
- Access Level: Public / Registered / Special

Information
- Contact's Position:
- E-mail:
- Street Address:

5. Add the **Information** you want to register for the new contact, including their **Contact's Position**, **E-mail**, and **Street Address** (if necessary).

6. Select the appropriate **Parameter** radio buttons to **Show** or **Hide** information on the frontend of the site.

Chapter 5

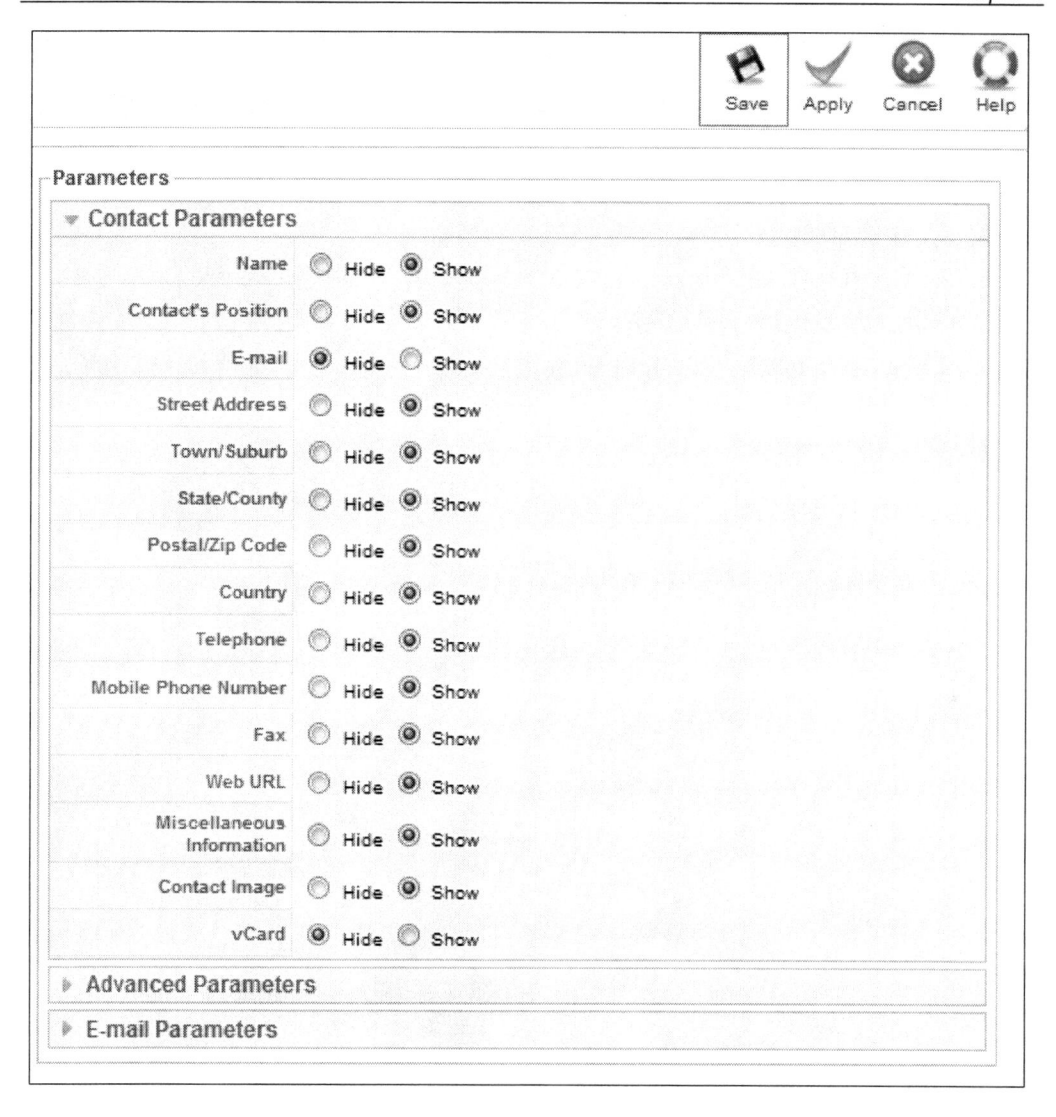

7. You can apply the settings within the **Advanced Parameters** and the **E-mail Parameters** as well, in order to add icons to the contact page and filter the e-mails.
8. Click **Save**.

User Management

Adding a new customer manually

We'll add a new customer to the Party People registered users list, the same way as we added a new administrative user.

1. Navigate to **Site | User Manager**, then select **User Manager** in the top menu.
2. Click the **New** button.
3. Add in the details for your new user as shown in the following screenshot.
4. Select the **Registered** group.
5. Click **No** to **Receive System E-mails**, as they are a customer and not an administrator.
6. Save the new user.

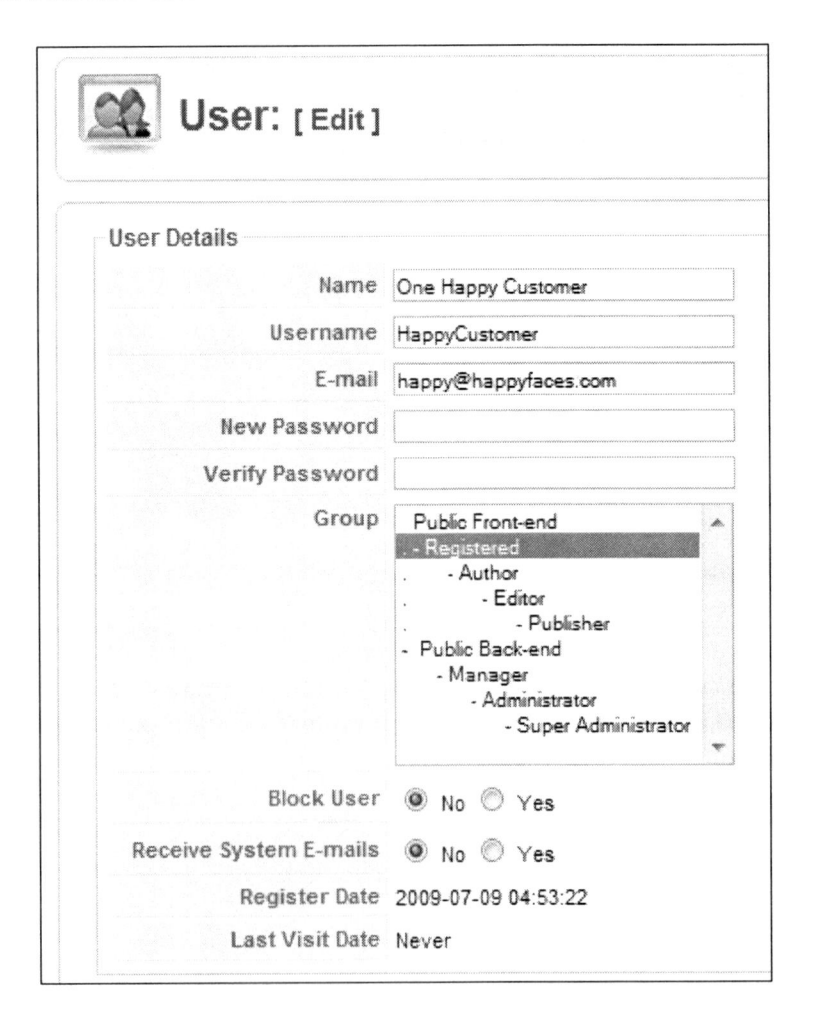

User: [Edit]

User Details

Name	One Happy Customer
Username	HappyCustomer
E-mail	happy@happyfaces.com
New Password	
Verify Password	

Group	Public Front-end
	- Registered
	   - Author
	     - Editor
	       - Publisher
	- Public Back-end
	  - Manager
	    - Administrator
	      - Super Administrator

Block User	● No ○ Yes
Receive System E-mails	● No ○ Yes
Register Date	2009-07-09 04:53:22
Last Visit Date	Never

Editing existing users

User details can be edited through the **User Manager** quite easily.

Editing a user profile

Let's edit a Party People user's e-mail address in the **User Manager**.

1. Click the checkbox next to the user and click the **Edit** icon at the top right of the screen, or click on the name of the user in the list on the **User Manager** screen.
2. Click on the **E-Mail** text box and replace the existing with the new e-mail address.
3. Click **Save**.

Also, if your site has numerous users, it would be time consuming to have to work your way through all of the names in the list. To make the process of locating a username in this case easy, use the filtering options at the top right of the **User Manager**, as shown:

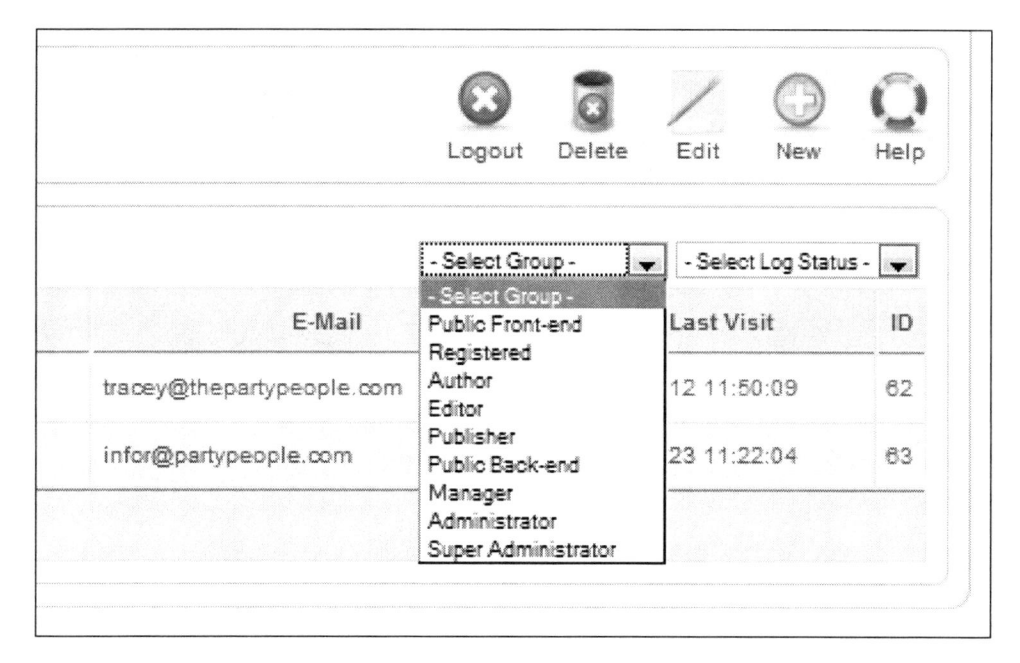

Updating the linked contact details

Within the user profile, you will also find a link to update the contact details of the user if they are listed as a site contact.

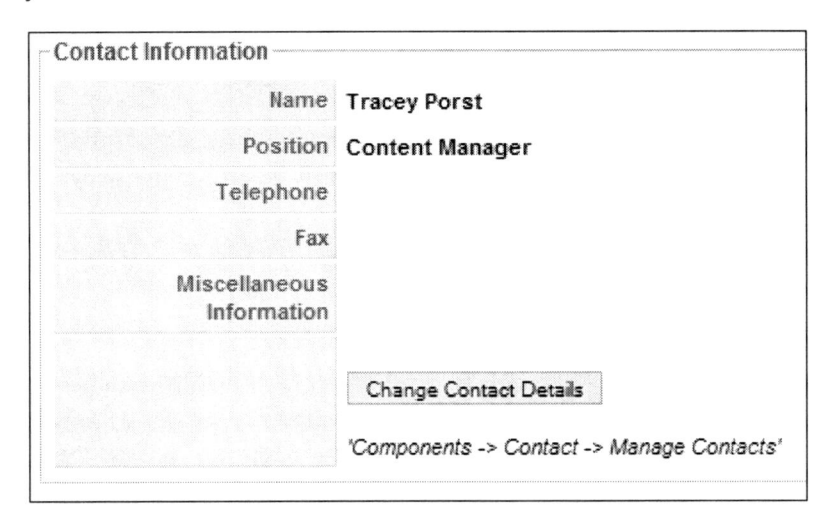

Contact Information	
Name	Tracey Porst
Position	Content Manager
Telephone	
Fax	
Miscellaneous Information	

[Change Contact Details]

'Components -> Contact -> Manage Contacts'

To update the user's contact details:

1. Click the **Change Contact Details** button under the **Contact Information** section to view the contact profile details of the user.
2. Update the profile details within the **Contact** profile information as shown in the following excerpt from that screen.

Chapter 5

Contact: [Edit]

Details

Name:	Tracey Porst
Alias:	name
Published:	○ No ● Yes
Category:	Contacts
Linked to User:	Administrator
Order:	1 (Tracey Porst)
Access Level:	Public / Registered / Special
ID:	1

Information

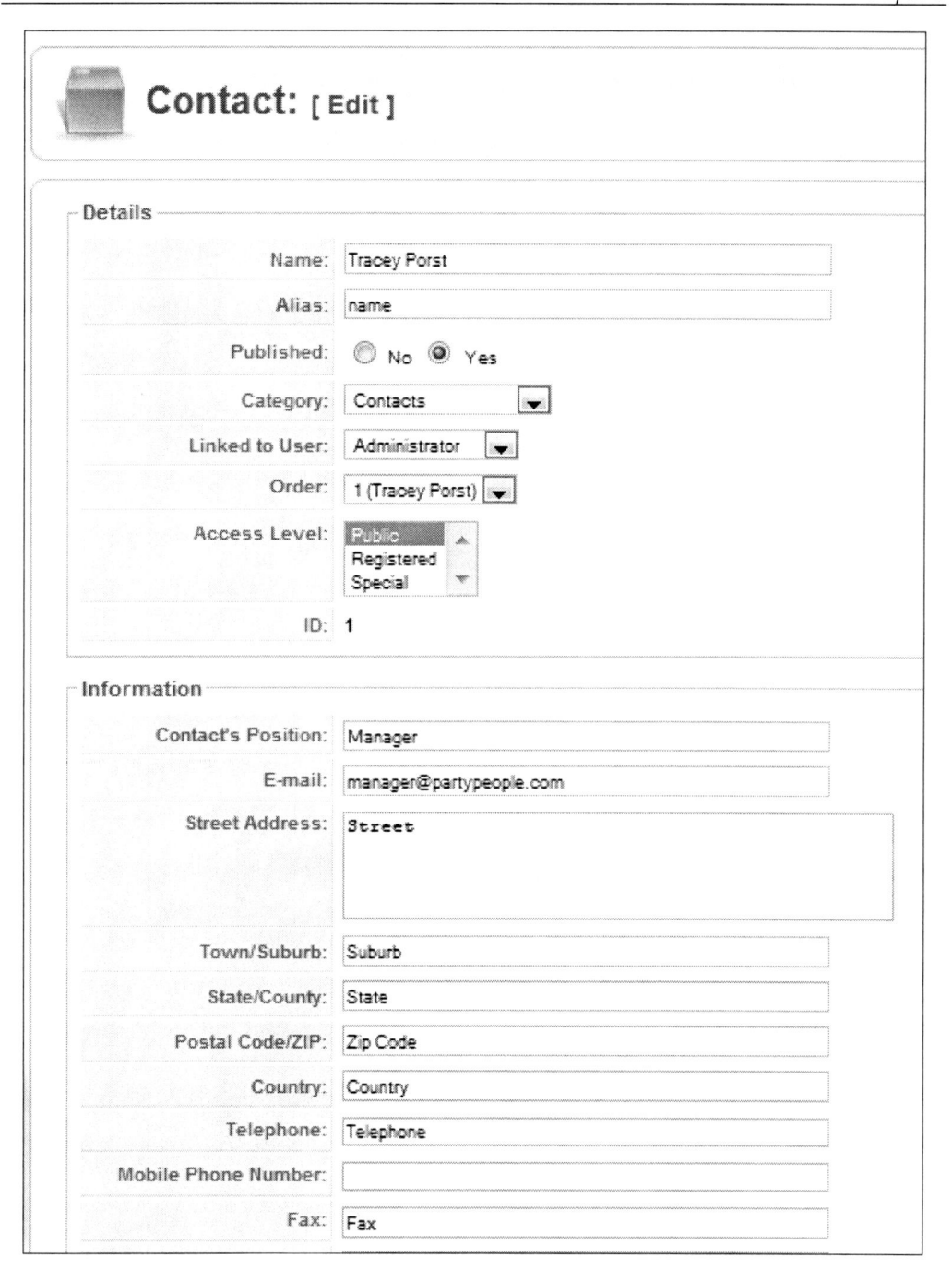

Contact's Position:	Manager
E-mail:	manager@partypeople.com
Street Address:	Street
Town/Suburb:	Suburb
State/County:	State
Postal Code/ZIP:	Zip Code
Country:	Country
Telephone:	Telephone
Mobile Phone Number:	
Fax:	Fax

3. Click **Save**.

User Management

Resetting a username and password

As mentioned, registered frontend users can do this for themselves using one of the links in the **Login Form**. Otherwise, we can use the **User Manager** again to edit the user's profile details. You can do this especially for the backend users, following the given steps:

1. Navigate to the **User Manager** screen.
2. Select **User** and open the profile screen.
3. Enter the new password in the **Password** input box. Then verify it.
4. Save the change when you're done.

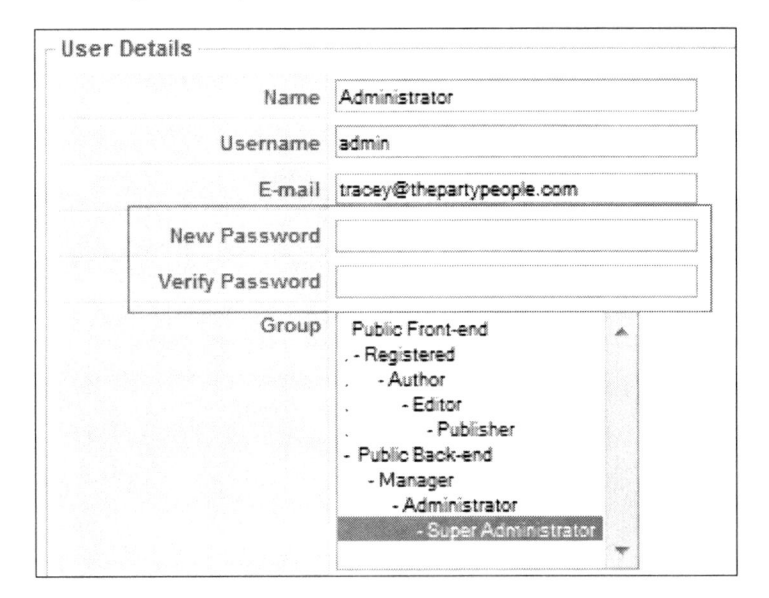

Dealing with problematic users

There may be times when you will need to block a user's access to the site. In fact, some spam bots can register themselves and you can find yourself with a list of oddly named users as a result. In this case, you would simply delete them.

However, if you have a particular individual user to deal with, the best method for handling them is to disable the account rather than deleting it altogether.

You can also use this to suspend an account as a temporary measure. The account can easily be reinstated at a later date, which is more efficient than re-establishing the account from scratch if you simply delete it.

Deleting a user

If you find yourself in the position of having to delete a user, follow the given steps:

1. Navigate to the **User Manager** screen, through the **Site | User Manager** menu or click the **User Manager** icon on the administration control panel.
2. Use the **Filter** drop-down list as shown in the following screenshot if you have many to choose from, and select the checkbox to the left of the user's name.
3. Click the **Delete** icon at the top right menu to remove that user profile.

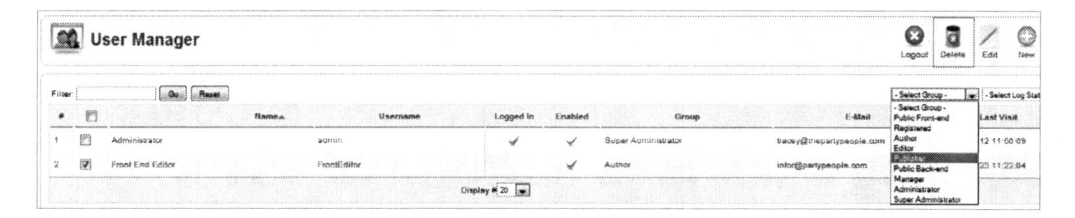

You will have noticed in the **User Manager** that user registrations are either *enabled* or *disabled*, the green ticks or red crosses indicating the user's status.

Blocking a user

If you find yourself having to suspend a user profile, prevent any activity by blocking them.

1. Navigate to the **User Manager**.
2. Filter your user listing if you have many, and click the green (enabled) tick under the **Enabled** column to disable the particular account. Changing the tick to a cross immediately disables the account and the user will not be able to log in from that moment.

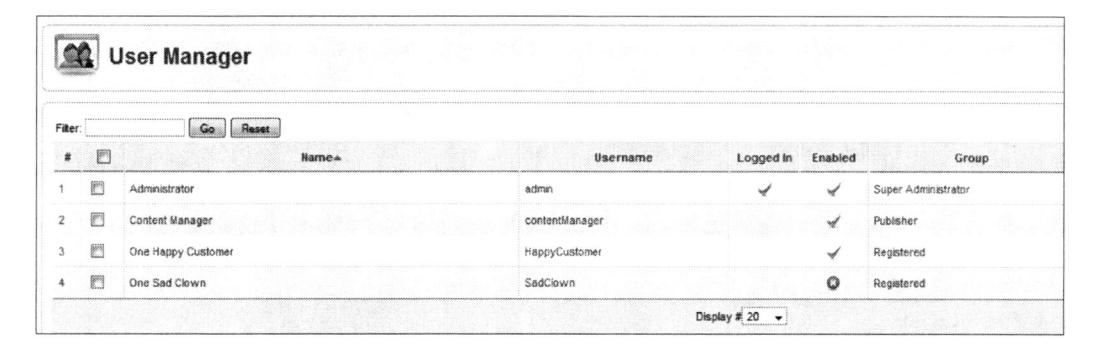

User Management

Note that only Administrators and Super Administrators can do this.

What if a new user can't log in?

It may be that the user has not activated their account because they have not followed the link in their activation e-mail. Alternatively, these e-mails can sometimes be blocked by the user's spam filter, which will send it directly to a junk e-mail box. In the first instance, ask them to check there first. However, if this is not the case, you can quickly enable their account if it is disabled. Activate the user account by the following steps:

1. Navigate to the **User Manager**.
2. Click the red (disabled) cross to immediately enable the account.

Sending e-mails to a group of users

As a Super Administrator, you can send an e-mail to a particular group of users.

To do this:

1. Select **Tools | Mass Mail** from the top menu.
2. Type in your e-mail **Subject** and the body of the message into the input boxes as shown in the following screenshot.
3. Click on the **Parameters** icon to set some consistent details for every e-mail sent. This could be the name of the website, or a signature at the end of the e-mail.
4. Also note some of the special e-mail settings:
   - **Mail to Child Groups**: Selecting this option means your e-mail will be sent to the user group selected and all of the child groups within. For example, if you send the e-mail to the **Public Back-end** group, the e-mail will be sent to all members of that group who are registered as Managers, Administrators, and Super Administrators. Otherwise, you can select just **Manager**. Using this option allows you to send the e-mail to a broader group.
   - **Send in HTML Mode**: This means sending the e-mail with special code to allow the recipient's e-mail client to display any HTML content.
   - **Group**: Select the user group the e-mail should be sent to. Work in conjunction with the **Mail to Child Group** function.

- **Recipients as BCC. Adds a copy to site e-mail** : This means all recipients will be included as **BCC** (**Blind Carbon Copy**) entries. This means none of the recipients will see each other's e-mail address and, as many e-mail routers treat e-mail without a **To** entry (because all of the recipients are in BCC), the site e-mail address will be used in the **To** entry box.

5. Click the **Send Mail** icon to send the e-mail to your recipients.

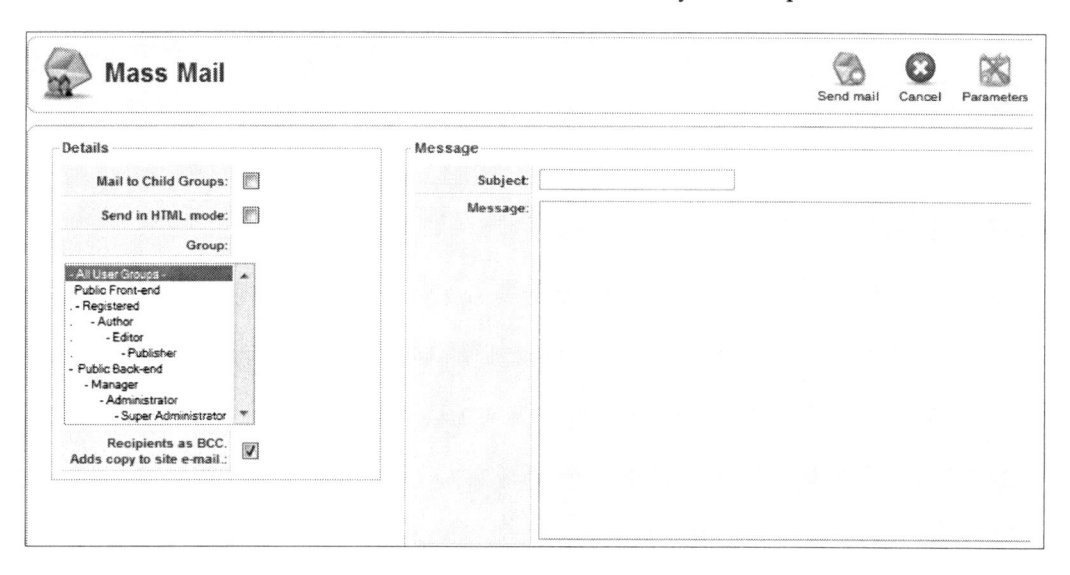

Sending a private message to a user

Also note that private messages can also be sent to any backend users. Note that these messages are not actually e-mails, but messages sent within the scope of the administration interface only. A protocol for checking these would be good practice.

1. Click on **Tools**, then the **Write Message** link.
2. Select your recipient, enter the subject, and type in your message.
3. Click **Send**.

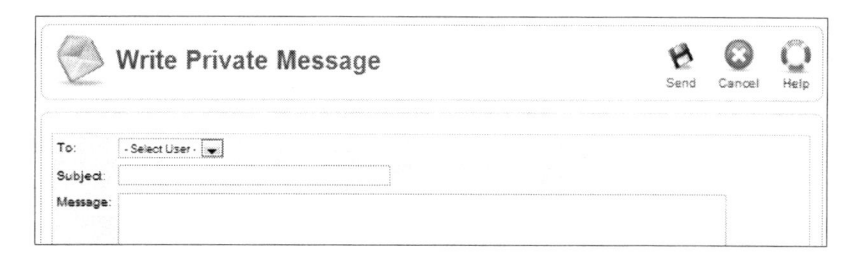

Summary

In this chapter, we looked at how the user management system within the administration interface allows you to effectively manage your website users and their profiles. There are many add-on third party extensions you can use to make this process even more functional, such as the powerful Community Builder component. The ability to undertake key administrative tasks, such as what we have covered in this chapter, is important and once you understand these fundamentals, you can build on your skill level to address tasks within any of the add-on extensions available.

Chapter 6, *Making Your Site Popular* covers search engine optimization tips and tools. Making your site popular and improving its search engine ranking is as important as managing your users. As mentioned in this chapter, making your site interesting to your target audience can turn casual visitors into registered users. Making your site perform better in search engine results can increase the number of casual visitors who land on your site.

6
Making Your Site Popular

As we know, search engines help us find websites and, theoretically, those with keywords and descriptions in the code that most closely match the words you type into the search box will appear ranked in order of their compatibility to your search query.

This chapter outlines:

- How search engines find websites based on keywords and page descriptions.
- How you can apply them to your website and increase the chances of a better ranking in the index page of a search engine result.

We'll also look at some ways you may be able to improve the success of your search engine ranking, using the Party People website to show you how.

So the question is, how do you get your site at the top of the listing page? Unfortunately, there isn't an easy answer to this one and there are no guarantees about making it to the top of the list either.

Overview of Search Engine Ranking

Without going into the finer details, search engines all work differently but they do follow some general processes that enable them to search for and retrieve a list of websites. Their search is based on the keywords and descriptions hidden within the code of the page, known as the "metadata." By running a program on their server that sends page lookup requests to websites, the search provider can index the results into an **organic** listing of links based on what they find. These programs are sometimes referred to as crawlers, spiders, or robots. A part of that process is to look for new content within websites. An **organic** listing is the list of links to sites on the results page that the search engines deem relevant based on order of relevance (without considering whether they are paid placements or not).

You may have also heard the term **Search Engine Optimization** (**SEO**). It refers to how web developers can make a website rank well when a search engine returns its results. There are many theories about how to achieve a prominent ranking, but the consensus is that updating your pages with well-written content regularly will always improve the chances of a better result. Visit `http://en.wikipedia.org/wiki/Search_engine_optimization` if you are interested in learning more.

What is metadata?

Descriptions and keywords are used to reflect the content within your site and are located within the metadata HTML tags of the site page. You can add them to your site, especially to Articles using the Article Manager interface. The key is finding the right words to define the content of the page, as well as words your target user might type into the search engine box. The combination of well-chosen keywords and what the user types in is what brings the results to a search engine.

There are various techniques around (for example, "word stuffing", where keywords are repeated many times) that try to trick the search engines into giving the website a better ranking. However, these tactics are identified fairly quickly, as the technology employed by the crawlers is vigilant. Tactics like these can also lead to a site being blacklisted.

If Google blacklists a site, it's because they have detected automated traffic being sent to them from a computer on someone's network, which indicates to them that there is suspicious activity coming from that site. You'll know if your site has been blacklisted as a **This site may harm your computer** message is displayed in the search index results where your site details appear in the ranking. If a user clicks the link anyway, they are taken to a special warning page, telling people this site will harm their computer. From your point of view, it's important to acknowledge the terms of service that Google provides (see `http://www.google.com/accounts/TOS` for full details). If your site has been marked as a potential threat, you have the right to address the reason with Google and find out why.

General strategies for SEO

There are many businesses that specialize in Search Engine Optimization techniques, but defining your own keywords and phrases allows you to contribute to your site's ranking as well. Brainstorming ideas, including phrases, words, and adjectives can produce some good results. Remember to consider who your target audience is and try to pre-empt what words they might use to try and find you.

In this section, we'll look at some strategies you can implement to help your site in the SEO rankings.

Updating content frequently

Making sure the content within your site is fresh and of interest to your core target audience is a good way to get started. Frequently updated sites can achieve better indexing results.

Write well and make your Articles text based. Search engines prefer words over images. If you include images, you should also include a description of them or make them link to another site or Article. Include keywords in your written content and use them in your metadata information.

Link building

Reciprocal links are very helpful. They are links to other websites, which link back to your site—outbound links that are reciprocated with inbound links to you. Google considers site popularity as part of its ranking process, so sites with lots of hits are often found at the top of the index page as well.

Remember to have the outbound links open in a separate tab or window. You don't want to lose your viewer to another site, because they may not come back to you. When the viewer closes the external site, your site will still be open and they may just take another look around before leaving. This also increases the amount of time they spend on your site, which helps as well. We'll look into this further when we look at Google Analytics.

Adding an external link to an Article

Let's embed an external link within an article on the home page of the Party People website. The link text will be the name of a catering company, rather than typing in the actual website address. You can also embed an image within your article to make this your link as well.

1. Create a new Article, using the Article Manager. Refer to Chapter 3, *Managing Images and Videos* if you're not sure on how to do this.
2. Type in the paragraph of text, including the words that will be the actual link to the external website.
3. Select the text to apply the link to and click the **Insert/Edit Link** icon in the text editing toolbar to open the dialog window.
4. Type the website address into the **Link URL** box including the **http://www**.
5. Select **Open Link in a new window** in the **Target** box.

6. Type in the **Title** for the link, for example **Delicate Delights**.
7. Leave the **Class** for now.
8. Click **Insert** to add the link to the Article.

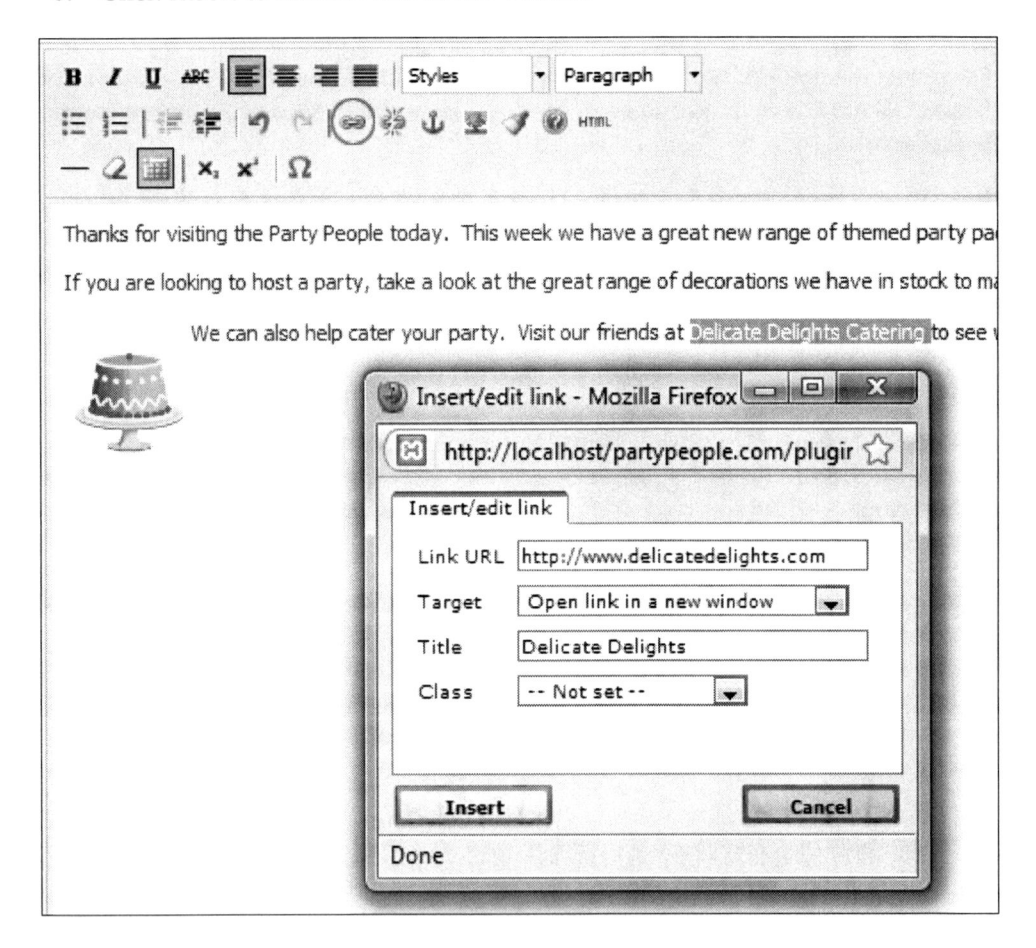

Adding an internal link to an Article

Cross linking your Articles also makes it easier to find related material on your site and there is an extension available to do this. We'll add a link from the same Article to the **What's New in Store** section using the Linkr component. If you don't have this component installed, then we can also add the link manually.

The following steps show how to link to an Article using Linkr:

1. Open the Article using the Article Manager.
2. Select the text or image you want to link from.

3. Click the **Linkr** button at the bottom of the text editor.
4. Navigate to the Article in the pop-up box that appears.
5. Click **Configure link**.
6. Choose **same page** for the **Page target**, as this is an internal link.
7. Click **Get link** to apply the link to the text.

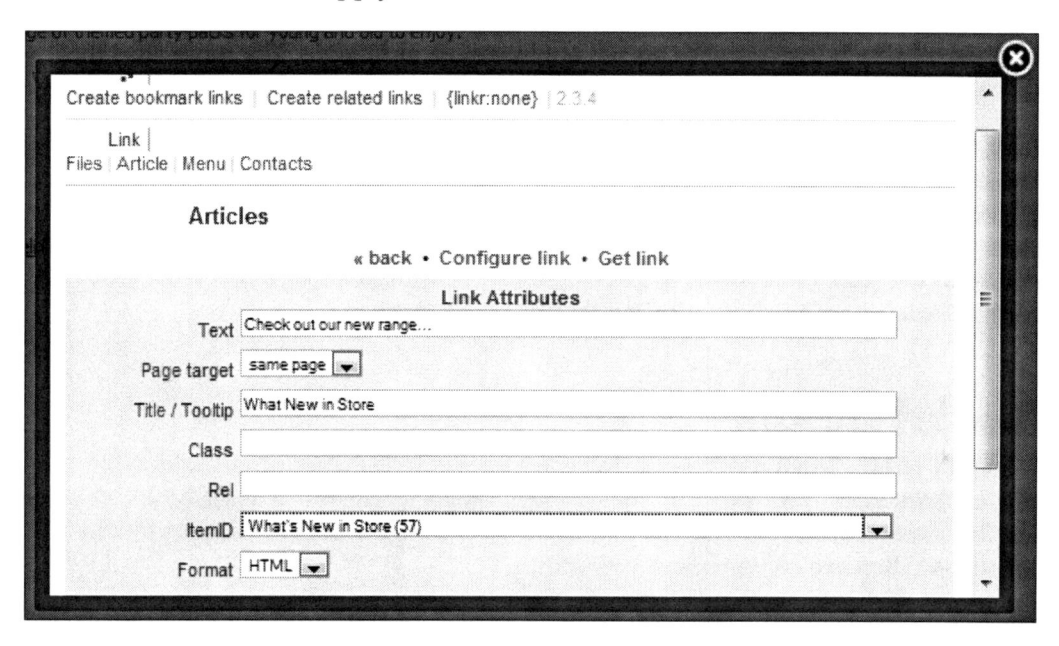

The following steps are given to add a link manually:

1. Navigate to the existing Article from the frontend of the website.
2. Copy the URL for the link from the browser address window.
3. Open the Article in the Article Manager from the administration interface.
4. Select the text or image you want to link from with the text editor.
5. Click the **Insert/Edit Link** icon in the toolbar.
6. Paste the URL into the **Link URL** box.
7. Select **Open link in same window** for the target.
8. Add the **Title** and click **Update**.

You can also ensure your Article titles are links as well. This works when you have a **Read More** link from an Article on the home page.

Posting links with your web address to any forums or bulletin boards you visit can also help. While I don't advocate signing up to everything and anything just for this purpose, it can be a good way to spread the word if you pick the right forum, one that is relevant to your needs.

Link popularity is important to search engines such as Google. The more sites that link to yours can mean a much better ranking.

Also, Google provides a free service called Google Analytics which you can use to analyze the traffic to and from your site. Google AdWords is another useful application that includes a tool that identifies keywords you can use to add to the metadata page and potentially help with improving your search engine ranking. You will need to set up an account with Google to access these tools. We'll work through setting these up, using the Party People site as our example.

Social media

While it's not the intention here to delve too deeply into the whole social media phenomenon, you have probably heard the term social media to describe websites like Facebook, Twitter, or Digg to name a few, as well as applications like RSS to collect and disperse content from websites.

The Internet today is considered to be in its second generation (Web 2.0) because it's content is largely user generated, which is partly due to the development of social networking websites. This means the Web has become collaborative and can now be used to provide a voice for people who may not have had one. If you want to know more about how it all started and the various forms it took, take a look at `http://en.wikipedia.org/wiki/Social_media` for more detailed information.

Essentially, these websites provide the tools for anybody who is inclined to express and comment on opinions, as well as share images, videos, or articles they have found that can be of interest to others. It's about creating relationships within an online community.

These new social networking tools are now very popular and can easily be integrated into a Joomla! website to help bring new visitors to it.

Using social media for marketing

Developing a marketing strategy using social media offers you the potential to bring the attention of the masses to your products and services, at very little or no cost to anyone— you or the user.

> This vast public medium offers you links, attention, and potentially a lot of site traffic. If you can think creatively about how you can use these free services, you have the ability to make your website profitable. The idea is to build up a network of followers, who are either willing to purchase from you or recommend your site to others. The more support you build, the more the word spreads.

Following is an overview of some popular social networking websites. You can integrate your profiles with them into your Joomla! website with a third-party extension. One highly rated non-commercial extension is called "Stalker", which we'll look at later in this section.

Facebook

Launched in 2004, Facebook is host to a global network of users who create profiles for themselves that include photos, videos, and information about their personal preferences. You might think it's just for kids, but in fact it's a widely used social and professional networking tool that you can use to promote your business or cause.

You can use Facebook as part of your own online marketing strategy by:

- Creating a profile of yourself to connect to friends and associates. This can be useful for building relationships and establishing a new line of communication with like-minded individuals. Based on the theory of six degrees of separation, you can find new friends who are friends of your friends, and who can potentially pass on your message to others.

- Updating your *status* to indicate that you have something to share with your *friends*, such as a new business venture. It also gives you an opportunity to collaborate, or promote your cause.

- Creating a special interest Facebook group and inviting your associates and other Facebook users to join it for discussions, collaborate on a project, or promote your interests or cause.

- Purchasing advertising space that is targeted towards particular users. Facebook has a section dedicated to advertising at http://www.facebook.com/advertising/. Create an ad that promotes your business or organization, that reaches literally millions of people.

Facebook has been recognized as one of the most trusted companies for privacy. While this may be the case, it's best to not include too much personal information and consider what you want everyone to know about you.

Visit `http://www.facebook.com` to set up a profile and get started.

Twitter

"Twittering" has become a verb, thanks to this social networking and "microblogging" website (such is the influence it has had on popular culture recently). Like Facebook, anyone who creates a profile can encourage "followers", that is, those who follow your "tweets" and keep up-to-date with your activities. Now, of course, celebrities and ordinary folk alike use it to do business.

You can use Twitter to:

- Post 140 character status updates for your followers about your latest news and information.
- Add a link to your website or some new material that you have added.
- Add photos to your profile of some new products or events.
- Follow anyone whose status updates you're interested in.

Use Twitter if you don't want to set up a full-blown profile on Facebook, but would prefer to just let people know when and if you have something to tell them.

See `http://www.twitter.com/` for more details and set up a profile.

StumbleUpon

This is another social networking website that allows users to find and present other websites they think will be of interest, based on preferences in a profile you create. A browser toolbar button can be installed and whenever you click it, you will be taken to a website that matches your interests. It's like a personalized search engine that only presents you with websites based on your interests.

Importantly, each user has the ability to rate each website and, along with the millions of other people who rate the site, a profile is built of the most interesting sites. Further, you can share your sites with friends and colleagues.

All of this has the potential to generate interest and hits on your site, potentially increasing your ranking with search engines, and thereby increasing your chances of better revenue.

See `http://www.stumbleupon.com` and take a look at how it all works in detail.

Delicious

This is actually a social bookmarking site that has created a community of users who share, tag, and manage their bookmarked websites with others inside the Delicious (formerly del.icio.us) network. The idea behind it is to improve the way users uncover and share information available on the Internet.

There is potential for you as a website owner to ask your site visitors to bookmark your site within their Delicious profile, using a Joomla! third party extension.

When you add a new link to your Delicious profile, consider the tags or keywords you can apply to it, just as you would apply them to your website article.

See `http://delicious.com/help/getStarted` for more details.

Reddit and Digg

Much like StumbleUpon, Reddit and Digg are social news websites where users can post links to websites that other users can comment on by voting on the content. The links are ordered in terms of their votes and can be moved up or down in the order displayed on the home page.

See `http://www.reddit.com` and `http://digg.com` for more details.

RSS feeds

In technological terms, an **RSS** is a file format that is described as both a **Really Simple Syndication** or a **Rich Site Summary**. Briefly, it's an application that allows subscribers to receive information from websites on a regular and ongoing basis, in full or summarized format. Website owners can include a feed from their site and invite subscriptions or subscribe themselves and include a display of the feed within their website. The core Joomla! application includes a module for displaying RSS feeds on your site, the installation of which is covered in Chapter 8, *Menus, Modules, and Components*.

Social media on your site

You can set up links to any of these social networking profiles and an RSS feed into and out of your website using the Stalker module. To show you how it works, we'll look at it within the Party People website environment. If you would like to install this component, you will need to download the zipped file from `http://www.nicktexidor.com/joomla-modules/download/18-stalker`. Then you can upload it using the installation procedure in the administration backend of your website. More on extensions and installations will be covered in Chapter 8, *Menus, Modules, and Components*.

Making Your Site Popular

Customizing Stalker

To show you how to change the parameters of Stalker, we'll customize this module on the Party People website.

Log into the administration of your Joomla! site, using the **Extensions | Modules** links from the top menu to see the module details and parameters, as shown in the following screenshot:

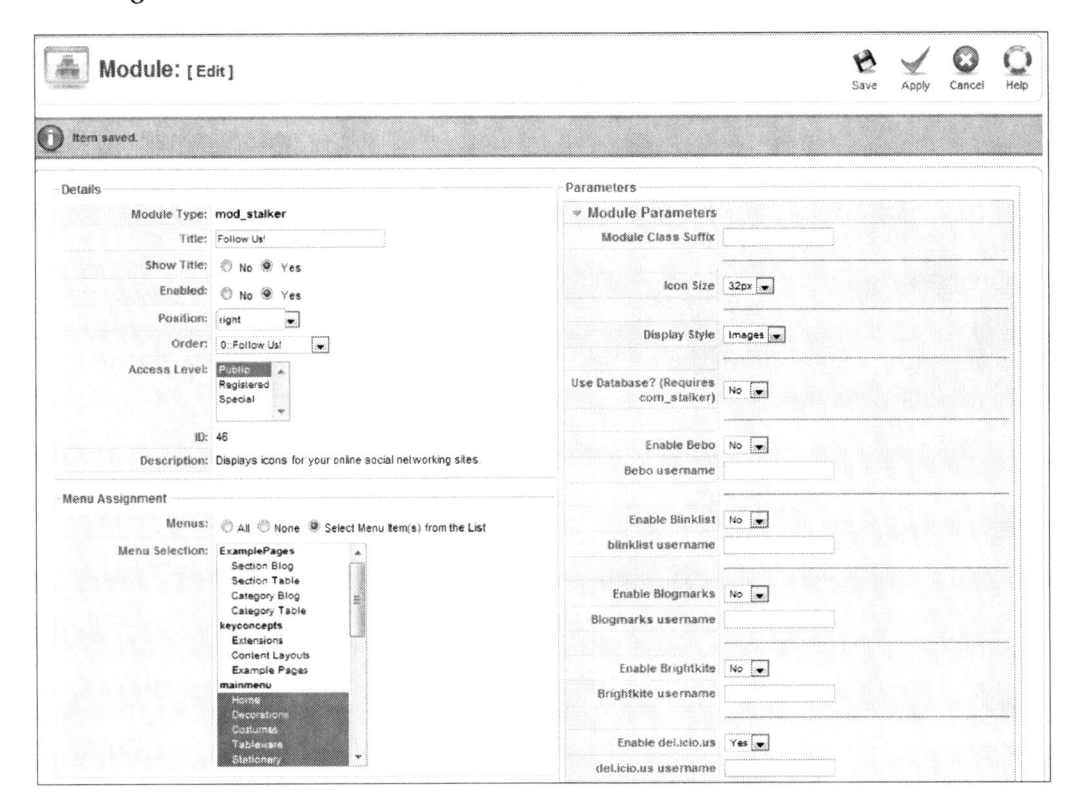

In the **Details** section:

1. Click in the **Title** textbox and give the module a new name. We chose **Follow Us** to be more indicative of its purpose. However, note that the name of the actual module itself won't change; it will still be **mod_stalker**. Select the **Yes** radio button for **Show Title** if you want to show the new title on the frontend. Select the **Yes** radio button for **Enabled**.
2. Choose the position of the module in the frontend interface layout from the list of positions in the drop-down menu for the **Position**. We chose **right** as there are already elements displayed on the left and this module will balance that out visually to some degree.

In the **Menu Assignment** section:

1. Select the **All** radio button to display the module on the page of the site. Or choose a select few only by choosing **Select Menu Items...**, click the first and then press *Ctrl* and click to add the rest. **None** means don't show the module on any menu items.
2. Within the **Parameters** section is where you enable each of the links to your social media profiles so the icons for each will appear on your frontend.

As you can see, there are a number of others you can use, as well as those mentioned in this section.

To add your details:

1. Select the profile you want to display from the list.
2. Choose **Yes** from the **Enable del.icio.us** drop-down menu.

Type or copy in the username for each profile, as shown in the following screenshot:

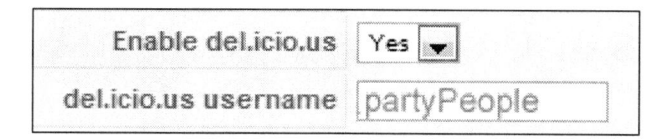

Enable del.icio.us	Yes
del.icio.us username	partyPeople

When you have made your selections, click the **Save** icon at the top right of the screen to save your changes.

When the module is enabled, the frontend of the website presents the logos for each of the social networking sites we have created profiles on, as shown in the following screenshot:

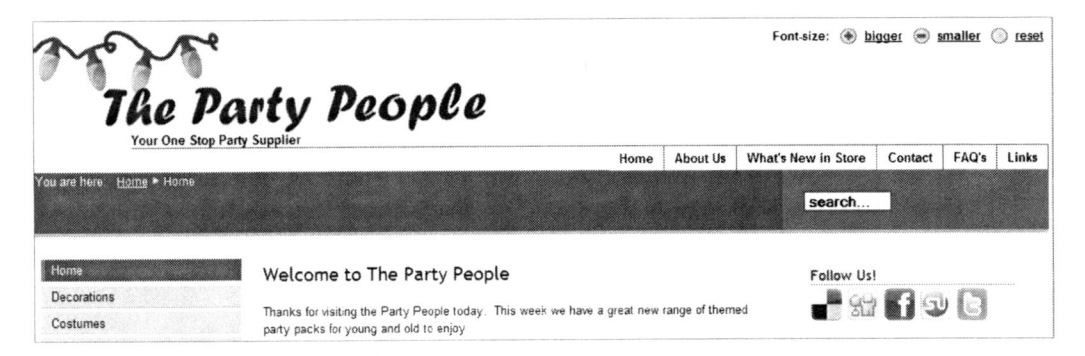

The logos are the actual links to your profiles. That is, the first icon is a link to your profile in Delicious, the second is to Digg, the third to Facebook, the fourth to StumbleUpon, and finally to your Twitter profile.

Remember, these also contribute to the number of links you have from your site which assist with search engine ranking.

Making the most of Google

Setting up a user account with Google means we can use the Analytics and AdWords applications, among many others that are available.

Setting up a Google Account

The steps to set up a Google account are as follows:

1. Navigate to `https://www.google.com/accounts/` and click the **Create an Account Now** link, as shown in the following screenshot:

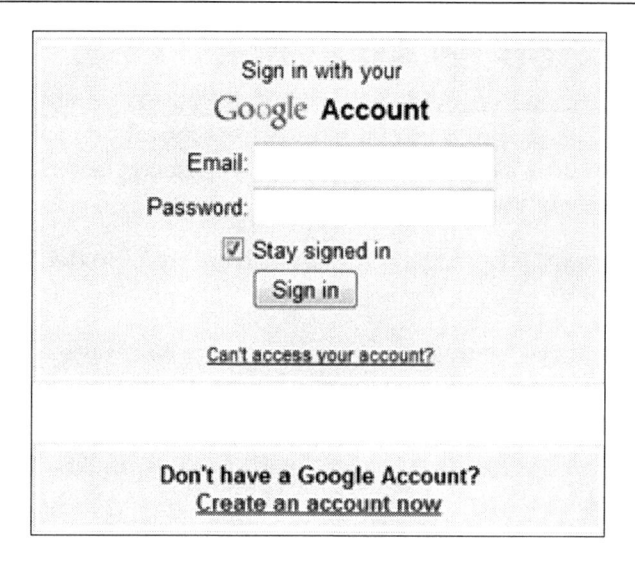

2. Work through adding details and ensure you understand the **Terms of Service** and **Privacy Policy**.
3. Make a note of the username and password.
4. Click the **I Accept Create my Account** button to complete the setup.

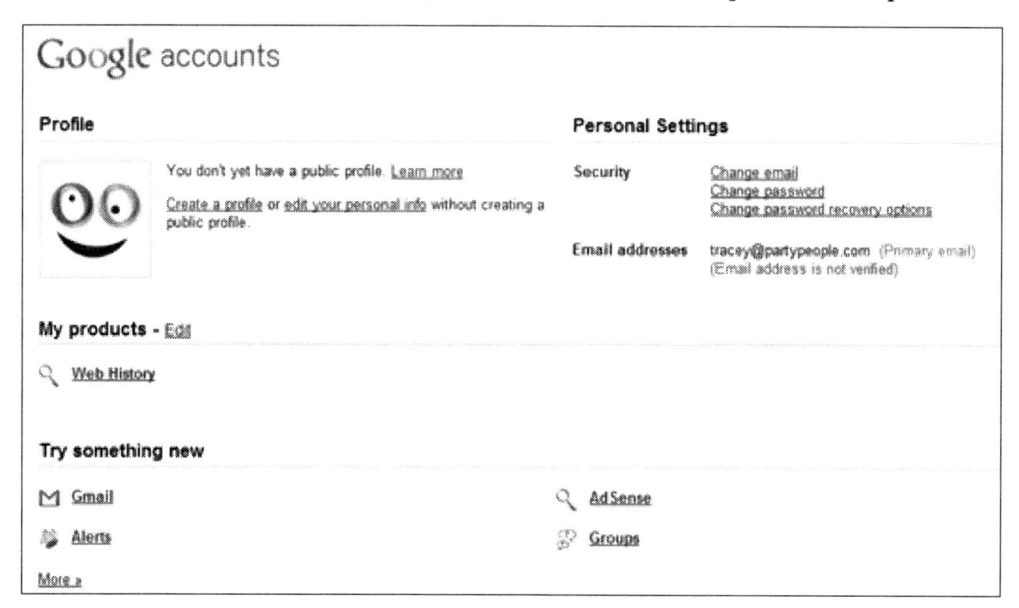

You can go on and add further details to build up your profile as well. For now though, we have established an account, so let's add the Google Analytics application to our Google profile.

Setting up Google Analytics

Using Google Analytics will provide you with data reports on who is interacting with your website. This includes tracking how users found your site, which pages they viewed, and for how long (information which you can use to further enhance your user's experience of your site).

Now that we have our Google Account, we can set up Google Analytics to track our site.

1. Navigate to `http://www.google.com/analytics/index.html` and click the **Sign Up Now** button under **Access Analytics,** as shown in the following screenshot.

2. Sign in with your Google Account details as prompted to land at the **Getting Started** page.

3. Click the **Sign Up for Google Analytics** button.

4. Add the details for the site and, if you agree to the terms of service, select the checkbox and agree to the **Terms of Service** as prompted.

5. Copy the tracking code as instructed and paste it somewhere for safe keeping. We need to add this to a page in our website. To do this, we add this code to a template file through the administration interface. Templates are files containing code that controls how the site is presented at the front and backend. If you would like to know more about templates and how they work for Joomla! go to `http://docs.joomla.org/Templates`.

6. Navigate to the Control Panel and select **Extensions | Template Manager**, as shown in the following screenshot:

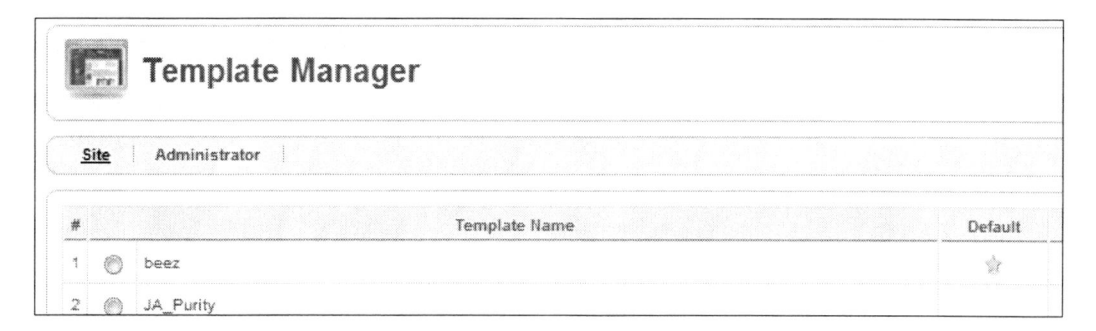

```
Template Manager

Site | Administrator

#    Template Name                    Default
1    beez                             ☆
2    JA_Purity
```

7. Click the name of the default template to access the **Template Edit** screen.
8. Click the **Edit HTML** icon at the top right to open the **Template Editor**.
9. Scroll down to the very end of the code until you can see the **</body>** tag and click just in front of it, as shown in the following screenshot.
10. Paste the code from Google Analytics here.
11. Click **Save**.

```
         </div><!-- footer -->
    </div><!-- all -->

    <jdoc:include type="modules" name="debug" />

<script type="text/javascript">
var gaJsHost = (("https:" == document.location.protocol) ? "https://ssl." : "http:/
document.write(unescape("%3Cscript src='" + gaJsHost + "google-analytics.com/ga.js'
</script>
<script type="text/javascript">
try {
var pageTracker = _gat._getTracker("UA-            );
pageTracker._trackPageview();
} catch(err) {}</script>
</body>
</html>
```

When you log back into your Google account, you will see a link to **Analytics** under the **My Products** heading that will take you straight to your analytics overview. After 24 hours, you can view the reports generated based on the traffic to your website. There is a page of detailed information on how to use the application at http://www.google.com/support/analytics/.

Research keywords

Relevant keywords and descriptions are very important for search engine rankings. They are what the crawlers use to index the results of their search to retrieve the results list.

There are many online tools available to help in identifying keywords and phrases. Google Adwords has a keywords tool which can help you generate keywords for your site around the URL address or the content.

Google's keyword tool

We can use the keyword tool to get some ideas about keywords applicable to your site and apply them to the metadata of our site files.

1. Navigate to your **Google accounts** page and there will be a heading **Try something new** with a link to **AdWords** that you can click on. If you already have an **AdWords** account, the link should already be under **My products**.

2. Click **Get keyword ideas** under the **Learn About AdWords** heading on the home page for **AdWords**.

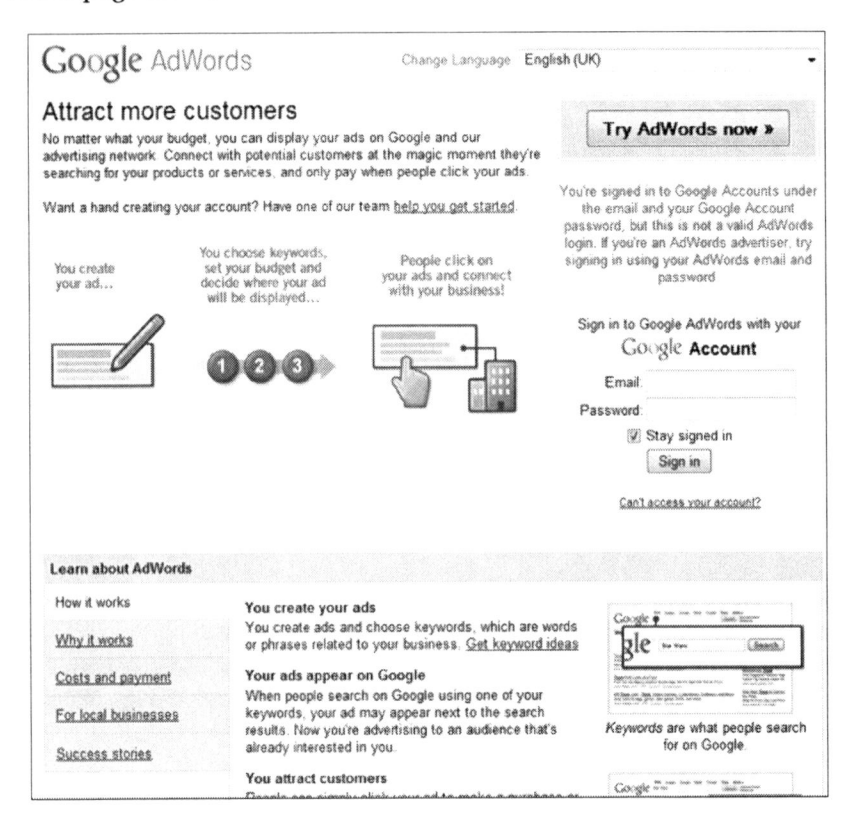

3. Click either **Descriptive words or phrases** or **Website content** to generate some keywords.
4. Enter the details under the second column based on your choice of words and phrases or website content.
5. Click **Get keyword ideas** and wait for the results!

From the table of keywords you generate, use the global search volume and other data to analyze which words or phrases have the highest "hit rate." From there, use them in your Articles and site metadata.

Adding lots of content

Include as much text-based content as you can within your site! The crawlers seek out words, so the more you have, the more chance you have of being found.

Include as many keywords as you can in the body of the text, at least one or two per paragraph as a guide.

Pay per click traffic

Ever noticed those "sponsored links" listed on your Google search result page? They're links to websites where the owner has bid on keywords that represent their site the most. When a user happens to search using one of these keywords, their site is listed under the sponsored links column, alongside the organic listing. Only when the user clicks the sponsored link, does the website owner pay anything.

Broadly, this is a new marketing model for the online environment, using contextual advertising. Many consider it successful as a short-term marketing strategy because of its immediate results.

Keyword tips

The following are some tips to keep in mind:

- Add keywords in upper or lowercase, as the indexing process is not case sensitive, so "Hat" will yield results for "hat" or "HAT."
- Use phrases as well as single words. People don't always type in a single word anymore. For example, "how do search engines work" will yield a more specific response than single words.
- Always use commas to separate the words and phrases.
- Use active words which encourage doing something or an activity.

- Know your target audience. Consider who they are and what words they would apply to your business or organization to try and find it.
- Do some research on how many searches there are for your keywords and phrases. There are many online tools to assist you with this. This is especially important if your site relies on new traffic. Try Wordtracker at `http://freekeywords.wordtracker.com/` for a free easy-to-use tool.
- Keep your keywords to 200 words maximum. Any more, and the search engine may interpret it as an attempt to flood the metadata and consider the site as spam.

Creating a new, search engine-friendly Article

Let's put all of this information to use and create a new, search engine-friendly article for the **Costumes** section of the Party People website. We'll add text, an image that links to another website, and some metadata.

As we know, the page metadata holds a brief description of the page and the keywords applicable to the content. While this information is not compulsory when creating/editing an Article, it makes good practice to include them.

Use the **Title** of your Article to add meaningful keywords, as this can also be helpful in better search engine ranking. Add a title that describes and defines the content of the Article. You can choose not to display the **Title** on the frontend of the site if it doesn't make any sense to the end user, by clicking the radio button in the **Parameters** section.

As mentioned, make the title linked as well.

First, we'll follow the given steps to set up the Article:

1. Navigate to **Content | Article Manager** from the top menu.
2. Click the **New** icon to open a new article.
3. Type in the name, section, and other details as you would for an Article.
4. Type in the text for the article. Remember to include easy-to-scan, targeted information that your target audience is interested in. Make some words bold so they stand out and catch the reader's attention.

Next we'll add an image, format it, and make it a link to an external website:

5. Click the mouse at the beginning of the second paragraph where we'll add an image into our text to break it up and make it easier on the eye.
6. Click the **Image** button under the textbox to add an image. Navigate to the media manager folder and select the image.
7. Select the image within the text so that we can make it sit to the left of the text; otherwise, the text will sit underneath the image, leaving a large space around the image.

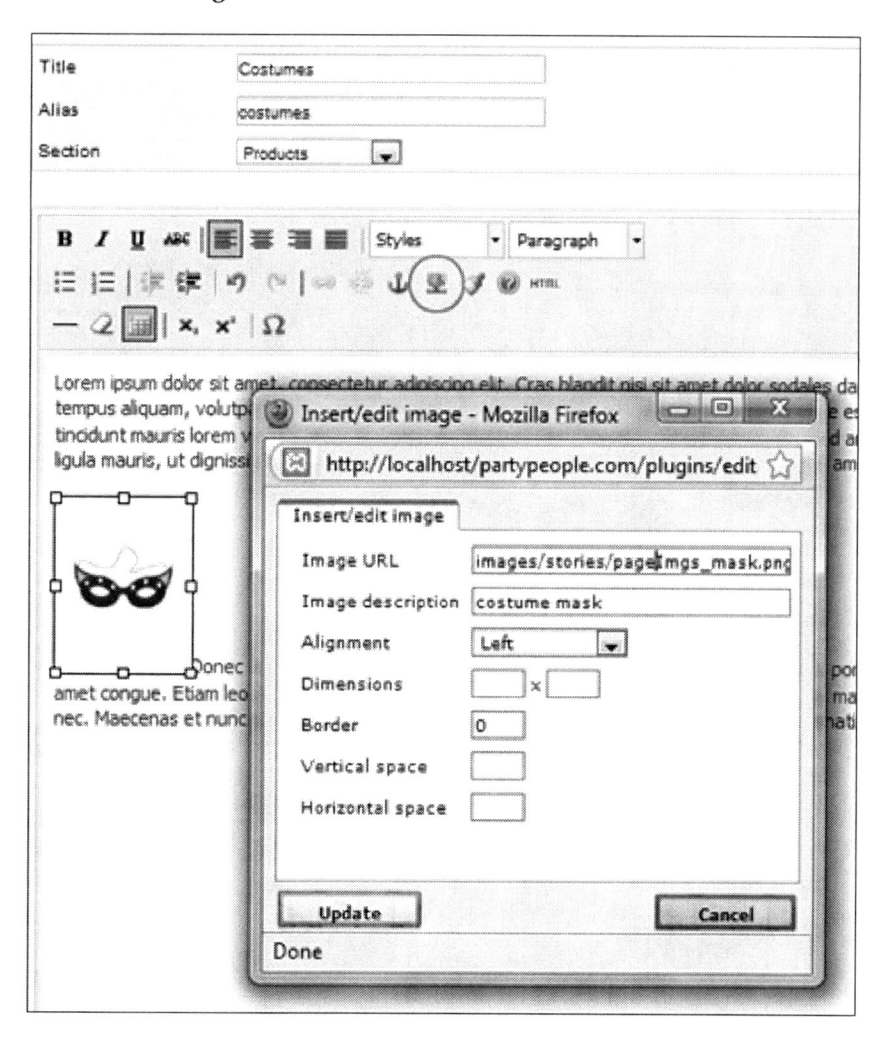

8. Type in a description for the image and select **Left** for the **Alignment**.
9. You can set the **Dimensions** of your image, if you wish to, or you may leave it.
10. Typing a number such as 1 or 2 will add a border around the image of that pixel width. We'll leave it as 0, as we don't want a border.
11. Leave the **Vertical space** and **Horizontal space** input boxes blank. These add padding around your image.
12. Click **Update** to save the changes.
13. Select the image again and click the **Insert Link** icon on the text editing toolbar.

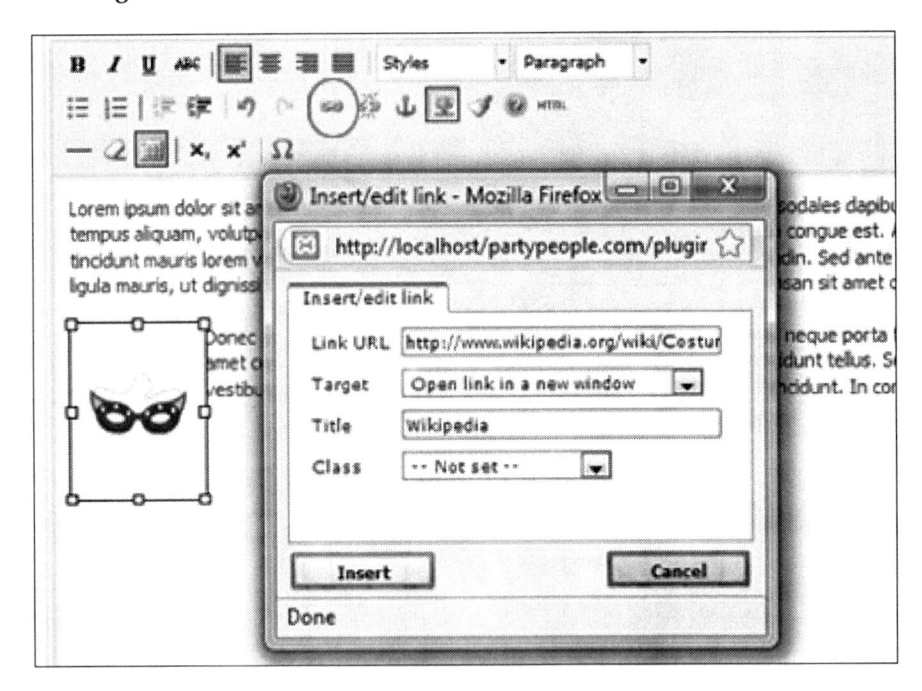

14. Type in the full URL link, including the **http://** at the beginning.
15. Select **Open link in a new window** for the target and type in the title of the link.
16. Click **Insert** to save.

Now, we'll add the metadata to the Article. Click **Metadata Information** in the right pane:

17. In the **Description** section add a brief, concisely written description of the page content. The information here will usually appear in the search engine listings. Using a few well-chosen words works better than a long-winded (not entirely relevant, but let's hope its useful) paragraph.
18. Type a brief description of the article's content into the **Description** box under the **Metadata Information** section.
19. Type in the keywords and phrases identified as the most relevant to your article, using commas to separate them.
20. Save the article.

The following screenshot shows the **Metadata Information**:

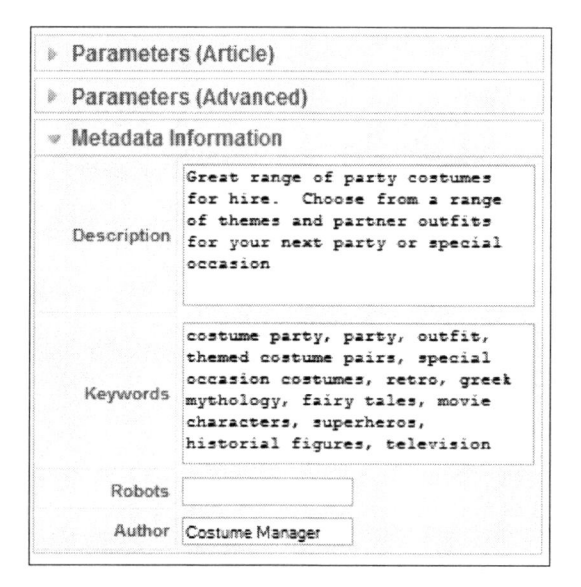

Summary

Though there is no exact science for getting your site to the top of the index page, it's certainly achievable. Use the free tools that Google offers to your best advantage, and keep up-to-date with the traffic landing at your site. Examine and act on the data Google provides and use it to keep your site focused on your target audience. Adding pertinent and active keywords, phrases, and descriptions to your Articles is something you can do to make a difference to the validity of your site.

Adding links to your pages will help them get noticed, and it's also a good way to network within your community. Online spaces provide as much opportunity to get to know like-minded and interested parties as much as the real world does.

Using social networking websites can offer you more in terms of building a community of followers, who can promote your products and services free of charge.

Now that we have implemented and reviewed a number of measures for making your site more search engine-friendly, in Chapter 7, *Security–Recovery and Precaution* we look at improving its security. Now that you have been working on making your site more interesting to your target audience and more search engine-friendly, all this new interest should be generating some new visits. Making it secure with all of this new interest is important in terms of making it less susceptible to malicious attack.

7
Security—Precaution and Recovery

While Joomla! itself is a robust framework, in this chapter, we'll focus on some practical ways to reduce the likelihood of hackers compromising your Joomla! website, along with information on how to recover your site if necessary.

The idea behind this chapter isn't to give out loads of technical information, but to offer some accurate security advice and references to further resources. By knowing some important background information, you will be in a better position to facilitate an understanding between yourself and an experienced Joomla! developer, should you need to engage someone to assist you or even enter into a thread on a discussion forum on an issue.

While this is practical advice, a serious compromise however, can mean that you will need to reinstall your site from a backup. Chapter 4, *Backing Up Your Website*, covers backing up your site in detail.

In this chapter, we'll look at:

- Precautions to make it harder for hackers to compromise your website
- How to recover from a malicious attack
- What to do if your site is exploited

Precautionary measures

There are a number of measures you can take to make it more difficult for malicious events to compromise your website. While none are 100% guaranteed, these measures will certainly make it a lot more difficult for them. There is information available if you would like to know more about the type of attacks that occur, such as "SQL Injections" (http://en.wikipedia.org/wiki/Sql_injection) or "mail injection" attacks, which basically exploit any security vulnerabilities within a PHP/MySQL framework.

While Joomla! is a secure content management system, there is always a chance that it can be compromised. However, if the security of your site has been carefully planned, then the risk is reduced considerably.

Keeping up-to-date

The Joomla! team responds very quickly to security exploits and hosts an administrator's checklist at http://docs.joomla.org/Category:Security_Checklist. It contains a list of links to pages with details on precautions, beginning with the implementation of the site, right through how to recover your site. It will help to get you started on the way towards understanding and learning about security issues. While this detailed list of measures and techniques are especially important for a web developer, you need to understand in general terms what is involved—and the consequences if these security measures have not been performed.

The Joomla! security forum also contains a post called **Has your site been compromised?** at http://forum.joomla.org/viewforum.php?f=432. Read through this as well. Also, make sure you have read through and understood the general advice presented in the forum.

Online security is a broad topic, but if you understand some of the broader concepts and possibilities, then you are on your way to taking the right precautions.

Upgrade to the latest version of Joomla!

The single most important thing an experienced Joomla! developer will tell you to do here is to install an upgrade patch when it is released, depending on which version of Joomla! you're running. Patches are issued frequently in response to new threats.

> It is important to note here that an upgrade patch is different from a migration of your site to latest version, say from version 1.0 to 1.5.14. The upgrade patch is relatively minor in terms of process (not importance). An upgrade patch will often include security upgrades and fixes for any bugs that are discovered subsequent to the last upgrade.

Localhost environments

Before installing an upgrade to your live site, it is advisable to test the process on a local copy (mirrored) of your site, which is a common practice for many developers. You set this up yourself on your computer as well, by installing a localhost server application, such as WAMPP or XAMPP (http://www.apachefriends.org/en/xampp.html), which are both free to download and install. However, some background knowledge of the setup is required, so you should read through the documentation on the respective websites for more information.

It is a good practice to test any major changes to your site before going live with them, to ensure no major problems arise and if they do, correct them before going live. It's beyond the scope of this chapter to provide detailed instructions on setting up a localhost environment, but you can read more on the topic at http://www.veoh.com/collection/screencasts/watch/v1802750A7Mnpe7z, where there is a short video tutorial, or have a Joomla! developer set it up for you.

Also, if the core modules of your Joomla! site have been customized (which isn't recommended), your web developer will need to transfer the customized code to the upgraded version of the Joomla! site and test whether it still works.

Installing the upgrade patch

Patches are supplementary software code usually bundled into a compressed file that is installed within the original framework. They come in .zip, .tar.gz, and .tar.bz2 formats. For the purpose of our instructions, we'll download a ZIP file into a Windows Vista operating system. Apple users can follow along using their MAC OS operating system procedures as well.

You can install the patch directly to your live site, but remember to do one thing—make a backup of your site files and database.

Security – Precaution and Recovery

We'll upgrade the Party People website from version 1.15.12 to 1.15.14 with a patch. Follow these steps to download the patch ZIP file to your local computer and then install the patch to the live site. We'll be jumping back and forth between your local hard drive and the web browser for this procedure.

1. Open the administration control panel to check which version of Joomla! your site is running on, which is shown at the top right of the Control Panel.

2. Navigate to the Joomla! download page at http://www.joomla.org/download.html and click the **Download other Joomla 1.5.x packages** link.

3. Scroll through the **Filename** column until you find the ZIP file to upgrade from version 1.15.12 to the latest, which is version 1.15.14 at the time of writing.

4. Click **Joomla_1.5.12_to_1.5.14-Stable-Patch_Package.zip** from the list to download it to a folder on your hard drive. I have created a new folder called **patchUpgrade** within my locally hosted version of the site.

5. Create a backup of your site. It's really important that you do this, just in case something goes wrong. Refer to Chapter 4, *Backing Up Your Website*, for details on how to do this if you haven't already.

6. Unzip the 1.5.14 patch file into the new folder.

7. Log into the administration control panel and the Global Configuration section and take the site offline before installing the patch. When your site is offline, anyone who visits will see the following, which means you have to log in, in order to view the site.

[136]

> **Joomla!**
>
> **Party People**
>
> This site is down for maintenance. Please check back again soon.
>
> Username
> Password
> Remember Me
> Login

8. Go back to your hard drive and open an FTP program to upload copies of the patch files into the root folder of your site. You may have already done this when you created a backup for your site from Chapter 4, *Backing Up Your Website*. Otherwise, you can use a free FTP client called FileZilla for this purpose. You can download and install it from `http://www.filezilla-project.org/download.php`.

9. Select all of the files and sub-folders within the folders containing the patch files, not including the **patchUpgrade** folder itself, as shown in the following screenshot.

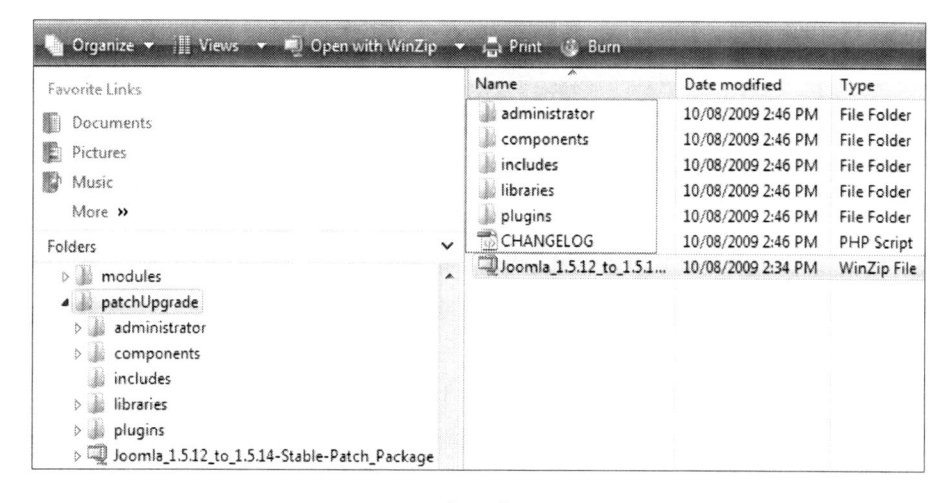

Security – Precaution and Recovery

10. Check that all the files and folders have been copied over to the server once the process is completed.
11. Review your site while it is still offline by logging in, to ensure it is still running smoothly.
12. Set your site online again through the Global Configuration panel.

Don't forget, if your site needs to be migrated from version 1.0x of Joomla! to latest version of Joomla!, it's advisable to have an experienced Joomla! developer do this for you.

Review your hosting account

The various hosting providers offer different levels of support, which can make a difference in the overall security of your site. There are a range of technical procedures developers can work through to check this, but they require a detailed knowledge of PHP programming language, its configuration, and server security.

Before considering a hosting provider, ask around to see if anybody else has used them before and whether they have a good reputation or not. Look for one that fulfills the following criteria:

- Implements a regular backup regime. Some hosting providers don't back up the site files as often as the more expensive ones do. You will need to weigh this up but you can, of course, create your own backups.
- Has proactively implemented measures to prevent hacking attempts to their clients' websites. Find out what they are and keep in touch by subscribing to their newsletter if they have one.
- Can offer you a dedicated server if your site is large. Most hosting services provide space on a server that also hosts other websites. This can put your site at risk if one site is compromised.
- Provides access to Raw Access Logs, which are discussed in the "What else should I do" section later in this chapter.
- Offers the best value for money in terms of security features.

Change the administration username and password

Change the administration username from "admin" and the password after you have logged in to the Control Panel.

1. Click the **User Manager** icon in the administration interface.
2. Select the **Administrator User**.

3. Type a new username into the **Username** box.
4. Type a new password into **New Password** and then **Verify Password**.
5. Click the **Save** icon to secure your changes.

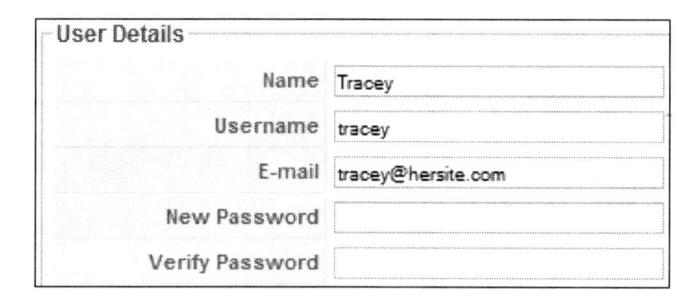

User Details	
Name	Tracey
Username	tracey
E-mail	tracey@hersite.com
New Password	
Verify Password	

6. Change passwords frequently, using a combination of letters, symbols, and numbers. It is best to avoid simple words just because you can remember them!
7. Don't use the same password or a variation of one for everything you need a password for.

Why change the administration username from "admin" to something else?

By changing this username to something trickier to try and guess, you greatly increase the difficulty for unauthorized users to access your profile and, therefore, the administration backend. The hacker then has a lesser chance of accurately guessing the username and password to gain access, which is a lot more difficult than just having to work out only the right password.

Even with access to the administrator folder restricted to specific IP addresses, a hacker still has the potential to log in through the frontend and cause damage by editing the site through there.

It makes good sense to ensure the login is as difficult as possible and change the administrator password regularly.

Reset the FTP login password

Within the administration interface, you can change the FTP password in the Global Configuration. These settings were established during the installation of your site, but you can change the password here.

1. Click on **Global Configuration** in the administration control panel.
2. Click the **Server** tab.
3. Enter a new password in the **FTP Password** input box and verify it.
4. Click the **Save** button.

Other precautions

Following is a brief list of some other areas that can be addressed:

1. Make sure your developer has installed the .htaccess file to the base directory of Joomla!
2. Avoid any beta versions of Joomla! third-party extensions, however useful they may seem, as some may not have been adequately tested.
3. Make sure your developer and/or hosting provider has protected the administrator folder in Joomla! so that only selected people can access that folder, based on the IP addresses of their workstations.

Installing and configuring jSecure authentication

There is an easy-to-install third-party plugin, highly rated by the Joomla! developer community that allows you to change the link to the administration control panel, making it difficult to find if you're a hacker wanting to cause trouble.

As you know, we access the control panel for the Party People website by typing in:

```
http://www.partypeople.com/administrator/index.php
```

Anyone can do this, which means potential hackers can do this too. Then, it's a matter of working out your username and password to get in.

As an additional security precaution, we'll download, install, and configure this plugin into the Party People website.

Downloading jSecure

The steps for downloading jSecure are as follows:

1. Navigate to `http://www.joomlaserviceprovider.com/downloads/` and under **Categories** select the **Joomla** link.

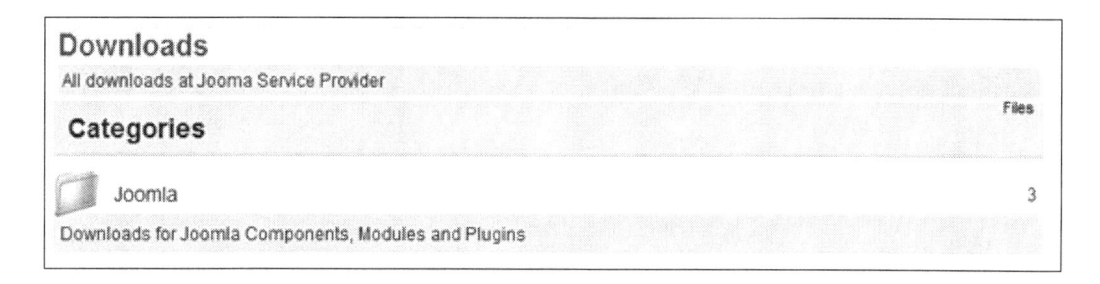

> **Downloads**
> All downloads at Jooma Service Provider
>
> **Categories**   Files
>
> Joomla   3
> Downloads for Joomla Components, Modules and Plugins

2. Click the **jSecure Authentication** link and then, on the next screen, the **jSecure Authentication Plugin for 1.5.X** link to access the ZIP file containing the installation files. Note this is the version for a Joomla! 1.5 version.

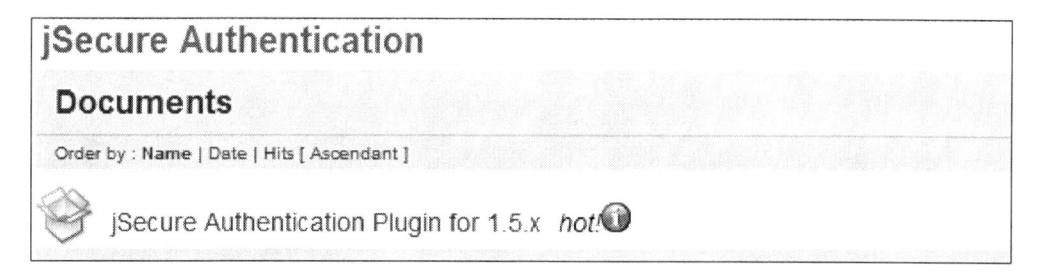

> **jSecure Authentication**
>
> **Documents**
>
> Order by : Name | Date | Hits [Ascendant]
>
> jSecure Authentication Plugin for 1.5.x *hot!*

3. Save the ZIP file to a space on your computer so you can upload it from the administration control panel. While writing this book, a local version of the Party People website was "mirrored" on the test machine's hard drive and the ZIP file was saved in the folder that was set up there.

Security – Precaution and Recovery

4. Note that in the following screenshot, you can see all of the ZIP files for the plugins and components installed in this site.

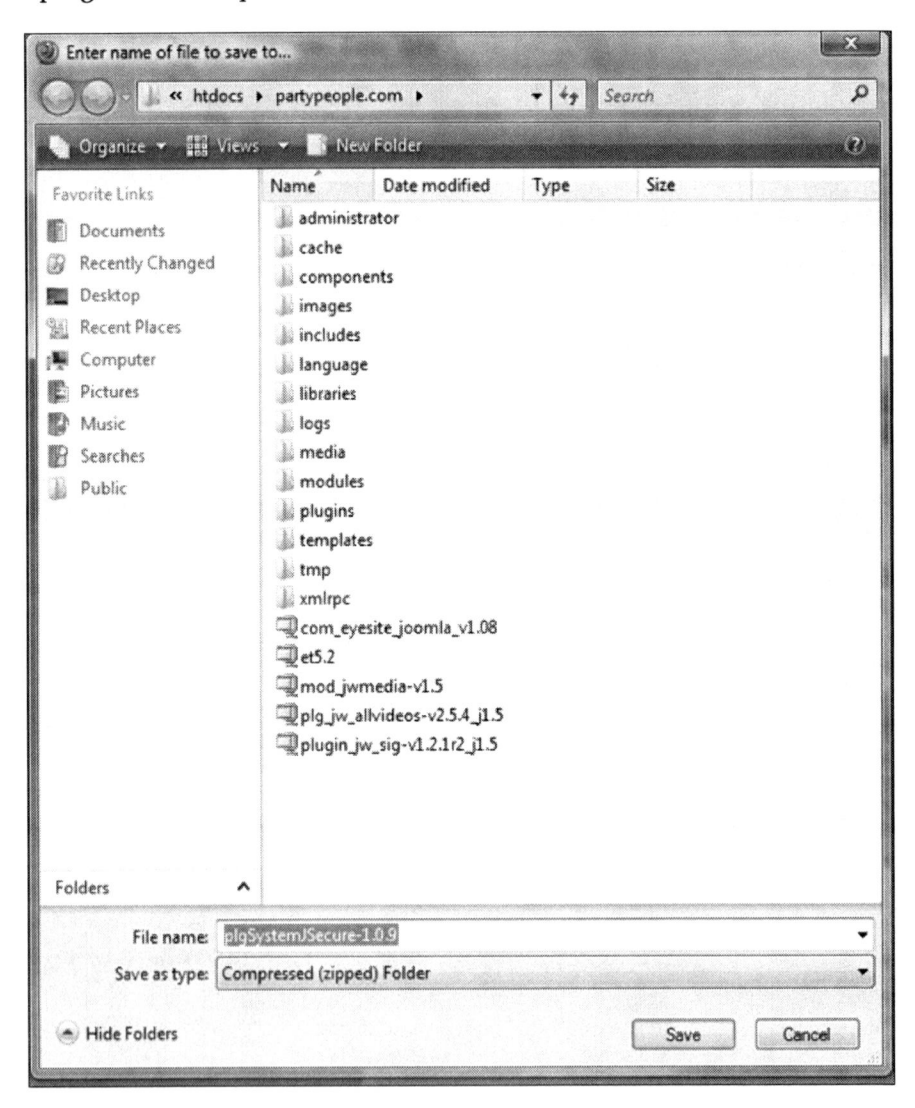

Installing jSecure through the administration control panel

The steps for installing jSecure are as follows:

1. Navigate and log into the control panel at http://www.partypeople.com.au/administrator.
2. Click **Extensions**, then **Install/Uninstall** from the top menu.

3. Click **Browse** in the **Extension Manager** screen and navigate to where you saved the **plgSystemJSecure-1.0.9** ZIP file on your hard drive.
4. Click the **Upload File & Install** button.
5. You should then see the **Install Plugin Success** message.

Configuring the jSecure Plugin to change the administration login URL

The steps are as follows:

1. Click **Extensions | Plugin Manager** in the top menu to access the **Plugin Manager**.
2. Click the drop-down menu in the **Plugin Manager** and choose the **Systems** plugin.
3. Click the link under the **Plugin Name** column to edit its parameters.

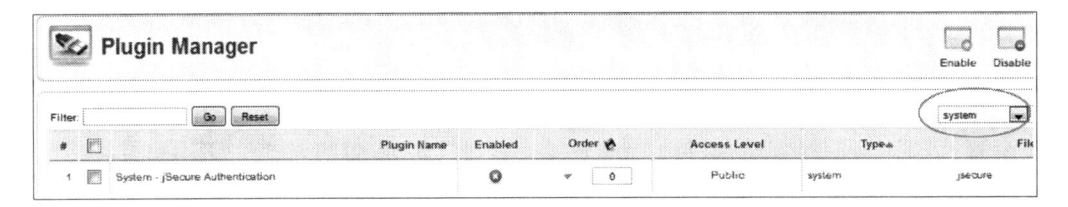

4. Click the **Yes** radio button to **Enable** the plugin. Leave the remaining **Details** at the default settings.
5. Change the **Key** under **Plugin Parameters** to a word you need to replace. In the URL string, we'll use **partyHats09**.
6. Click **Redirect to Index Page** for the **Redirect Options**. You can change this to another page using the custom redirect option. If so, you will need to add the path.
7. Click the **Save** button.

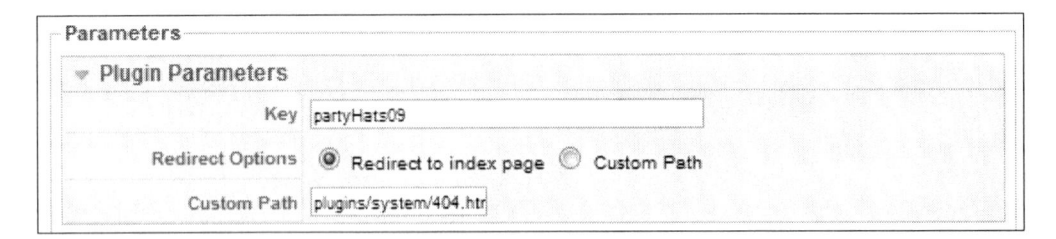

Navigate to your new administration login page; our page is now the following link:

http://www.partypeople.com/administrator/?partyHats09

> Note the "?" in the string. You will need to include this in yours as well.

Now, it's not so easy to locate the login to your administration page. Make sure you note the key you choose. If you lose it, it will need to be changed through the PHP MyAdmin control panel through your hosting provider. This means logging into the database and changing it from there.

Also, it's a good idea when you have successfully navigated to your new administration login to copy and save the new link, including the key and question mark, just in case.

What should I do if my site is exploited?

Firstly, don't panic. There are steps you can take to recover your site quickly if it's not a serious compromise.

Firstly, take your site offline until you have repaired the damage:

1. Log into the administration interface. If you can't do this, see the next section and then come back to do this.
2. Click the **Global Configuration** icon.
3. Select the **Site** link at the top left.
4. Click **Yes** for **Site Offline**.
5. Add a suitable message or leave the standard one in **Offline Message**.
6. Click the **Save** icon.

If it is a serious breach, such as the site is being used to send spam, pop-up ads are appearing, or your visitors are being redirected to another (possibly offensive) site, then the best option is to reinstall your site from a backup and have your server space checked for malicious scripts, but we'll consider this later.

Help, I can't log into the administration panel!

An example of a minor attack that occurred on a site I built, where hackers posted an article to the home page that included some graffiti-like tags. When I attempted to log into the administration panel to remove it, I couldn't get in.

This is the result of hackers changing the administration password. Follow these steps to reset it and log in again:

1. Generate an MD5 hash value.
2. Reset the "admin" user password in the database.
3. Log into the administration interface.

Each of the previous steps are explained in the following sections.

Generate an MD5 hash value

A what? It's a string of characters that represent a word/sequence of characters you choose for the new password.

1. Download the **HashCalc** application from `http://www.slavasoft.com/hashcalc/overview.htm` to generate the string for your new password.
2. Unzip and install the program on your hard drive.
3. Type a word you would like to use as your password in the **Data** box. Leave **Data Format** as **Text String**.
4. Select the **MD5** checkbox.
5. Click **Calculate** at the bottom to generate the MD5 value to be used in resetting your administration password within your Joomla! database.
6. Copy and paste this value somewhere so you can refer to it again in the next stage.

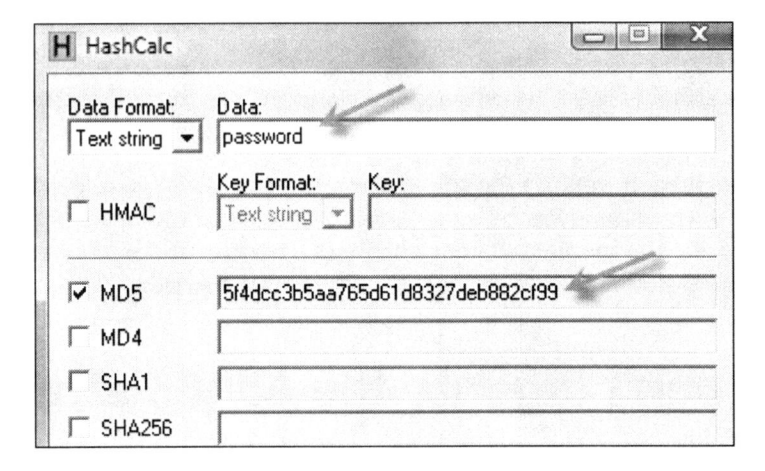

Reset the "admin" user password in the database

If you have changed your Super Administrator username from "admin", then select that username. For our purposes, we'll assume it's still "admin".

1. Log into your Control Panel on your hosting account.
2. Click the **phpMyAdmin** icon.

3. Select the database for your website.
4. Scroll down the list of tables and select the **jos_users** table. Click the **Browse** button. Note that **jos_users** is the default table prefix, which can be changed by the developer.
5. Select the row for the super admin account by selecting the checkbox on the left. If you have more than one, select just one.
6. Click the pencil icon to edit this record.
7. Copy and then paste the MD5 hash value you generated into the password **value** field. Note that you must paste the hash value into the field, not the actual password it represents.
8. Click **Go** to save the record.
9. Exit the phpMyAdmin interface.

Log into the administration interface

To log into the administration interface, follow the given steps:

1. Navigate to the address of the administration interface of your site in your browser, for example, http://www.yoursitename.com/administrator.
2. Type in the administration username and the new password you chose to represent with the MD5 hash. This time type in the word, not the hash code. You will be able to access the administration panel with this new password from now on, unless you decide to change it.

Just as in my example, it may be the hackers who have created and published a new article. If you can still access the administration interface, follow these steps to remove it. To delete any offensive article:

1. Select **Article Manager** in the administration interface.
2. Scroll through the list of articles to locate any that you have not created. You could also enter one of the words from the title of the Article into the filter textbox.
3. Click the box to the left of the offending article and then the **Delete** icon to delete the Article.

What else should I do?

Just because you have deleted an offending content item, don't assume that is all they have left for you. Follow these steps to check for further damage.

Check for any new or suspicious files

Check for any newly created or suspicious-looking files on the server, which you can access through the Control Panel for your hosting account. Check especially for strange PDF files or any new file with a different extension through the rest of the site. They may contain code that might execute some further nastiness at a later stage.

Looking for these can be like looking for the proverbial needle though, and sometimes the code is buried deep within the page. Having an experienced Joomla! developer search and delete them for you is the safest option.

Run diagnostic scripts

Your developer can run particular scripts that detect when files were created or modified. They require detailed knowledge of how MySQL databases work, so it's best to have someone with background knowledge do this for you.

Advise your hosting provider

A good Internet service provider will care that a site on their server has been exploited. Further, if or when you are able to work out how your site was attacked, tell them this too. If your site lives on a server with many other sites, there is the chance the attack on yours came through another site on the same shared server (a stable mate). Having your site on a shared server should be avoided if possible.

Review the Raw Access Logs for your site

These are simple text files you can download from your hosting account Control Panel to see who has accessed your site, and determine whether there has been any suspicious activity. You can download a zipped version to your local computer and open it in a plain text editor.

To download the information:

1. Log into your Control Panel account.
2. Click on the **Raw Access Logs** icon.

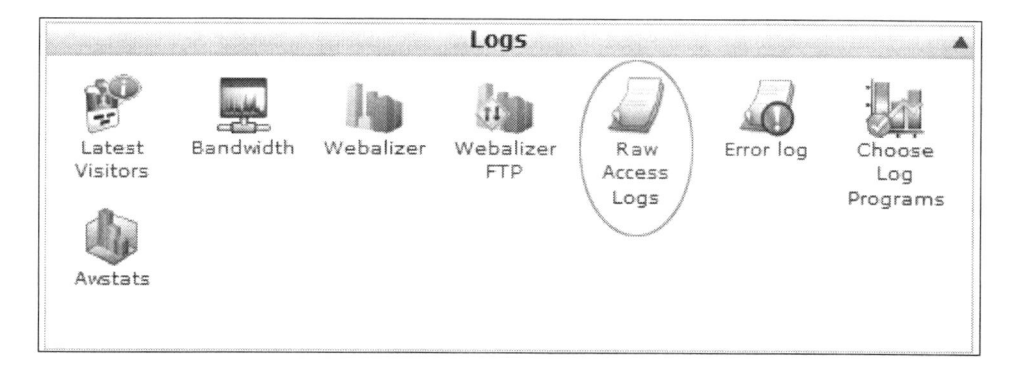

3. Select the site you require the information for and download the file, probably in a zipped format. Save it on your hard drive or storage media.

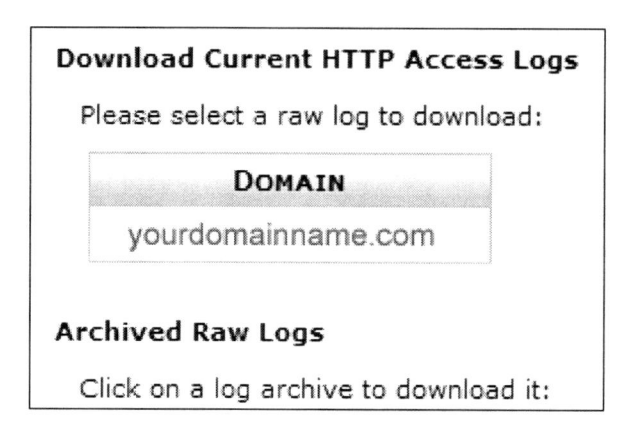

4. Navigate to the zip file and unzip it. Open the file in a plain text editor, for example, Notepad.

The information you see will appear like numerous lines of code. Scan through each line and see if there are any suspicious names or words amongst them. You can send this to your hosting provider, who can use it to determine who has bypassed their security measures and hopefully stop them from doing so again.

How do I recover my site after a serious compromise?

If your whole site has been brought down or it's doing things it's not supposed to, such as sending out spam e-mail for example, there is a good chance the hackers have found their way into your hosting account and corrupted core operating files. In this case, it's best to delete the existing site files and rebuild or reinstall everything from a backup. Chapter 4, *Backing Up Your Website*, has details on backups and restoring your site.

If you don't already have a reliable backup process worked out, build one into your administrative activities.

Summary

While we have attempted to cover as much as possible about security and precautionary measures, they are only a select number of the security issues that can arise. There are many ways that a site can be compromised. However, if you follow these proactive steps, hopefully, you can minimize the possibility and/or react quickly if there is a compromise.

In this chapter, the focus has been on taking precautions rather than reacting to an event, because the emphasis should be on good administrative practice. Preventing a disaster is far better than having to go through the process of having to recover your site. Having a regular backup routine is very important to the recovery process, and will allow either you or your developer to reinstall quickly, and get the site up and running as soon as possible. While a minor incident can be dealt with in-house, a serious compromise of your site is best dealt with by an experienced Joomla! security expert.

In the next chapter on extensions, we'll look at a number of the highly rated and popular third-party extensions that can be added into the Joomla! core framework, as well as guidelines for installing them.

8
Menus, Modules, and Components

Chapter 1, *Exploring Your New Joomla! Website* briefly outlined what components, modules, and plugins do in terms of the general framework of your Joomla! website. In fact, there are many third-party commercial and non-commercial extensions you can build into your site to extend its capabilities. In this chapter, we will look at applying some of the key components and modules that are a part of the core Joomla! installation, as well as look at an overview of some third-party extensions including the following:

- VirtueMart: For shopping cart and catalogs
- JCal Pro: An events calendar
- DOCman: To update and manage files
- Letterman: To send newsletters

We'll look at how these new features can be added as links to existing menu structures in order to present content in the frontend.

Using the Party People website once again, we will do the following:

- Extend the top menu with a link to an FAQ page, using the Menu and Module Managers
- Build a web links page with the Web Links component and add it to a frontend menu
- Add an advertising banner with the Banners component
- Add a rotating, random image display to the frontend
- Install a component called JobGrok to show you how it's done

Menus, Modules, and Components

Extending a menu with a new link

The Menu Manager allows us to update any of the menus published to the frontend of our website, so we can add a link to a new page, re-order the links, or remove them as needed.

We'll add a new link to the Party People's top menu. This menu is global, that means it appears on every page and provides access to what we've decided as being consistently relevant information. We want to add a new link called "FAQ's" which links to a section that provides details on delivery times, warranties, and so on to the customers.

Adding a new menu item is a two-step process. Firstly, we'll create a new Article with the information and then add the link to the menu using the Menu Manager.

Creating the Article

We'll create the new Article in the same way as we have done previously.

1. Click **Content | Article Manager** using the top menu of the administration control panel.
2. Click **New** to create a new Article for the FAQ information.
3. Type in **FAQ's** for the **Title**. Leave the **Alias** blank.
4. Type in the remaining details as you have for the previous Articles.
5. Save your Article.

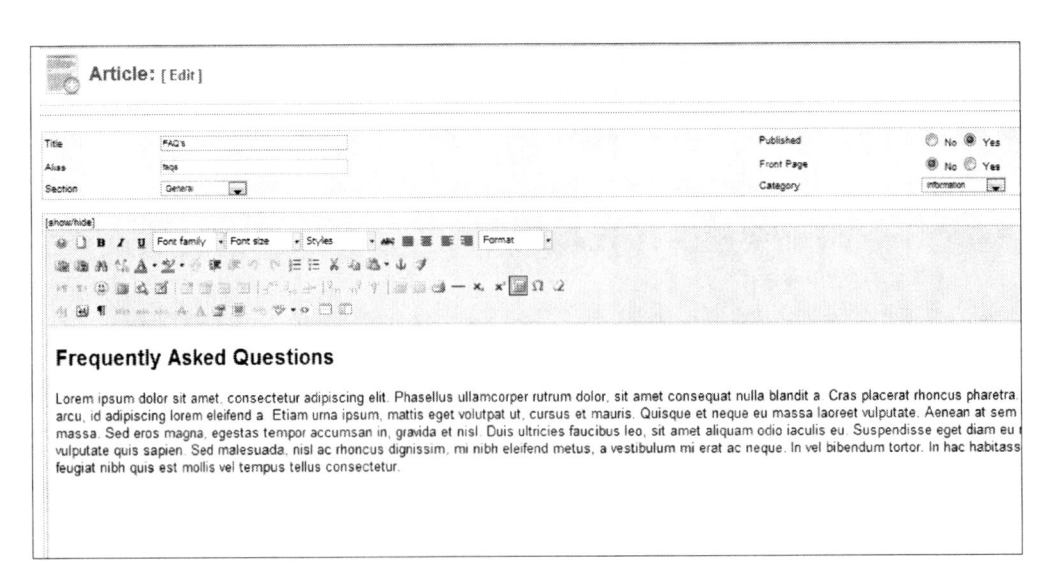

Chapter 8

Next, we'll add the actual link to the menu itself.

6. Navigate to **Menu | Menu Manager** using the top menu.
7. Click the **Menu Items** icon for **Top Menu** to see the list of existing links within the top menu. These will correspond with what we see on the frontend of the website.
8. Click the **New** icon in the top-right contextual toolbar to view the **Select Menu Item Type** tree structure.

| 3 | ◎ | Top Menu | topmenu | |

9. Select **Articles | Article Layout** under the **Internal Link** heading, as shown in the following screenshot, as we are adding a link to a single article. The **Article Submission Layout** link allows users to add articles.
10. Also, note that you can add to any one of the items that appear in this directory tree, including other components and so on.

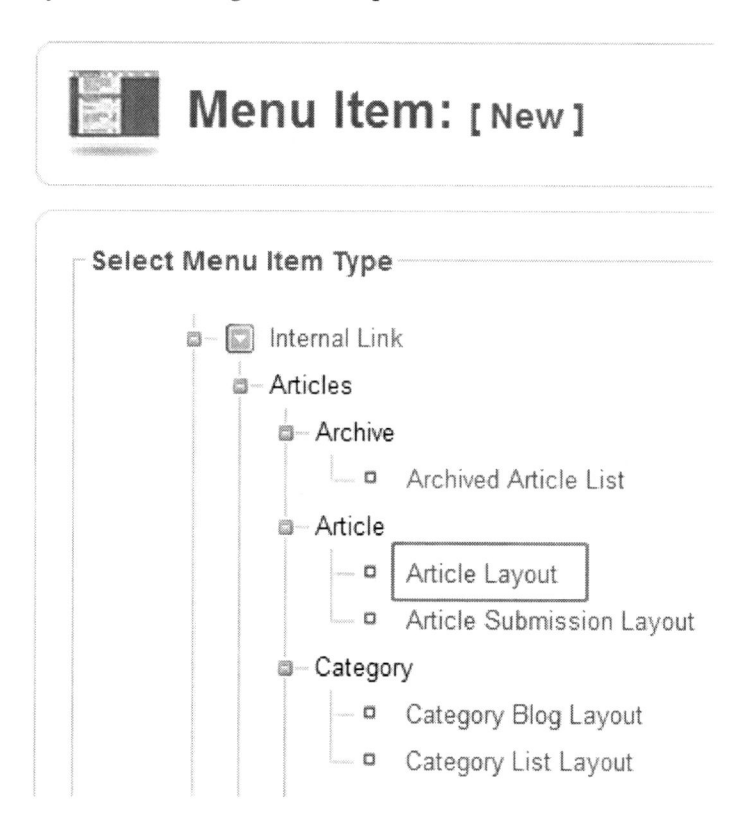

Menu Item: [New]

Select Menu Item Type

- Internal Link
  - Articles
    - Archive
      - Archived Article List
    - Article
      - Article Layout
      - Article Submission Layout
    - Category
      - Category Blog Layout
      - Category List Layout

Menus, Modules, and Components

11. Type in the title of your new menu item, that is, **FAQ**, as it should appear on the frontend of the website.

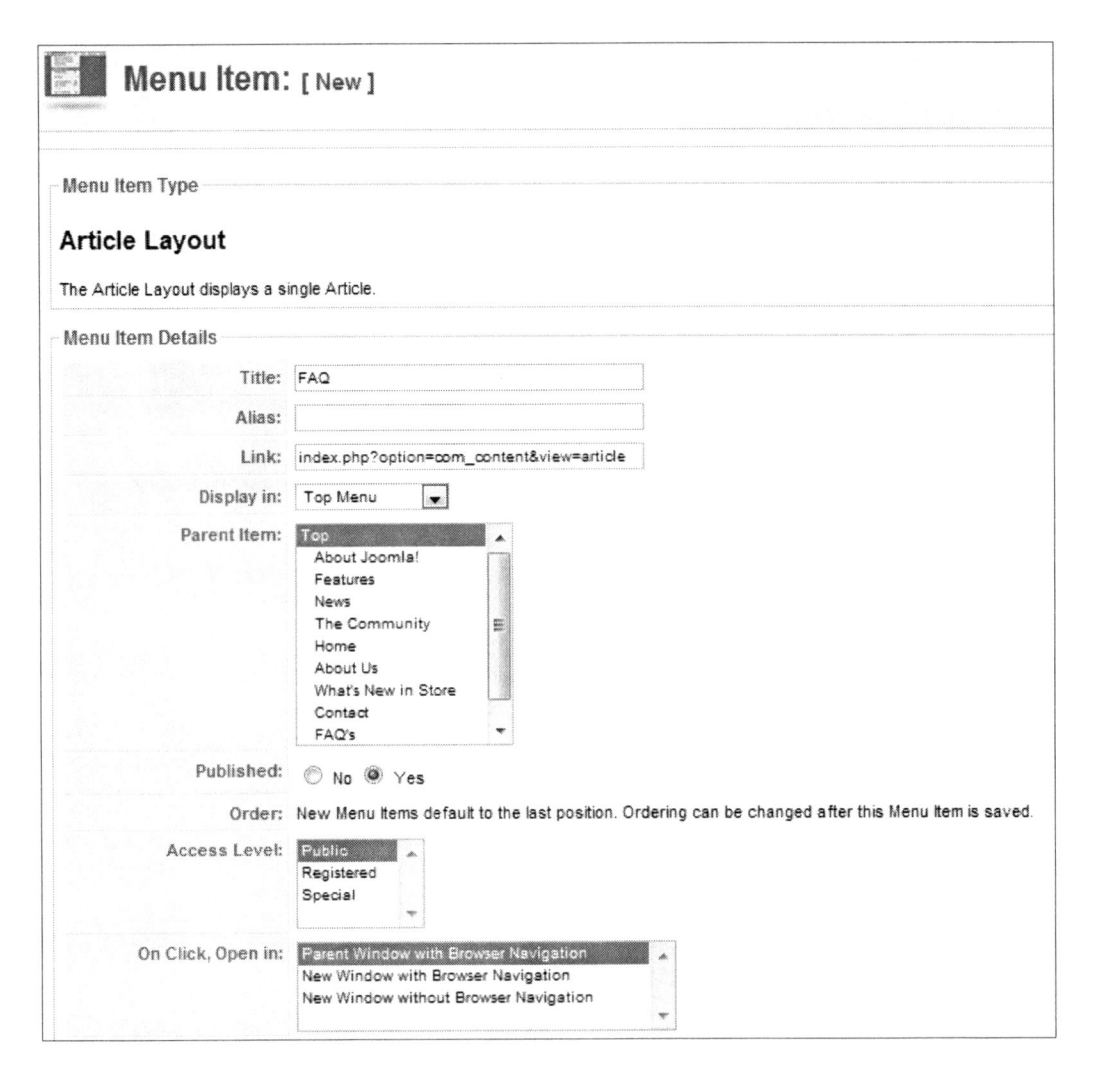

Menu Item: [New]

Menu Item Type

Article Layout

The Article Layout displays a single Article.

Menu Item Details

- Title: FAQ
- Alias:
- Link: index.php?option=com_content&view=article
- Display in: Top Menu
- Parent Item: Top / About Joomla! / Features / News / The Community / Home / About Us / What's New in Store / Contact / FAQ's
- Published: ○ No ● Yes
- Order: New Menu Items default to the last position. Ordering can be changed after this Menu Item is saved.
- Access Level: Public / Registered / Special
- On Click, Open in: Parent Window with Browser Navigation / New Window with Browser Navigation / New Window without Browser Navigation

12. The **Display in** box should default to **Top Menu**.
13. Click **Yes** for **Published** if not already set.
14. Leave the **Access Level** as **Public** so that every visitor to the site can see it.
15. Leave **On Click, Open in** at **Parent Window with Browser Navigation** to open the article within the existing window.

[154]

16. Navigate to and select the Article to be displayed under the **Parameters–Basic** section, as shown in the following screenshot. Note that you can also filter the Sections and Categories to make it easier to locate the article you are looking for.

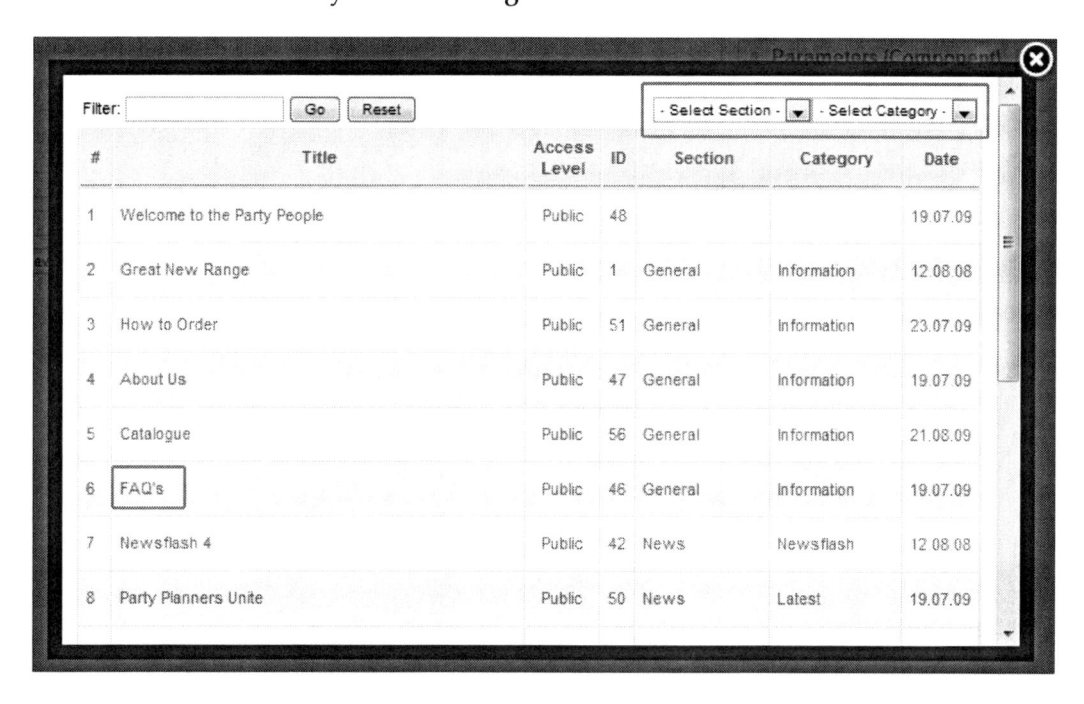

17. Within the **Parameters** section, we'll leave the **Component** and **System parameters** as they are for now.
18. Click **Save** to add the new menu item.

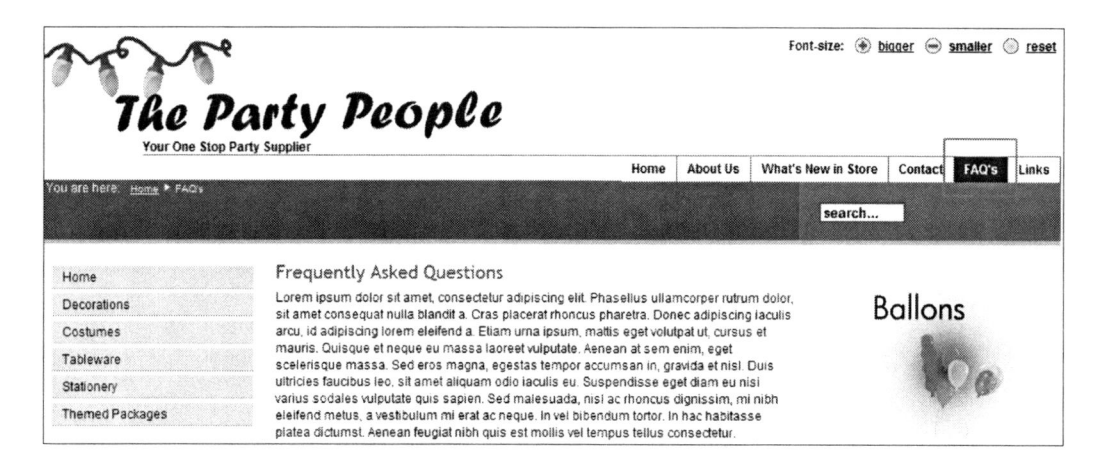

Reordering menu items

You can also reorder the menu items as they appear on the frontend of the site.

1. Navigate to the **Menu Manager**.
2. Select the menu item to be moved and click the green up and down arrows in the **Order** column, until the order is how you would like it to be.
3. Click the computer disk **Save** icon next to **Order**.
4. View the frontend to check your changes.

Removing a menu item

You can do this quickly using the Menu Manager.

1. Navigate to the **Menu Manager** from the top menu.
2. Click the checkbox next to the menu item to be moved.
3. Click the **Unpublish** icon on the top menu. This doesn't actually delete the item but removes it from the menu. It can be re-published later if needed.

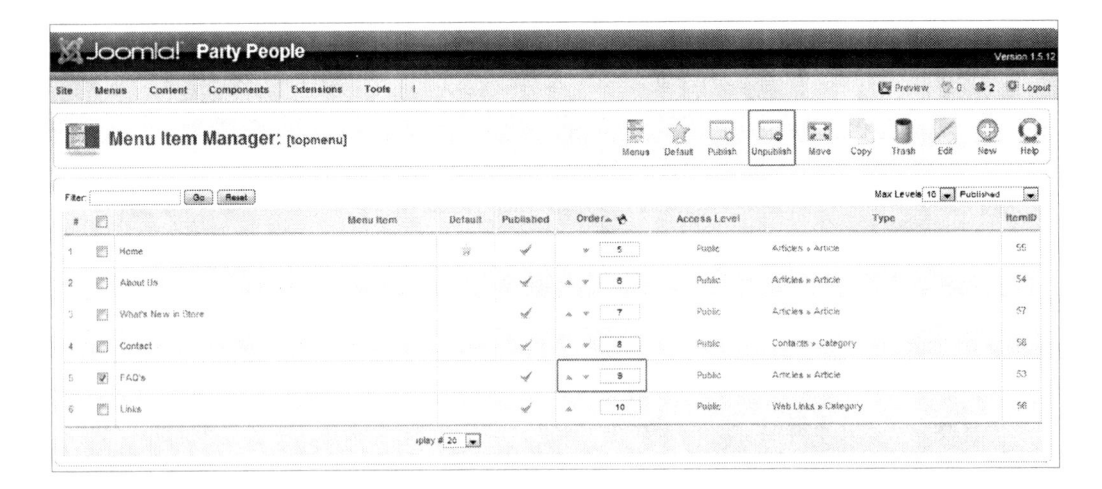

While we are thinking about menus, let's add a **Links** item to the top menu of the Party People website using the Menu Manager again and the Web Links component.

Adding Web Links

In Chapter 6, *Making Your Site Popular*, we looked at how having links to other websites can assist with your search engine ranking. Within the Joomla! framework, there is a Web Links component which can be enabled to create a section with a list of links to external websites. Perhaps you can use this if you belong to a group of affiliated organizations and would like to acknowledge them. You could arrange a link swap arrangement where you all have links to each other on your sites.

Within the Party People website we'll add a Web Links section. We'll begin by setting the global parameters for the list of web links, so they appear consistently. Then, we'll add a category for each link to slot them into and then add the actual links. Finally, we'll add a link to the Web Links list in the Party People top menu using the Menu Manager.

We'll add a list of links to the charitable organizations supported by the Party People website.

Setting the Web Links global parameters

It's a good idea to establish default values of the Web Links component upfront using the global parameters so that they appear consistently, and so that you won't have to establish individual settings every time you add a link. You can also decide on a number of presentation factors upfront too.

The following steps are given to set the global parameters:

1. Select **Components | Web Links | Links** using the top menu.
2. Click the **Parameters** icon to open the Global Configuration window and work through the options.

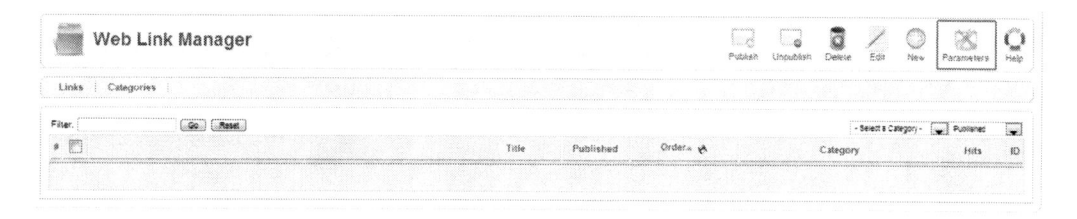

Menus, Modules, and Components

3. Click the **Show** or **Hide** option in the **Description** box in the Global Configuration section of the window, as shown in the following screenshot. When we add a new link, we can add a custom description of the link.

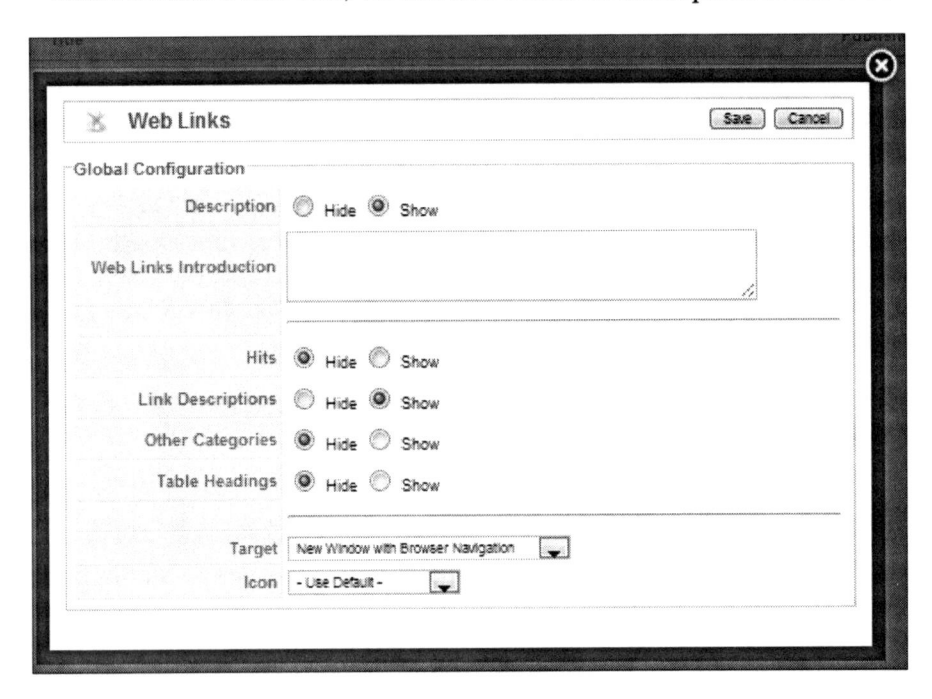

4. Type in some optional text for display above the first category of links for **Web Links Introduction**. Decide whether to reveal the number of times your link has been clicked on the frontend web links page. Click **Hide** or **Show**.
5. Select whether to display the individual **Link Descriptions**.
6. Click **Hide** or **Show** for **Other Categories**. If you have more than one category, you can show all of them as listed or linked.
7. Click **Hide** or **Show** for **Table Headings**. These are the column headings for your display page. If you don't have a large list, click **Hide**.
8. Click the drop-down menu for **Target** and decide how the link should open:
    - **Parent Window with Browser Navigation**: The external site loads within the same window as your site. This means taking the user away from your site, and potentially not having them return.
    - **New Window with Browser Navigation**: The linked site appears in its own window with its own navigation. This would be the preferred option if you don't want to lose the user, as the window with your site in it remains open.

Chapter 8

- **New Window without Browser Navigation**: This is the same as the previous option, but without the standard browser navigation icons.

9. Click the drop-down menu to choose an icon that will appear to the left of the Web Links URL addresses. You can add your own through the Media Manager if none of the standard ones suit.
10. Click **Save**.

Adding a Category of links

Now as the parameters are set, to further help keep things organized, create a Category in the Web Links component. Click on the **Categories** link in the Web Links Manager, as seen in the earlier screenshot, under the **Web Links Manager** heading.

Click the **New** icon to create the new Category.

1. Type in **Charities We Support** for the name of the category with the Party People site, as shown in the following screenshot.

[159]

Menus, Modules, and Components

2. Click **Public** so that anyone who visits the site can see the list. You can select who can see the links by clicking the following:
    - **Registered**: They are seen only by those registered with the site.
    - **Special**: For viewing only by those users who have Author status or higher.
3. Click **Save** to add your new Category.

Note that we can also type in a description and an image for this Category.

Adding the links to the Category

Now we'll add a link to the **Charities We Support** category.

1. Click **Links** in the **Web Link Manager** screen.
2. Click the **New** icon to open the **Web Link** screen.

3. Type in **RSPCA Australia** into the **Details** box.
4. Click **Yes** for **Published**.
5. Select the **Charities We Support** from the drop-down menu selection for Category.
6. Type in the URL to the link, that is, `http://rspca.org.au/`.
7. Select the order of the link as first, which is the only option when it's the first web link.
8. Select **Use Global** under the **Parameters/Target** section.

9. Type in a brief **Description**.
10. Click **Save** to add the link to the list in the Web Link Manager.

Editing and deleting web links and Categories

Using the Web Links Manager also allows you to update the links you have added.

To edit your links and Categories:

1. Navigate to the **Web Links Manager** through the top menu.
2. Select **Links** or **Categories** to view the list.
3. Select the checkbox to the left of the **Link** or **Category** title.
4. Select **Publish**, **Unpublish**, **Delete**, or **Edit** as required.

However, remember that if you delete a link, it's gone and there is no warning. Consider unpublishing it instead.

Okay, now for the fun part.

Adding the web links page to the (top) menu

Now that we have the web links ready to go, let's add the **Links** item to the top menu of the Party People website.

1. Navigate to the **Menu Manager | Top Menu** using the top menu.
2. Click **New** within the **Menu Manager** for **Top Menu** to reveal the **Menu Item** category tree.

Menus, Modules, and Components

3. Click **Web Links** to open the sub category and click **Category | Category List Layout**. The other options are:
   - **All Categories | Web Link Category List Layout** to show a list of all the Web Link categories.
   - **Web Link | Web Link Submission Layout**.

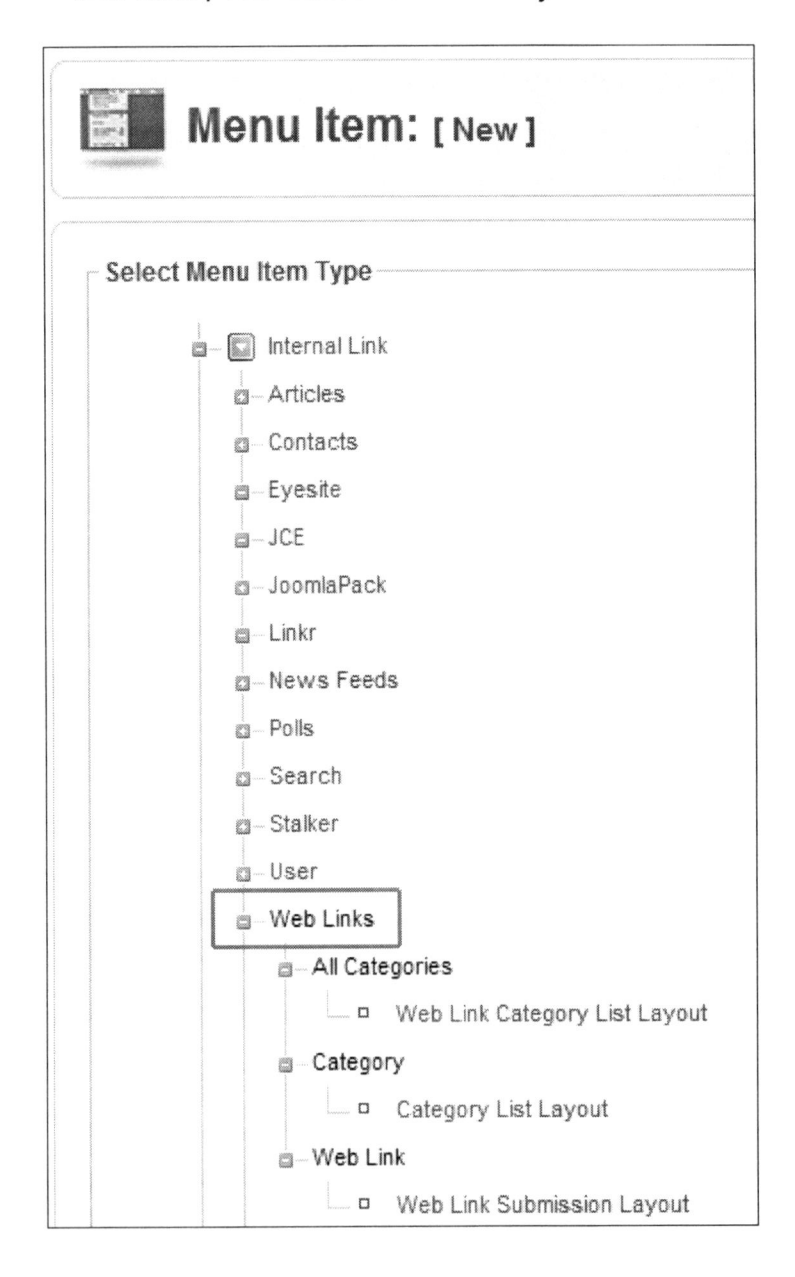

Menu Item: [New]

Select Menu Item Type

- Internal Link
  - Articles
  - Contacts
  - Eyesite
  - JCE
  - JoomlaPack
  - Linkr
  - News Feeds
  - Polls
  - Search
  - Stalker
  - User
  - **Web Links**
    - All Categories
      - Web Link Category List Layout
    - Category
      - Category List Layout
    - Web Link
      - Web Link Submission Layout

4. Type **Links** into the textbox as it will appear on the frontend of the website.
5. Leave the **Menu Item Details** as the default settings, including the **Display in** the drop-down box, as it should have **Top Menu** selected.

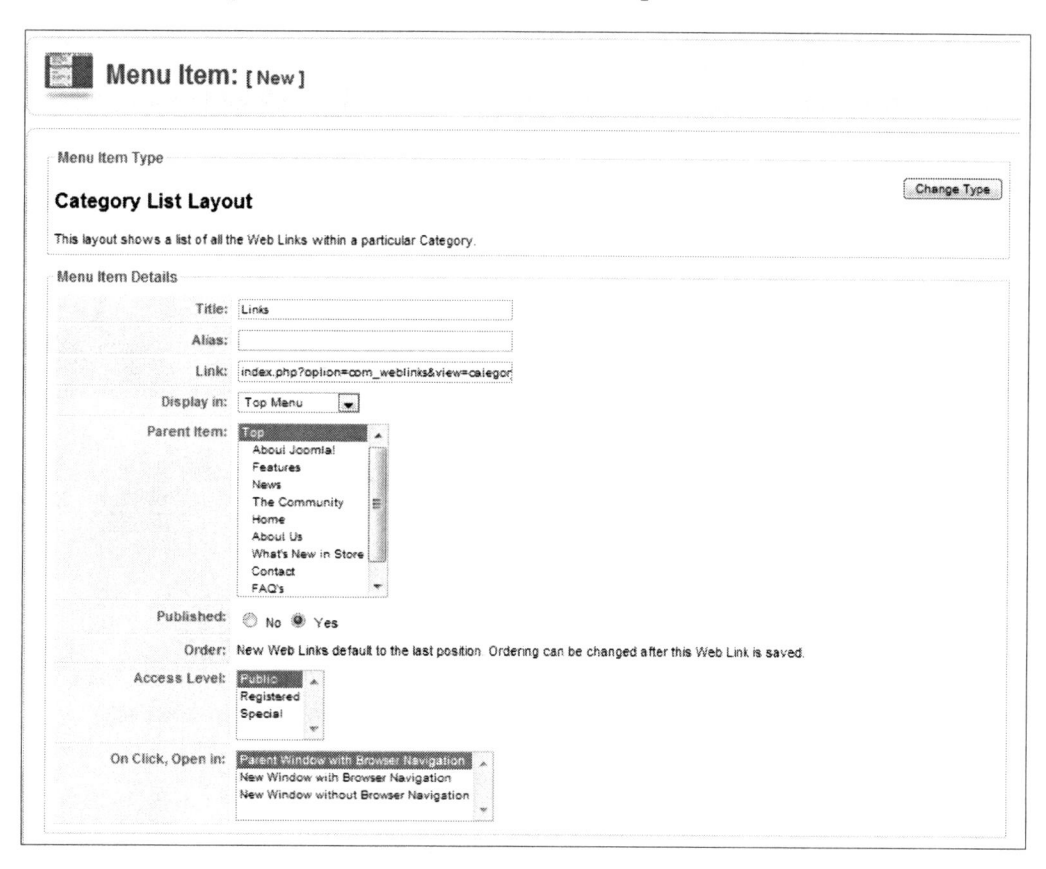

6. Confirm the **Category** under the **Parameters(Basic)** setting.

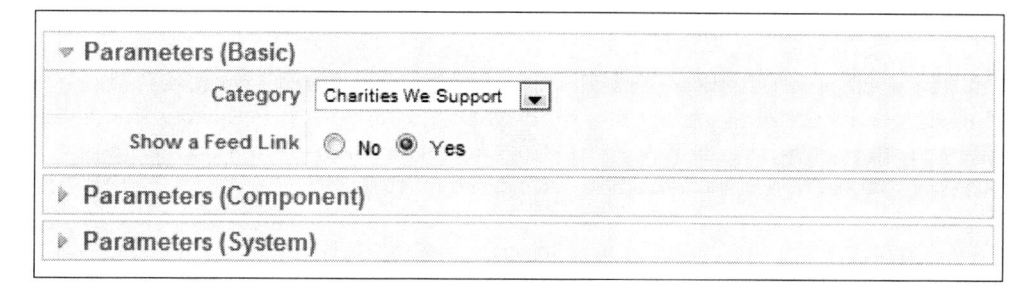

Menus, Modules, and Components

7. Open the **Parameters (Components)** section to view the settings we made in the global parameters of the Web Links component. We will leave these as they are; however, they can be changed if required and will override the settings made earlier.
8. Leave the **Parameters (System)** as they are.
9. Click **Apply** to save your work, but remain within the **Menu Item (Edit)** screen. We will check the updated menu on the frontend.

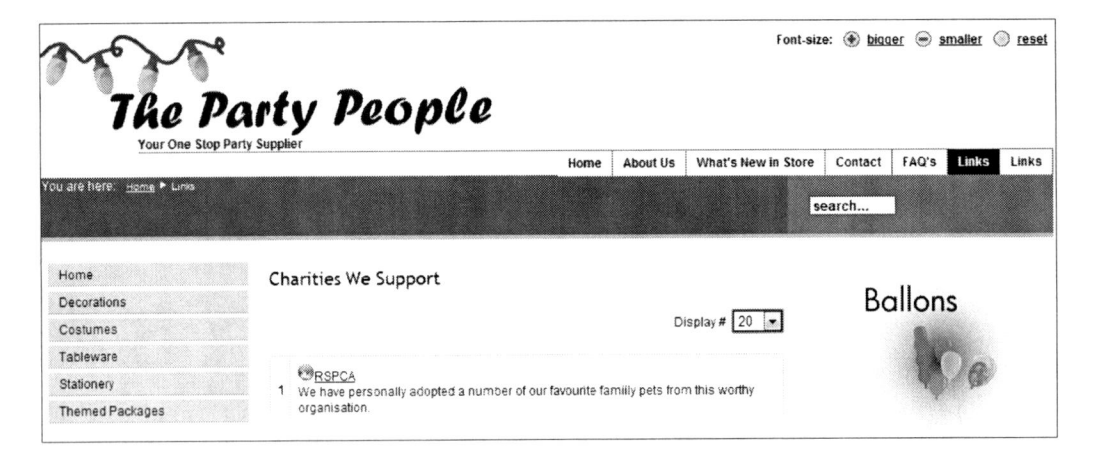

Its, all good, so go back and click **Save** to finalize your changes.

You can add any number of links and categories and publish them to your site.

Advertising banners

Do you have paid advertising on your website? If so, they are shown through the Banner component, which is enabled through the Modules section. Banners use a component and a module to function, and the module must be enabled to allow the component to show the banners.

Much like a real world banner, website banners generally have a narrow/tall or wide/narrow aspect ratio and fit into module positions built into the site template. When you set one up, you will need to know the dimensions of the banner image and it must be suitable for its position within the site layout.

Website owners can generate income from displaying an advertising banner, referred to as an "impression." When a user clicks on the banner ad, referred to as a "click through" and visits the advertiser's website, the original website owner is paid a commission. It goes further than this too, but the position of the advertisement within the website "real estate" is important and advertisers pay for their positioning.

Our Party People website doesn't have any banner advertising yet, so we will set this up and organize the banners to appear on certain pages. We won't add anything too distracting, as website users can use ad blockers to turn off the advertisement display altogether.

Setting up banner advertising

The first thing to do is to establish who is going to be accepted as banner advertiser on the site, then work out what the image will be and its dimensions. Once you have that sorted out, upload the image into the images/banners directory using the Media Manager.

Then, within the Banner component, we'll firstly have to add a Banner Category, a client, and their actual banner advertisement specifications. You can't add a banner to your site without a client or a Category.

The Party People will be advertising a banner for their friends at the RSPCA.

Let's begin with navigating to the Banner Manager through the **Components | Banner** link in the top menu.

Adding a banner Category

We need to establish categories for our Banners, just as we did for the Web Links. This allows you to organize and sort them if you have many.

1. Click the **Categories** link within the **Banner Manager**.
2. Click the **New** button to open the **Category** details screen.
3. Type **Charities** for the **Title**.
4. Leave the default options as they are for now.
5. Click **Save**.

Menus, Modules, and Components

The following screenshot shows two examples of **Categories** created for the Party People website.

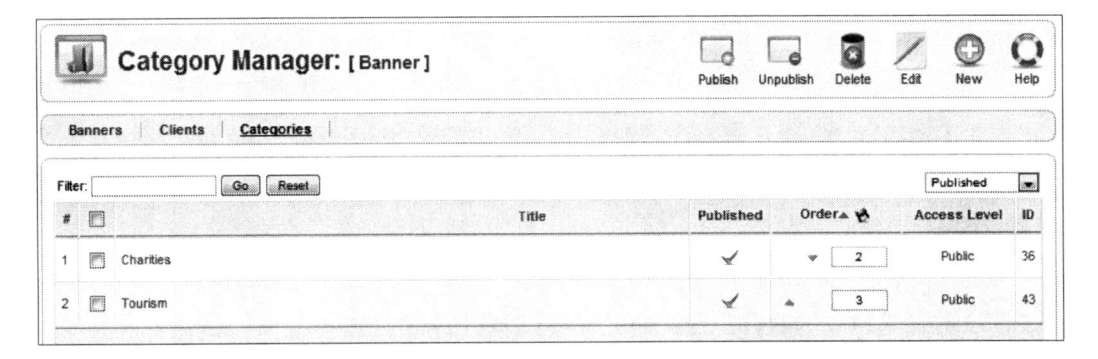

Adding a banner client

In order to display a banner we must have a client who would be the organization displaying their banner on the website, in our case the RSPCA.

1. Click the **Clients** link in the **Banner Manager** screen.
2. Type in the **Client Name**, **Contact**, and **Email**.
3. Click **Save**.

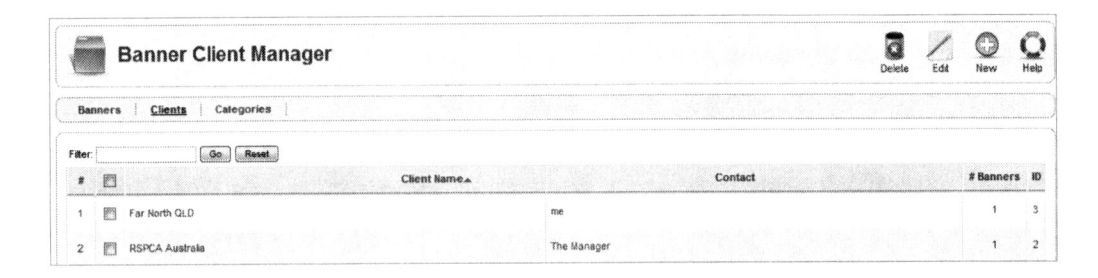

Now that we have the category and clients established, we can set the global parameters as well.

Setting the banner parameters

Just like we set the global parameters for the web links, we'll do the same for our banner.

1. Click the **Banners** link in the **Banner Manager** screen.
2. Click the **Parameters** icon to reveal the dialog window and choose to do the following:

- Enable the component to record the number of banner impressions on a daily basis.
- Record the number of "click throughs" on a daily basis.
- Leave the **Tag Prefix** blank for now; we'll look at this later.

3. Click **Save** for your changes.

Adding the banner

Now we have established the behind the scenes settings, we can create the actual banner and add it to the frontend of the website.

1. Click the **New** icon on top right of the **Banner Manager** screen.
2. Add the title **RSPCA** in the name box as it will appear within the Banner manager listing.
3. Click **Yes** to show the banner.
4. Make the banner sticky. A sticky banner is one that will displayed consistently and take priority over the non-sticky banners. If there is more than one sticky banner, they will be rotated. If a banner is not sticky, then it will not be displayed. Sticky banners can have a set number of impressions associated and once this expires, they are no longer displayed and the others are displayed. Impressions refer to the number of times a banner ad is downloaded, and therefore seen.
5. Type **1** for the **Order** of the banner display. This means the RSPCA banner will display first when there is more than one.
6. Select the **Category** and **Client Name** respectively.
7. Check **Unlimited** for the number of impressions purchased for this banner. The advertiser can pay for a certain number of impressions, that is, "click throughs" to their site.

Menus, Modules, and Components

8. Type in the full URL of the website to be clicked through to.
9. No clicks have been recorded yet, but it shows how many. It can also be reset.
10. Select the image to be displayed in this banner from the drop-down list. All these images are from the images/banners folder. Use the Media Manager to upload your banner images to this folder.
11. Type the width and height of the image to be displayed.
12. Type in any **Tags** if you want to match up this banner with a certain content Article. This allows you to display a banner based on the content of an Article viewed. Note that the **Search by Tag** parameter is set to **Yes** in the banner module. The tags are used to match keywords entered for an Article, which we can do in the next step.

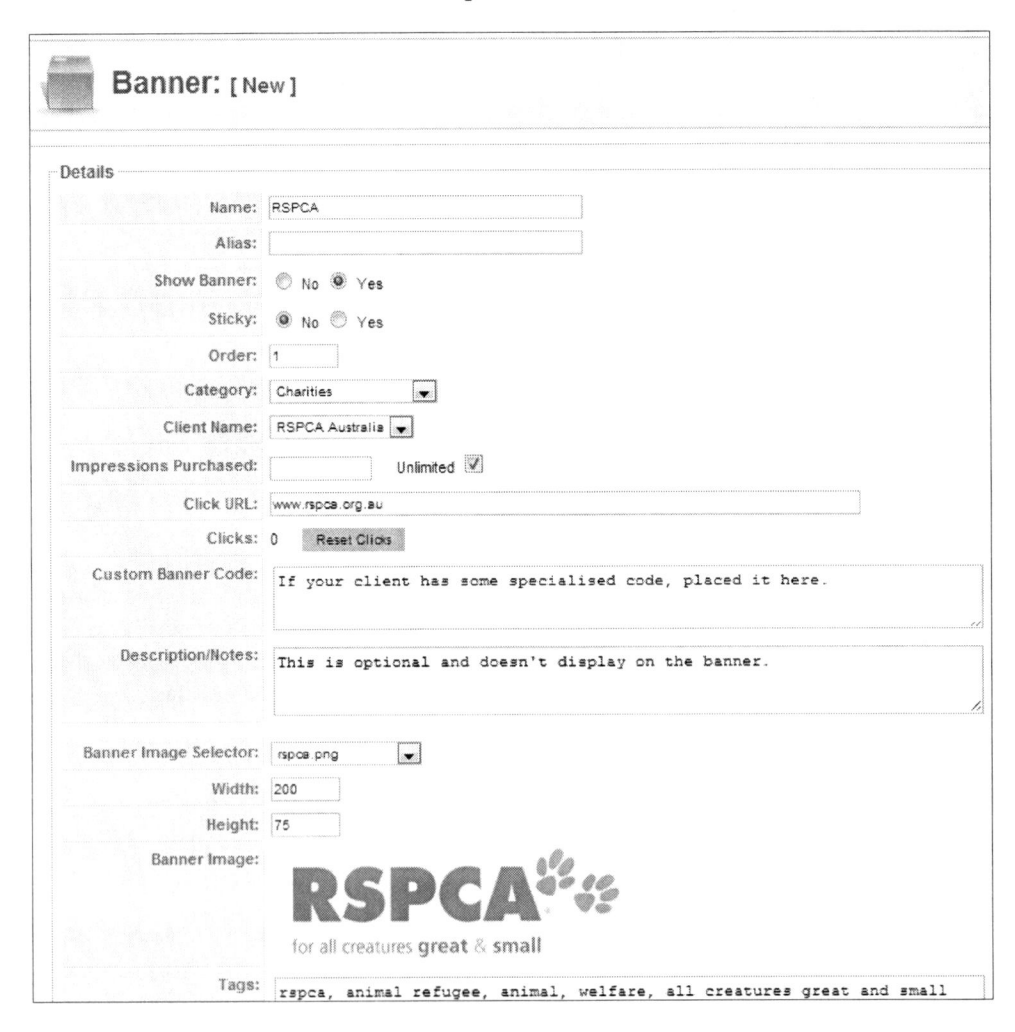

There is no customized code or descriptions required for this banners so these boxes can be left blank. If you do have some code or descriptions, add it in here as well.

13. Click the **Save** icon at the top right to save your new Banner.

In the **Banner Manager**, you will be able to see the details of your banners and sort them as well, as shown in the following screenshot.

Next, we need to move into the **Module Manager** to enable the banner.

Enabling the banner module

The banner module is a core module of the initial Joomla! installation, so you don't need to download anything to get it up and running. It can be uninstalled, however, but here we'll assume that it hasn't been and that is not enabled.

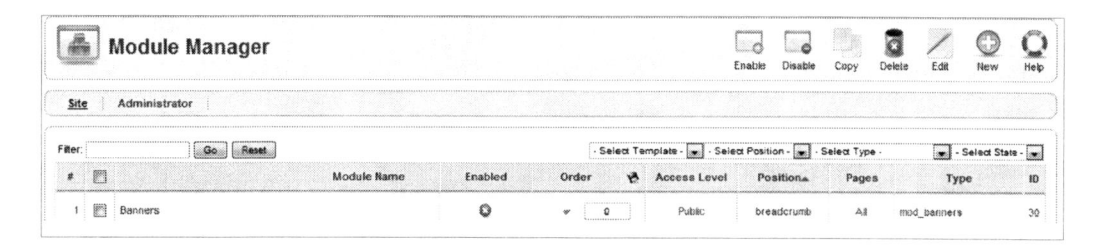

1. Click **Extensions | Module Manager | Site** to see the modules that appear on the frontend of the Party People website.
2. Click the **Banners** link under the **Module Name** column to open the Banner module editing screen.

Menus, Modules, and Components

3. Under the **Details** section, leave the **Title** of the module as **Banners**.

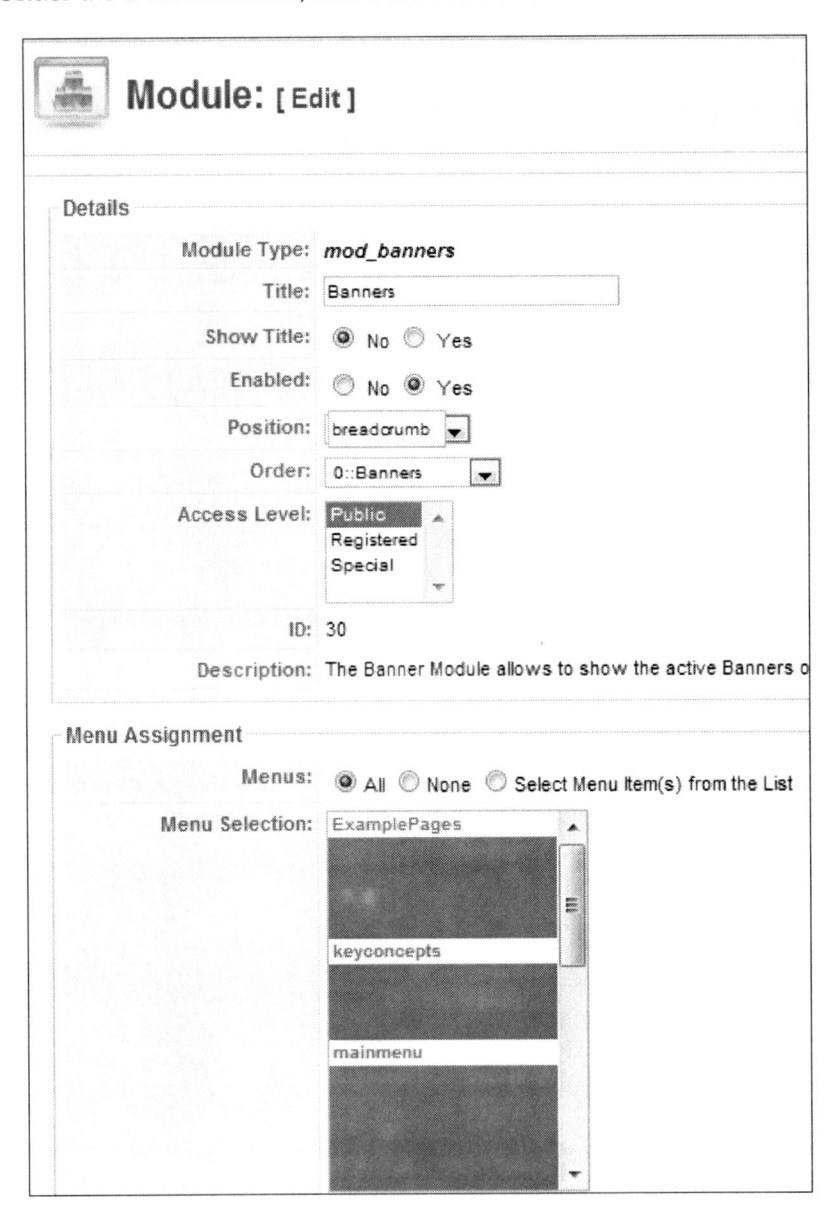

Module: [Edit]

Details

- Module Type: *mod_banners*
- Title: Banners
- Show Title: ● No ○ Yes
- Enabled: ○ No ● Yes
- Position: breadcrumb
- Order: 0::Banners
- Access Level: Public / Registered / Special
- ID: 30
- Description: The Banner Module allows to show the active Banners o

Menu Assignment

- Menus: ● All ○ None ○ Select Menu Item(s) from the List
- Menu Selection: ExamplePages / keyconcepts / mainmenu

4. Click **No** for **Show Title**.

[170]

Chapter 8

5. Click **Yes** to enable the module.
6. Open the drop-down menu to see the **Position** options. We will select **breadcrumb** for our website. The positions of these modules are determined within the template your website uses; the breadcrumb position sits under the logo in this template. Just make sure you turn off your breadcrumbs module!
7. Leave the **Access Level** as **Public**.
8. Under the **Menu Assignment** section, check the **All** radio button so that the banner ad appears on all menu item pages. **None** means it won't appear on any menu items. Alternatively, you can select which menu items it appears on if **Select Menu Item** is chosen.
9. Under the Module Parameters, select **New Window with Browser Navigation** so when the viewer clicks on the banner ad image, the website it links to opens in a new window, rather than yours.

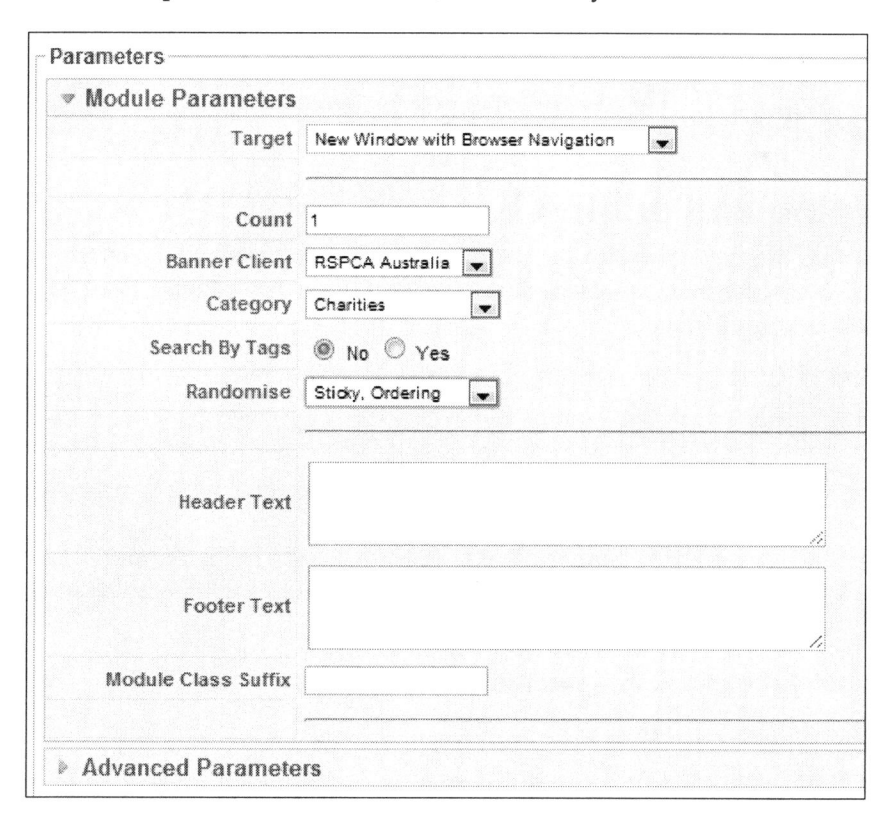

10. Type in the number of banner ads you have to display. We have two.
11. Select the **Category** and **Banner Client** for this banner.

12. Select **No** for **Search by Tags** on this occasion.
13. Select **Sticky, Ordering** for **Randomise**.
14. Click **Save** to set your module parameters and enable it.

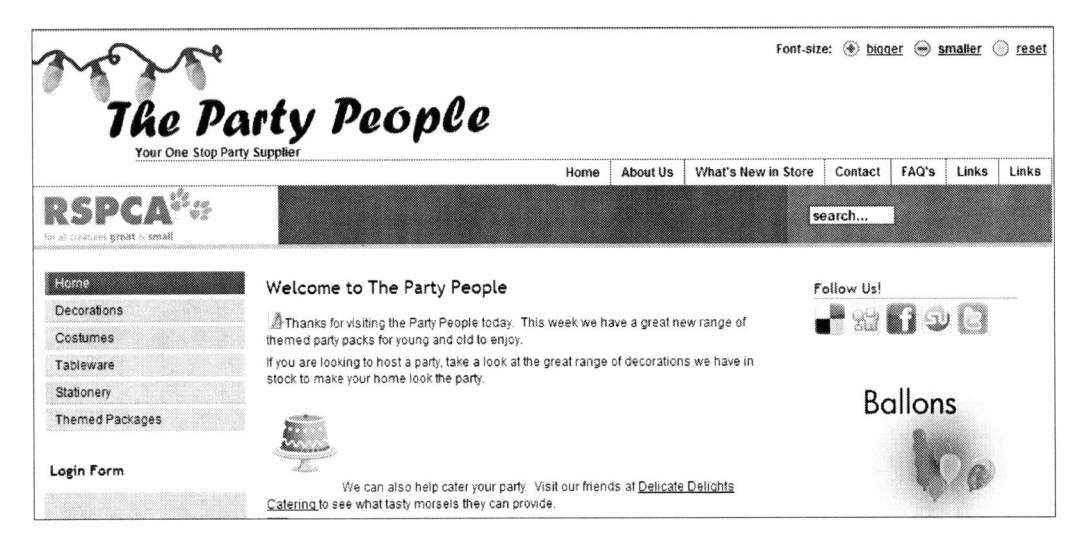

Managing and editing banners

In the Banner Manager you can see the number of impressions and click through generated by the banner, as well as sort them by **Category** and state (that is, **Published** or unpublished).

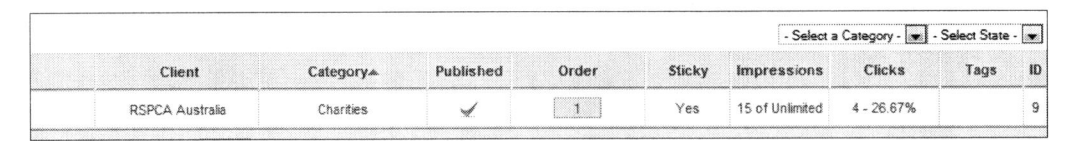

If you need to change your banner, then click on its name in the Banner Manager to open the banner edit screen and edit the details (as you did when you created the banner).

If the banner has expired, then you can delete it by:

1. Clicking the checkbox next to the banner name.
2. Clicking **Delete** to remove it. There is no confirmation for this, so be sure that it is to be deleted.

You can also manage the clients and categories of your banners in the Banner Manager as well.

Latest news module: Updating and adding

This module can present a list of the latest news that you may like your users to read. You add this as a list of links from a module position that you choose and decide how many articles to link to and in what order.

We will enable this module to add a "Party People News" item to the left column of the frontend layout.

Setting up the content

Firstly, we already have a **News** section and a category called **Latest** published. If you don't have them, create them or make sure they are published before you begin, or you will just have to do this later anyway.

1. Create a new Article and publish it within this Section and Category. Check back to Chapter 2, *Creating, Editing, and Organizing Content* if you aren't sure on how to do this.
2. Make a note of the Section and Category ID numbers, as you will refer to these shortly.

Enabling the module

Now that the content is ready, we'll enable the latest news module and customize it.

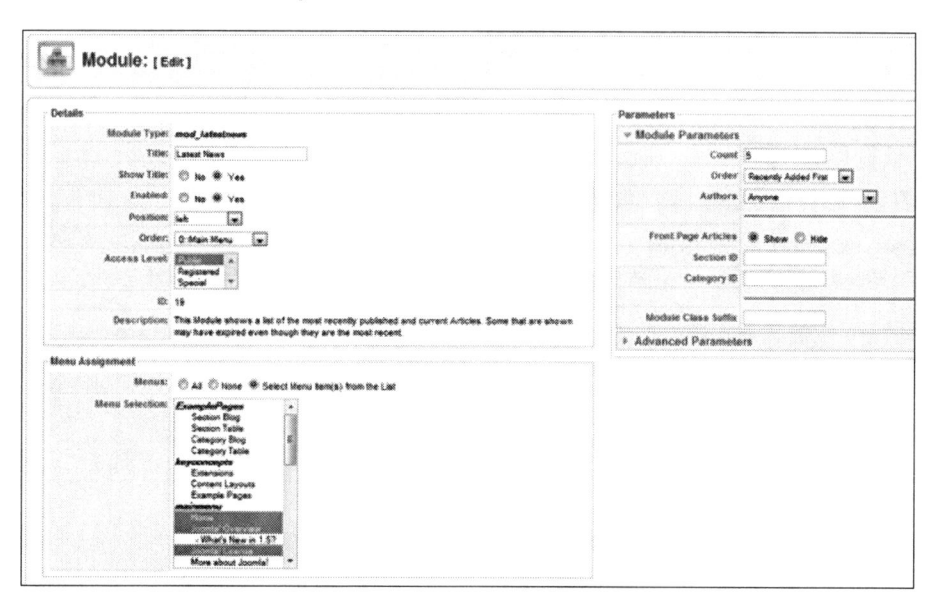

1. Navigate to **Extensions | Module Manager**.
2. Click the **Latest News** link under the module name column to view the module edit screen.
3. Type **Party People News** into the **Title** textbox. This now changes the name of the module from **Latest News** in the Module Manager list.
4. Click **Yes** for **Show Title**.
5. Click **Yes** to enable the module.
6. Click **Left** from the **Position** drop-down menu.
7. Select the hierarchy position for the module in the **Order** drop-down selection. Select the module you want this one to appear under.
8. Select **Public** for **Access Level**.
9. Click the **All** radio button under **Menu Assignment** so that it will appear consistently on each section of the frontend.
10. Type in **3** for the **Count** in the **Module Parameters** section. This shows the number of articles to display. We'll add three in anticipation of creating more Articles. This number can be changed as required.
11. Click **Recently Added First** for the **Order**. This ensures the most up-to-date information appears at the top of the link list.
12. Select **Anyone** so there is no **Author** filter.
13. Click **Hide** for **Show Front Page Articles**.
14. Type in the **Section ID** and **Category ID**.
15. Click **Apply** to save your changes.
16. Check if the frontend layout is okay and the links work. If so, save your work.

Managing your latest news

When we want to add more news Articles, we can simply create them and add them to the same Section and Category and the links will be added to the module.

If you want to reorder them, shuffle them up and down using the arrows and the **Order Save** icon as outlined earlier.

Random images module

The Party People website has a sequence of random images displayed in the right column that we want to update with new images. We can do this in two ways:

Change the files in the image folder

The steps to change files in the image folder are as follows:

1. Navigate to the Media Manager through the top menu: **Site | Media Manager** or click the icon on the administration control panel.
2. Navigate to the **images | stories | randomImages** directory where the images are stored.
3. Edit, upload, or move the images as needed. Chapter 3, *Managing Images and Videos* describes how to do this in detail.

The new images or adjustments will be displayed on the frontend of the site.

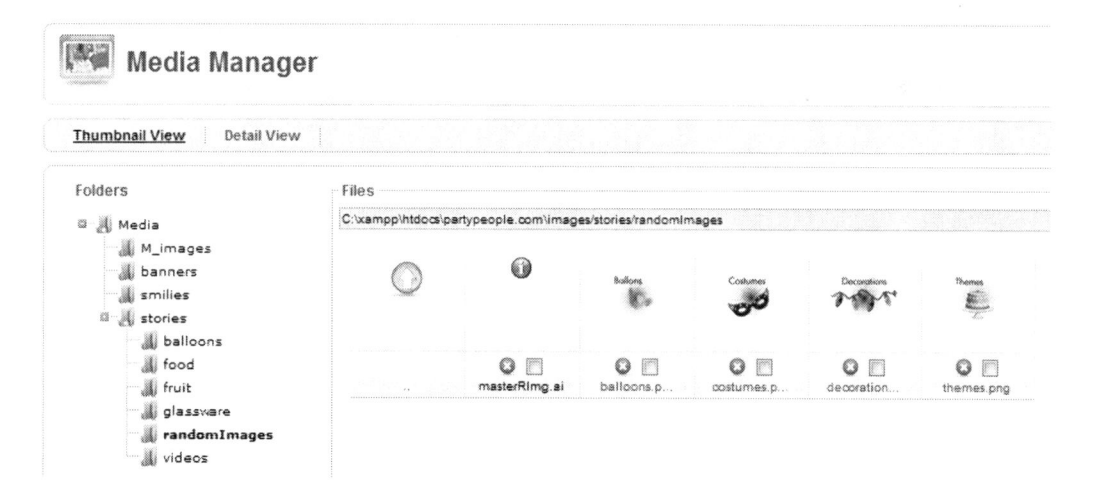

Redirect to a different image directory

The steps are as follows:

1. Click **Extensions | Module Manager** in the top menu to view the list of enabled and disabled modules installed on the site. Ours is enabled and in the right position, so we will sort the list to only display enabled modules in the right position.

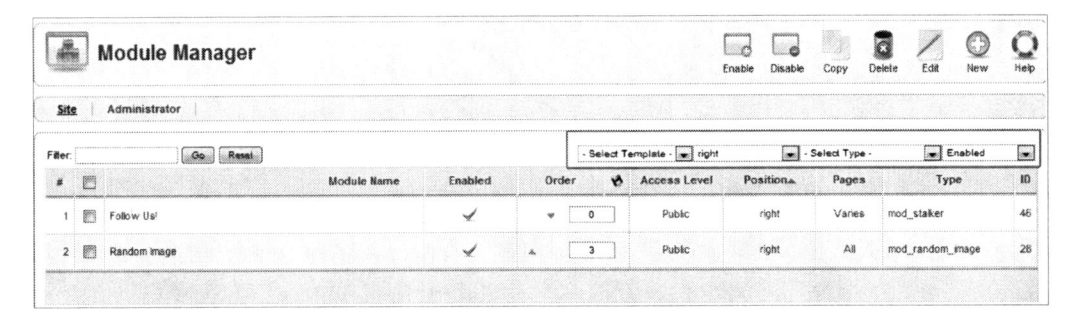

2. Click **Random Image** link under **Module Name** to view the module settings. Yours may be named differently, so watch out for this.

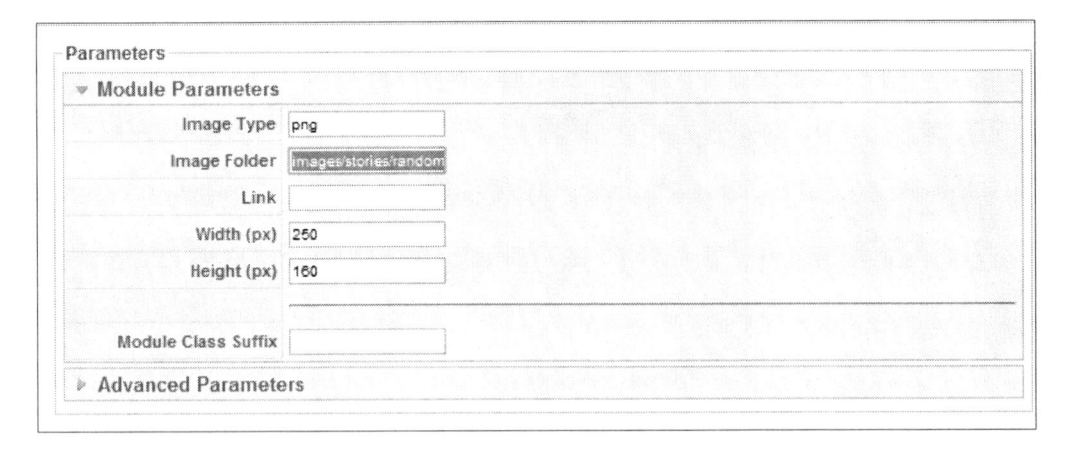

3. Type the name of the new folder in the **Image Folder** box. Be sure to type it exactly as it is, or the images will not show if the link is incorrect.

4. Click **Save**.

You can also change the following:

- The dimensions of the images displayed, by typing in the sizes in the **Width** and **Height** boxes. These are handy if your image file dimensions are large. Also, it means you won't have to scale them down with image editing software to fit them within the display area.
- The link to an external website, when you click the link.

Installing third-party extensions—modules, components, and plugins

Installing a third-party extension is not difficult in itself. However, some are more complex than others in terms of setting up their parameters after they have been installed. The Joomla! development team hosts a section on the website for reviewing and downloading extensions at http://extensions.joomla.org/. Their purpose and benefits are outlined, and they are all categorized and reviewed by people who have installed them. Some are commercial, which means you must pay for them. Others are non-commercial, meaning they are free to download and use, but may require registration prior to download.

There is a large range of extensions available. One such component is the shopping cart application, VirtueMart. This is installed in the same way as any other extension. However, once installed, you need to configure it in order to display your catalog of items, along with the prices, shipping costs, and any other fees and charges.

It is also important to note that some third-party extensions work better than others and you should always avoid installing beta versions. If you choose to install one, check the reviews. Look for the **Editor's Pick** section on the extensions listing.

Position of modules

As mentioned in Chapter 1, *Exploring Your New Joomla! Website*, the position of content within your site is determined by whether it's contained within a component or a module. Content within components sits within the middle of the interface design, whereas module content generally sits to the left, right, top, or bottom of the components.

Where you choose to present your module content, is determined by the choice you make when you enable the module. Module positions themselves are determined by the template design. The template designer would have taken into consideration the "screen real estate" in terms of what's important for the user to see first (the top left being the prime position) which is why you will often see company logos here. It is beyond the scope of this book to begin tweaking templates to change module positions; however, it is worth pointing this out.

Plugins

As mentioned in Chapter 3, *Managing Images and Videos*, content plugins like EasierTube (http://joomlacode.org/gf/project/easiertube/) and Simple Image gallery (http://www.joomlaworks.gr/) make it possible to display videos and an image gallery on your website, without much trouble at all. You can download and install both the plugins to add them to your website. They sit around the perimeter of the main content, but can also be loaded into modules.

Plugins themselves add a level of functionality to your website by working in the background (executing some code actually) and responding to events that occur when a component tells them to do something. These events can be a system event, a content-based event, a user-based event, a contact event, or an editor event. These are all things your Joomla! developer is familiar with.

You probably won't have to do much with plugins at this level. If you want to add some specialized feature to your site that requires one, talk to your developer to have them install one for you.

Installing an extension

We'll install an employment/jobs listing component to the Party People website called JobGrok. It displays a list of available jobs, to the potential applicants and allows them to send an e-mail to apply for the position. This is great for a business with a small human resources department, or a small business wanting to advertise a position, without the expense of a consultancy or advertising externally.

Firstly, we need to download the ZIP file with the component files from the developer's website at http://www.jobgrok.com/home/downloads/file/view/14/1.html. However, note that registration is required to download this component.

1. Download the ZIP file from the developer's website onto your local hard drive.

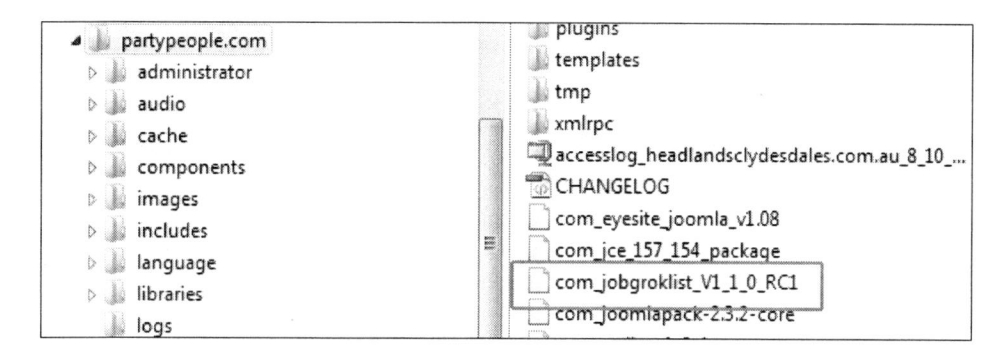

2. Log into the administration panel and navigate to the **Extensions | Install/Uninstall** section.

3. Click the **Install** link and click **Choose File** to select the zipped file that you previously downloaded, and upload it into the administration framework.

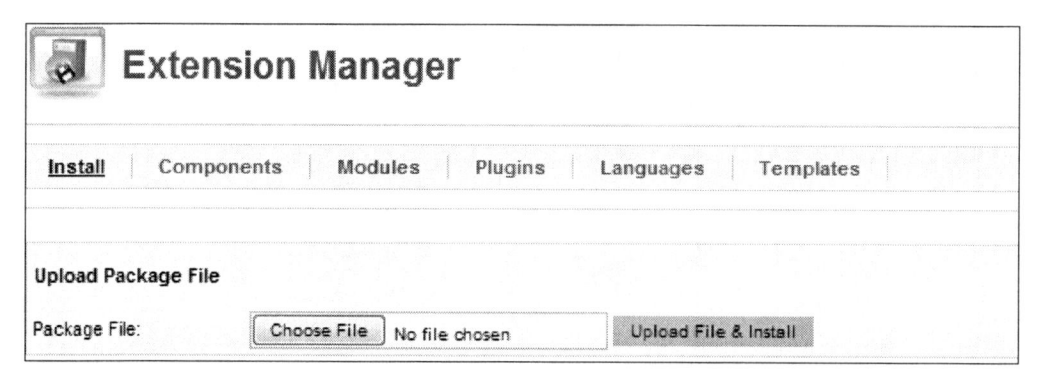

4. Select the file from your computer and click **Upload File & Install**. You will see a message that says **Install Component Success** when this is complete.

That's all you need to do in order to actually install a component. This is a component; you won't need to enable it like you would need to enable a module or plugin. Instead, navigate straight to the **Components** menu and select **Job Grok Listing**, as shown in the following screenshot, to begin setting up the parameters.

Configuring the component

Content within the various components are all different and will have their own set of parameters. The JobGrok component includes a number of global parameters that can be configured upfront, making managing the content within it more efficient. You can see how it should look at the developer's website: http://www.jobgrok.com/products/demo.html.

Chapter 8

To access the component parameters, follow the given steps:

1. Click the **Component | JobGrok Listing** link in the top menu.
2. Click the **Parameters** icon on the top right toolbar of the **Postings Manager**.

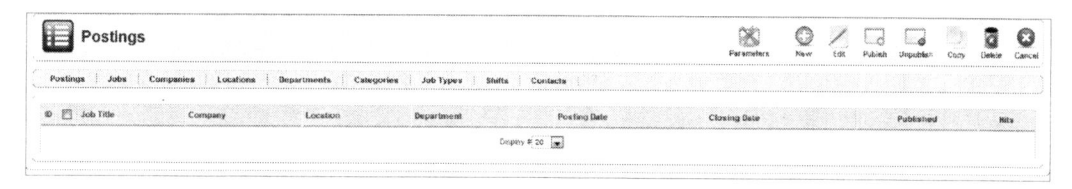

3. Set up your job listings, beginning with the company, locations, departments, and all of the other details.

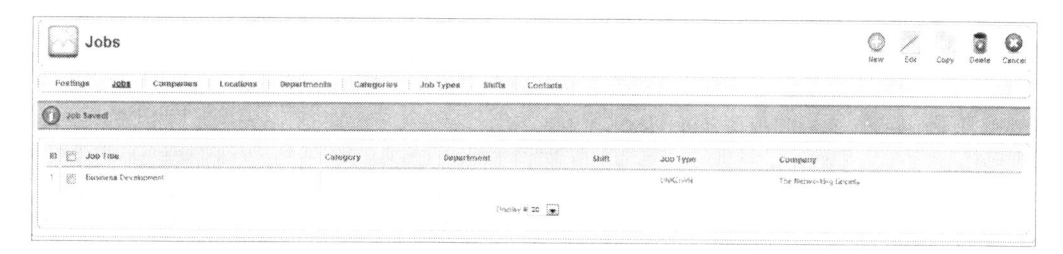

Then once you have all of these details, click on the **Job** link and create a new job.

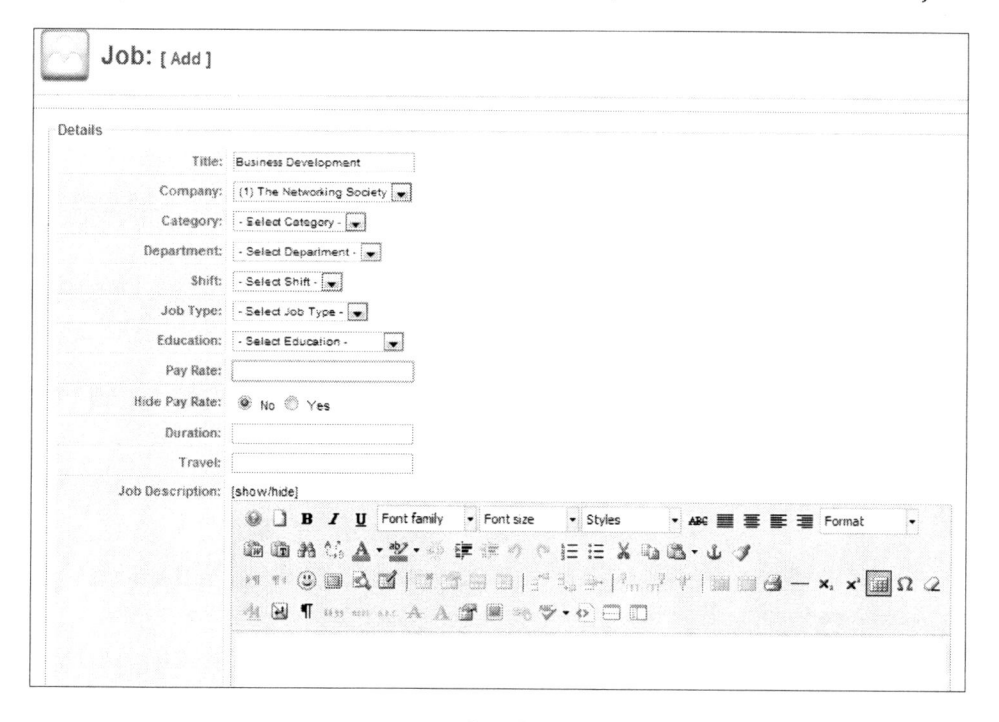

Adding the new component to a menu

Once you have the component set up, you will want the users to look at the content, so you will need to add a link to it from a menu. We do this in the same way as outlined earlier in this chapter, within the section on "Extending the menu with a new link".

This time, however, when you add a new menu item, you will see a link to the component in the directory tree, as shown in the following screenshot:

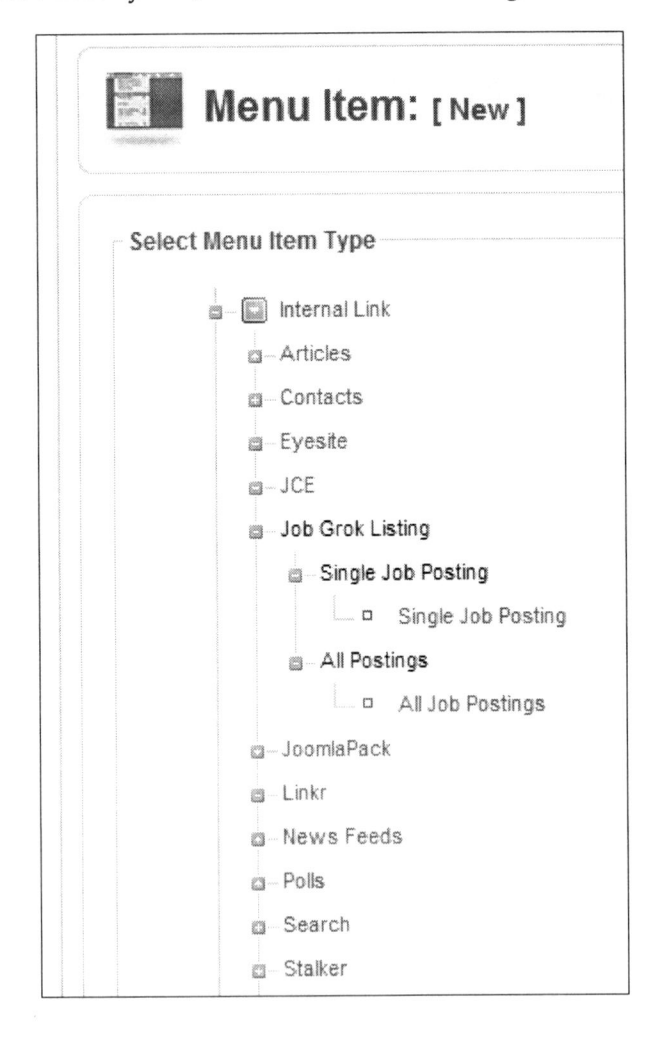

Menu Item: [New]

Select Menu Item Type

- Internal Link
  - Articles
  - Contacts
  - Eyesite
  - JCE
  - Job Grok Listing
    - Single Job Posting
      - Single Job Posting
    - All Postings
      - All Job Postings
  - JoomlaPack
  - Linkr
  - News Feeds
  - Polls
  - Search
  - Stalker

Select the option that suits your needs, and work your way through the new menu items screen. Set all of the parameters that you want displayed on the frontend as well.

Chapter 8

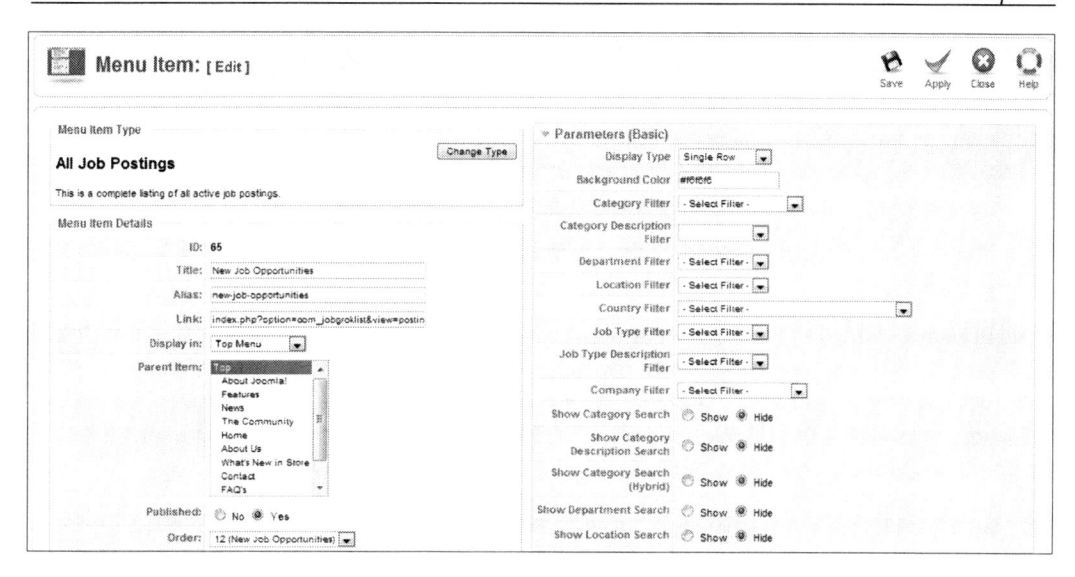

Once you have done that, save your preferences and you will see the new link on the menu you chose to add the link to, and how it will look within the site.

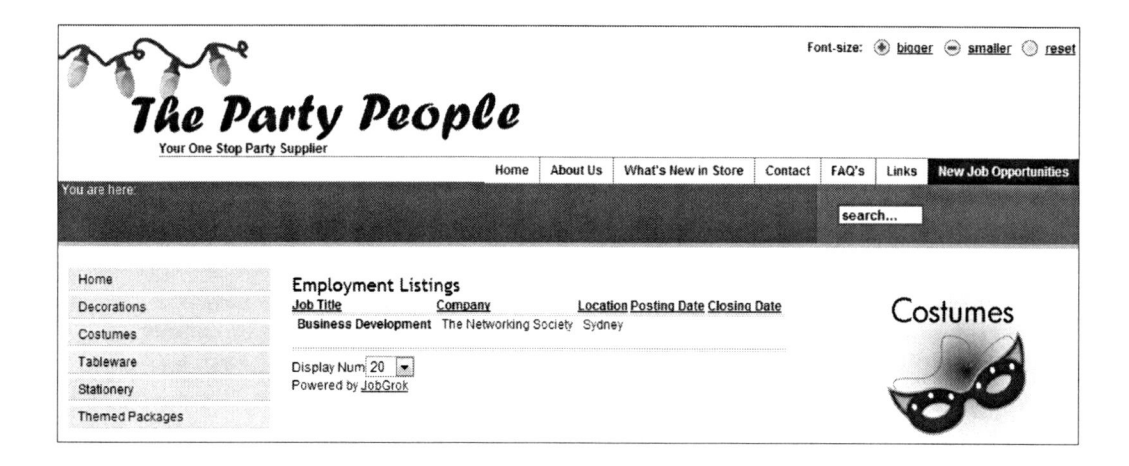

[183]

Additional third-party extensions

JobGrok is just one non-commercial third-party extension available to download. The following is an outline of some other popular and highly rated extensions available. As mentioned, you can visit the Joomla! extensions listing at `http://extensions.joomla.org/extensions` for a full overview of all the categories.

VirtueMart

This is a very popular shopping cart and catalog component that is free to download and install. You can use it not only for e-commerce applications, but also as a product catalog if you don't want to set up merchant account facilities or a PayPal account. You can upload images and descriptions into your catalog and potential buyers can contact you for details.

See details at `http://virtuemart.net/` for a full overview.

JCal Pro

This is a well-regarded events calendar component. It is a commercial extension that offers a number of options, including private and public calendars and multi-language options. It also has an easy-to-use backend management and can be configured to a number of themes. More details are available at `http://dev.anything-digital.com/JCal-Pro/Features.html`.

DOCman

Document uploading and downloading is made easier using this non-commercial component. Categories can be established for various document types and specific documents can be assigned to certain users as well. You can extend the core framework of this component, as there are also a number of add-ons to extend its basic functions. The developer's website at `http://www.joomlatools.eu/products/docman.html` has full details.

Letterman

This is an easy-to-use component that allows you to send newsletters with text and images from your website to subscribers. Newsletters are subscribed by users, who can be imported from other newsletter lists and managed through the administration backend. Visit `http://joomlacode.org/gf/project/letterman` to download the files.

Core modules

Within the core Joomla! framework itself, there are a number of useful modules that can be enabled, without the need to download any third-party files.

To access any of these modules, go to the Module Manager using the **Extensions | Modules** links in the top menu. There you will see the full list of modules installed within the site. Select the module you want to use by clicking the link in the **Title** column.

Following is a brief outline of what some of these core modules can do for you on your site.

NewsFlash

You can randomly display new articles, either one at a time, or a fixed number of them within a module position. Enable the module and start applying the details you require, as you have with the other modules that we have enabled throughout this book.

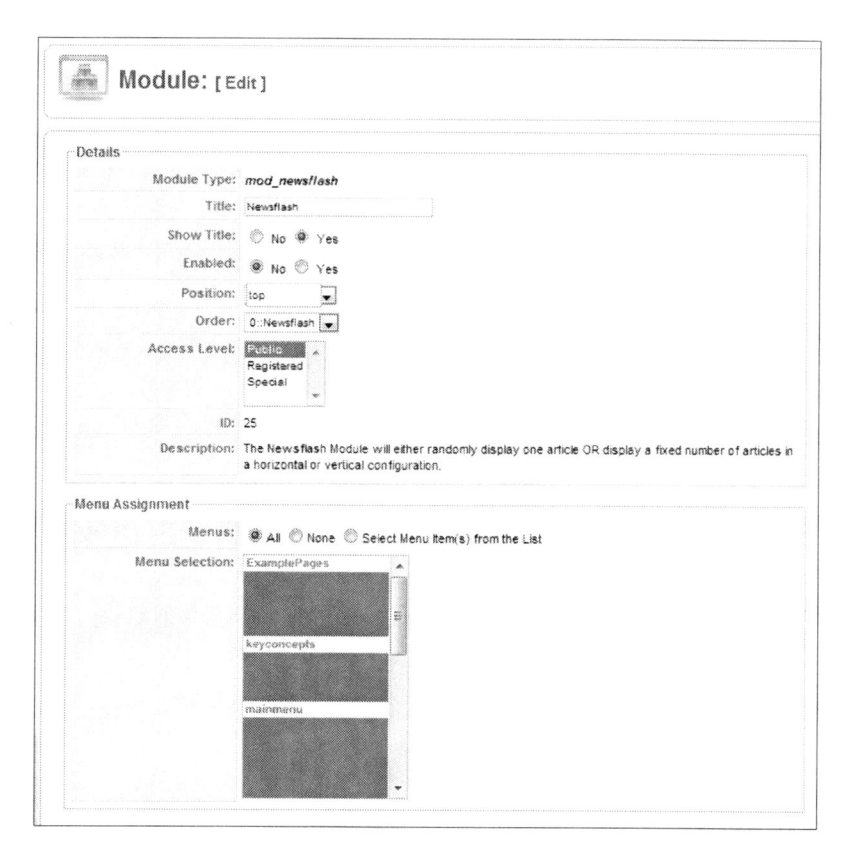

The parameters section allows you to select the category of article, how they are laid out, whether they contain images within the display, and whether to show a **Read More** link and so on.

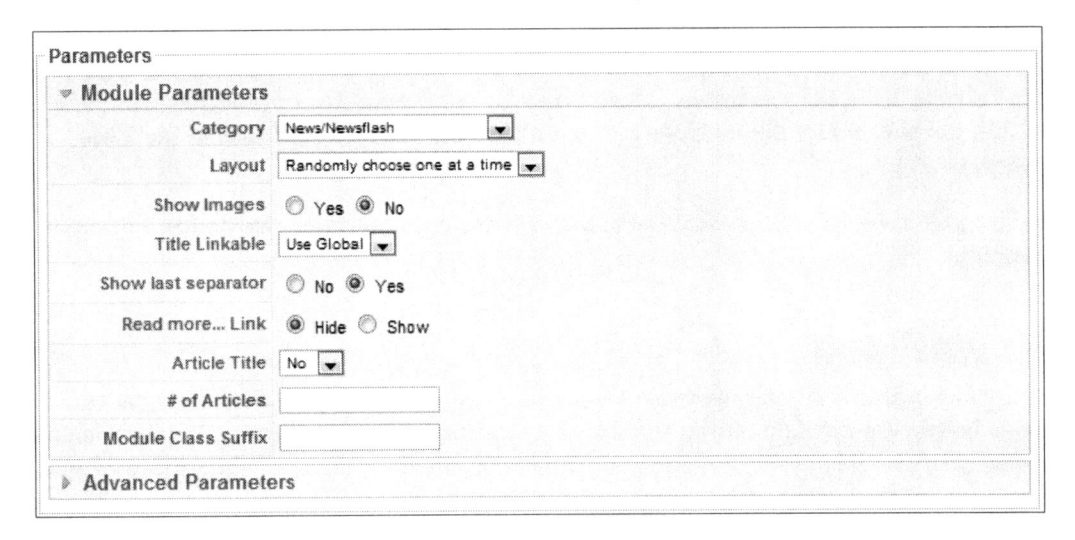

Who's online

This is a useful module to enable if you want to know who is accessing your website at any one time.

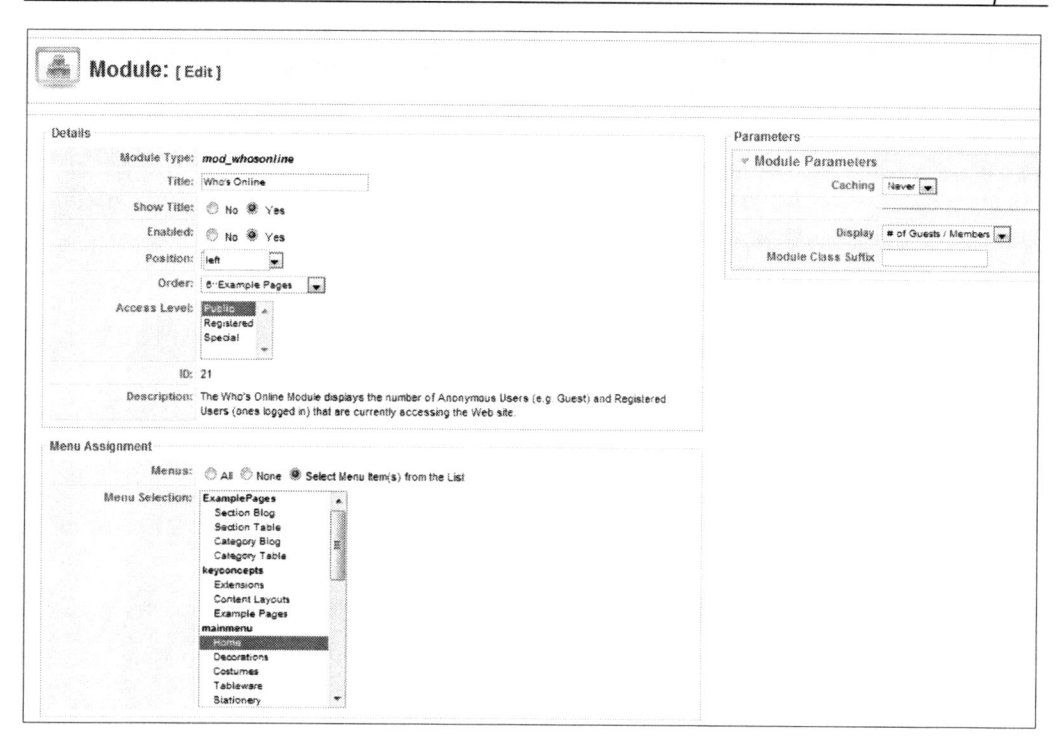

Note that with any of these modules, you can choose which menu items to display them on as well. So, if you only want to show the number of users online on your home page, select that option in the **Menu Assignment** section.

Polls

This module works with the polls component, where you set up a particular poll and then refer to it within the module. The edit screen allows you to choose which poll you want to display. Say you want to learn more about your user demographic on a certain issue, then set up a poll to pose a question, which they can answer quickly. (Always make it quick and easy and you will get a better response rate.)

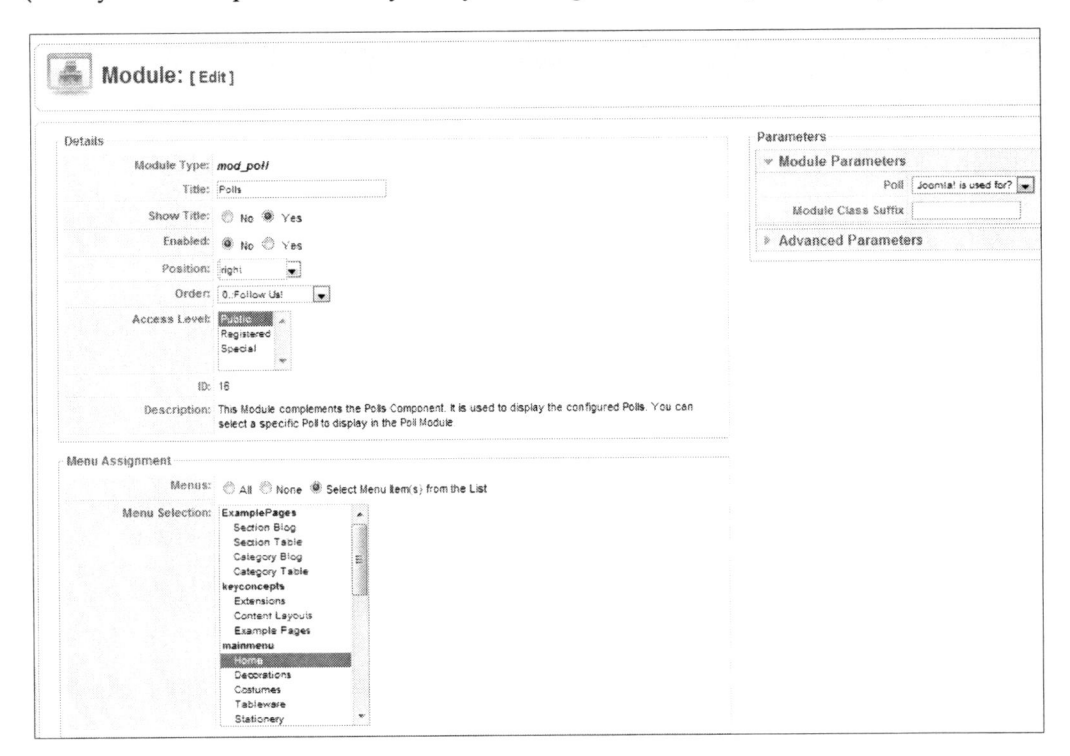

Feed display

This module allows you to show a syndicated RSS feed on your website. You add the URL to the website you want to feed through into your site and part of the text will be shown on your site. The section on "Social media" in Chapter 6, *Making Your Site Popular* looks at how having an RSS feed into your site can assist with search engine optimization.

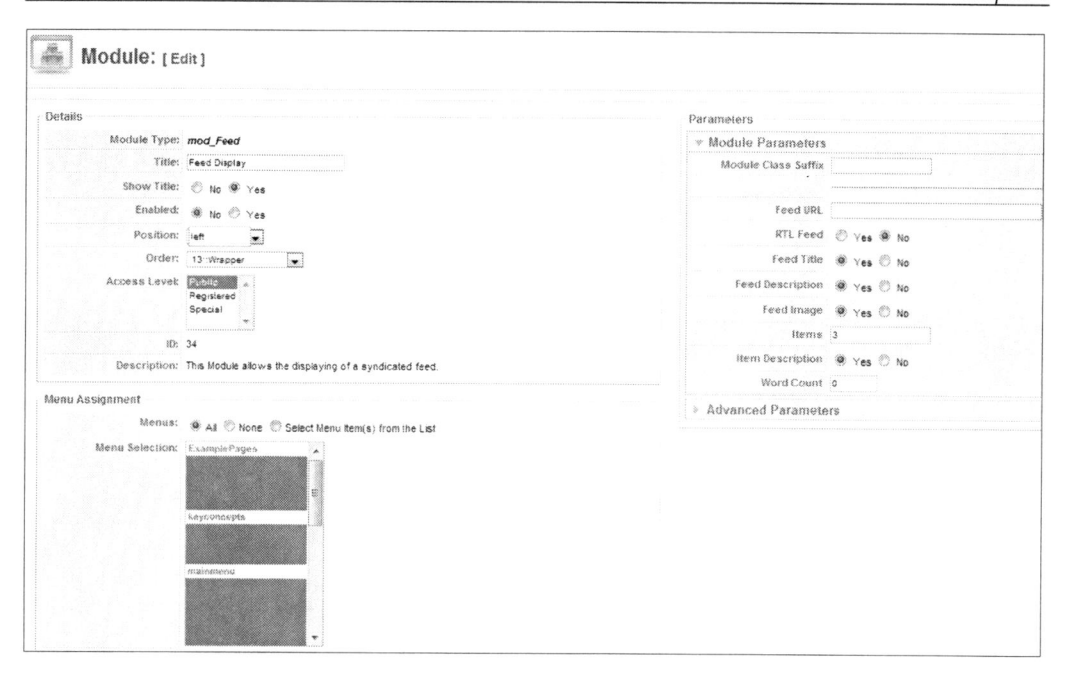

Summary

Using components and modules becomes more familiar each time you access them, as the manager screens are consistent in their layout and accessibility. Now you can add and manage these core features, and there are many more within the core Joomla! installation that you may find useful for your own website. Take the time to explore them, consider how you could use them, and check whether they fit into the framework of your website.

There is a great range of third-party components, modules, and plugins that can be downloaded and installed. Thanks to the community of developers, many are non-commercial and free to use, whereas others can be purchased and offer a greater range of options within them. The Joomla! extensions page at http://extensions.joomla.org/ is an endorsed repository of links to these third-party extensions. They are categorized and rated for popularity, editor's picks, and more.

Index

Symbols

.avi file 58
.gif file 52
.jpg file 52
.mov file 58
.png file 52
.swf file 58
.wmv file 58

A

Adidas site 24
administration interface
 component section 11
 content 10
 extension 11
 global menu bar 10
 help 12
 menus 10
 site 10
 tools 11
administration panel
 administration interface, logging into 147, 148
 admin user password, resetting 146
 diagnostic scripts, running 148
 MD5 hash value, generating 146
 Raw Access Logs, reviewing 149
 suspicious file, checking for 148
 unable, to login 145
advertising banners
 about 164
 adding 167, 169
 banner Category, adding 165
 banner client, adding 166
 banner module, enabling 169-172
 banner parameters, setting 166
 editing 172, 173
 managing 172, 173
 setting up 165
 setting up, steps 165-, 172
AllVideos plugin
 using 60
 video, changing 61
Article
 content, breaking up 37-39
 editing 33, 34
 editing, text editor used 32-34
 new content, adding 34
 opening 33
 page break, adding 38, 39
 Read More link, adding 37, 38
 table, adding 35, 36
 text, adding 35
Article Manager
 about 25
 Articles, filtering 26, 27
 column headings 27
 column headings, Access Level 28
 column headings, Front Page 28
 column headings, Order 28
 column headings, Published 28
 toolbar 28
 using 26
Article parameters 45
 Access Level option 45
 advanced parameters 46
 Author Alias option 45
 Author option 45
 Created Date option 45
 Finish Publishing option 45

metadata information 46
Start Publishing option 45
Audacity 65
audio files
  about 64
  third-party extensions, configuring 65, 68

B

Bakup Wizard
  using, for site files backup 74-76

C

content
  importance 21
  writing, tips 22, 23
Control Panel
  about 69
  advanced 71
  databases 71
  domains 71
  files 71
  link 72
  logs 71
  mail 71
  modules 70
  phpMyAdmin 72
  preferences 71
  screenshot 70
  security 71
  software services 71
copyright
  about 23, 51
  avoiding 23
core modules
  about 185
  feed display 188
  NewsFlash 185, 186
  pools component 188
  Who's online module 186, 188
Creative Commons web site 23

D

Delicious, social media 119
DOCman 184
downloading

jSecure authentication 141

E

EasierTube plugin 62
e-mails
  Group setting 108
  Mail to Child Groups setting 108
  private message, sending 109
  Recipients as BCC (Blind Carbon Copy)
    setting 109
  sending, to group of users 108, 109
  Send in HTML Mode setting 108
existing users, User Manager
  contact details, updating 104, 105
  password, resetting 106
  profile, editing 103
  username, resetting 106
extensions
  components 17
  modules 17
  overview 16
  plugins 18, 19

F

Facebook, social media
  using 117
File Transfer Protocol. *See* **FTP**
frontend
  authorization 40
  frontend content, adding for approval 41
  login form, editing 91
  publishing from 40
  users 90, 91
frontend users
  authors 90
  editors 91
  example 90
  publishers 91
  registered users 90
FTP
  about 76
  connection details 77
  details, entering 77

G

gallery, images
  dimensions, changing 56, 57
  updating, steps 55, 56
Google, social media
  account, setting up 122, 123
  Analytics, setting up 124, 125
Google Analytics
  setting up 124,125
GZipped format 73

H

home page
  content, guidelines 24
  content, managing 25
hosting account, reviewing
  about 138
  administration password, changing 138, 139
  administration username, changing 138, 139
  FTP login password, resetting 140

I

image
  .gif file format 52
  .jpg file format 52
  .png file format 52
  applying, to website 53
  downloading, precautions 52
  file size 52
images
  about 49
  adding 52
  deleting 54
  gallery dimensions, changing 56, 57
  gallery, updating 54-56
  uploading, steps 53, 54
installing
  jSecure authentication 140
  jSecure authentication, through administration Control Panel 143
  third-party extension 177-180
  third-party modules 177
  third-party plugins 178

J

JCal Pro 184
JCE text editor
  Choose a Text Color icon 40
  Code Edit icon 40
  downloading 39
  Edit the CSS icon 40
  Emoticons icon 40
  Paste from Word icon 40
  Search and Replace icon 40
  Select a Background Color icon 40
  Toggle Fullscreen Mode icon 40
JobGrok component
  configuring 180
  new component, adding to menu 182, 183
  parameters, accessing 181
Joomla! version, upgrading
  about 134
  localhost environments 135
  upgrade patch, installing 135-138
Joomla! website
  articles 12, 13, 21
  backend 8
  categories 12
  categories, creating 13
  Control Panel, accessing 8
  Control Panel, icons 9
  frontend 8
  global configuration screen 14
  operational settings 14-16
  organizing 12
  sections 12, 13
  uncategorized articles 14
jSecure authentication
  configuring 140-145
  downloading 141
  installing 140
  installing, through administration Control Panel 143

K

keywords, social media
  Google's keyword tool, using 126, 127
  researching 126, 127

L

latest news module
  adding 173, 174
  content, setting up 173
  enabling 174
  managing 174
Letterman 184
login form, frontend
  customizing 91
  Forgot your password link 92
  Forgot your username link 91
  new account registration 92

M

manual site backup
  about 71
  database backup, phpMyAdmin used 72, 73
  external FTP application used, files download 76, 77
  external FTP application used, files upload 76
  site files backup, Backup Wizard used 74-76
manual website restoration
  about 84-87
  archive file, creating 79, 80
  archive file, uploading 79, 80
  backing up, JoomlaPack component used 78
  kickstart.php file, installing 83, 84
  new database, creating 81-83
  new user, creating 81-83
  steps 77
Media Manager
  about 49, 50
  accessing 50, 51
  accessing, thumbnail view 50, 51
  new subdirectory, creating 51
menu extension
  Article, creating 152-155
  menu items, removing 156
  menu items, reordering 156
  new link, using 152
  new menu item, adding 152, 157

N

new account registration, login form
  allowing, steps 92, 93
  custom text, adding 94-96
  registered users, directing 96, 97
new user, adding as site contact
  about 98
  including, in list of contacts 99-101
  new contact Category, adding 98
  new customer, adding manually 102

O

organic listing 111

P

Party People website
  advertising banners 164
  latest news module, updating 173, 174
  random image, adding 175
  top menu, extending with link 152
  Web Links, adding 157
phpMyAdmin
  using, database backup 72, 73
precautionary measures
  about 134
  hosting account, reviewing 138
  Joomla! version, upgrading 134
  keeping up-to-date 134
  other methods 140
problematic users, User Manager
  account, activating 108
  blocking 107, 108
  dealing with 106
  deleting 107

R

random images module
  image folder file, modifying 175
  redirecting, to different directory 176, 177
Really Simple Syndication. *See* **RSS feeds, social media**
Reddit, social media 119

Rich Site Summary. *See* RSS feeds, social media
RSS feeds, social media 119

S

search engine 111
search engine-friendly Article
  creating 130
Search Engine Ranking
  metadata 112
  overview 111
security
  precautionary measures 134
SEO
  about 112
  general strategies 112-116
SEO, general strategies
  content, updating frequently 113
  external link, adding to Article 113, 114
  internal link, adding manually to Article 115, 116
  internal link, adding to Article 114-116
  link, building 113
site, recovering 150
social media
  about 116
  Delicious 119
  Facebook 117
  Google 122
  Google Analytics 124, 125
  Internet (Web 2.0) 116
  keywords, researching 126
  keyword, tips 127, 128
  multiple content, adding 127
  Reddit 119
  RSS feeds 119
  setting, up on site 119
  sponsored links 127
  Stalker, customizing 120
  StumbleUpon 118
  Twitter 118
  using, for marketing 117- 122
Stalker, customizing
  about 120
  details, adding 121
  Details section 121

Menu Assignment section 121
StumbleUpon, social media
  using 118

T

third-party extension
  DOCman 184
  installing 177-180
  JCal Pro 184
  JobGrok 184
  Letterman 184
  VirtueMart 184
third-party module
  installing 177
third-party plugins
  installing 178
toolbar
  about 12
  contents 12
  Help icon 12
toolbar, Article Manager
  Article, archiving 28
  Article, copying 30
  Article, moving 29
  Article, publishing 29
  Article, trashing 30
  Article, unarchiving 29
  Article, unpublishing 29
  Edit button 30
  Hide button 31
  New button 31
  Parameters button 31
tools, administration interface
  clean cache 11
  global check-in 11
  mass mail 11
  purge expired cache 11
  read message 11
  write message 11
Twitter, social media
  using 118

U

uncategorized articles 14
Upload File tool
  using 51

User Manager
  about 89, 97
  existing users, editing 103
  new user, adding as site contact 98
  new user, creating 97
  problematic users, dealing with 106
users
  about 89, 90
  administration users 91
  frontend users 90
  managing 97
  registering 90

V

video files
  .avi file 58
  .flv file 58
  .mov file 58
  .wmv file 58
  about 57, 59
  adding, cons 57
  adding, pros 57
  considering, points 59
  format, choosing 58
  uploading, AllVideos plugin used 60
  uploading, steps 60
  using 57
  versions 58
  YouTube video, updating 62
videos 49
VirtueMart 184

W

Web Links
  adding 157
  Category of links, adding 159, 160
  deleting 161
  editting 161
  global parameters, setting 157-159
  links, adding to Category 160
  page, adding to top menu 161- 164
What You See is What You Get. *See* WYSIWYG
Wired magazines web site 21
WYSIWYG 21

X

x icon 54

Y

YouTube video, video files
  dimensions, changing 64
  EasierTube plugin 62
  updating 62

Z

Zipfile
  accessing 141
  downloading 178
Zipped format 73

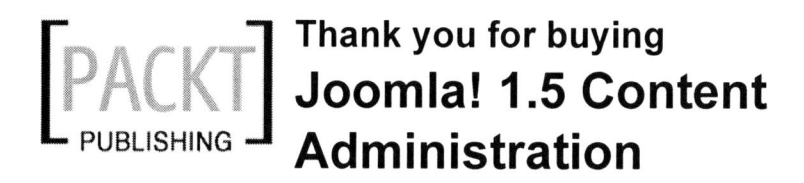

Thank you for buying
Joomla! 1.5 Content Administration

Packt Open Source Project Royalties

When we sell a book written on an Open Source project, we pay a royalty directly to that project. Therefore by purchasing Joomla! 1.5 Content Administration, Packt will have given some of the money received to the Joomla! project.

In the long term, we see ourselves and you — customers and readers of our books — as part of the Open Source ecosystem, providing sustainable revenue for the projects we publish on. Our aim at Packt is to establish publishing royalties as an essential part of the service and support a business model that sustains Open Source.

If you're working with an Open Source project that you would like us to publish on, and subsequently pay royalties to, please get in touch with us.

Writing for Packt

We welcome all inquiries from people who are interested in authoring. Book proposals should be sent to author@packtpub.com. If your book idea is still at an early stage and you would like to discuss it first before writing a formal book proposal, contact us; one of our commissioning editors will get in touch with you.

We're not just looking for published authors; if you have strong technical skills but no writing experience, our experienced editors can help you develop a writing career, or simply get some additional reward for your expertise.

About Packt Publishing

Packt, pronounced 'packed', published its first book "Mastering phpMyAdmin for Effective MySQL Management" in April 2004 and subsequently continued to specialize in publishing highly focused books on specific technologies and solutions.

Our books and publications share the experiences of your fellow IT professionals in adapting and customizing today's systems, applications, and frameworks. Our solution-based books give you the knowledge and power to customize the software and technologies you're using to get the job done. Packt books are more specific and less general than the IT books you have seen in the past. Our unique business model allows us to bring you more focused information, giving you more of what you need to know, and less of what you don't.

Packt is a modern, yet unique publishing company, which focuses on producing quality, cutting-edge books for communities of developers, administrators, and newbies alike. For more information, please visit our website: www.PacktPub.com.

Joomla! E-Commerce with VirtueMart

ISBN: 978-1-847196-74-3 Paperback: 476 pages

Build feature-rich online stores with Joomla! 1.0/1.5 and VirtueMart 1.1.x

1. Build your own e-commerce web site from scratch by adding features step-by-step to an example e-commerce web site
2. Configure the shop, build product catalogues, configure user registration settings for VirtueMart to take orders from around the world
3. Manage customers, orders, and a variety of currencies to provide the best customer service

Building Websites with Joomla! 1.5

ISBN: 978-1-847195-30-2 Paperback: 384 pages

The best-selling Joomla! tutorial guide updated for the latest 1.5 release

1. Learn Joomla! 1.5 features
2. Install and customize Joomla! 1.5
3. Configure Joomla! administration
4. Create your own Joomla! templates

Please check **www.PacktPub.com** for information on our titles

Joomla! Web Security

ISBN: 978-1-847194-88-6   Paperback: 264 pages

Secure your Joomla! website from common security threats with this easy-to-use guide

1. Learn how to secure your Joomla! websites
2. Real-world tools to protect against hacks on your site
3. Implement disaster recovery features
4. Set up SSL on your site
5. Covers Joomla! 1.0 as well as 1.5

Joomla! 1.5 SEO

ISBN: 978-1-847198-16-7   Paperback: 324 pages

Improve the search engine friendliness of your web site

1. Improve the rankings of your Joomla! site in the search engine result pages such as Google, Yahoo, and Bing
2. Improve your web site SEO performance by gaining and producing incoming links to your web site
3. Market and measure the success of your blog by applying SEO
4. Integrate analytics and paid advertising into your Joomla! blog

Please check **www.PacktPub.com** for information on our titles